Unveiling
Inequality

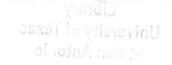

Unveiling Inequality

A World-Historical Perspective

Roberto Patricio Korzeniewicz and Timothy Patrick Moran

Russell Sage Foundation
New York

The Russell Sage Foundation

The Russell Sage Foundation, one of the oldest of America's general purpose foundations, was established in 1907 by Mrs. Margaret Olivia Sage for "the improvement of social and living conditions in the United States." The Foundation seeks to fulfill this mandate by fostering the development and dissemination of knowledge about the country's political, social, and economic problems. While the Foundation endeavors to assure the accuracy and objectivity of each book it publishes, the conclusions and interpretations in Russell Sage Foundation publications are those of the authors and not of the Foundation, its Trustees, or its staff. Publication by Russell Sage, therefore, does not imply Foundation endorsement.

Library of Congress Cataloging-in-Publication Data

Korzeniewicz, Roberto Patricio.
    Unveiling inequality : a world-historical perspective / Roberto Patricio Korzeniewicz, Timothy Patrick Moran.
        p. cm.
    Includes bibliographical references and index.
    ISBN 978-0-87154-483-4 (alk. paper)
    1. Income distribution—Case studies. 2. Equality—Economic aspects—Case studies. I. Moran, Timothy Patrick. II. Title.
    HC79.I5K68 2009
    339.2—dc22

                                                                        2009016777

The paper used in this publication meets the minimum requirements of American National Standard for Information Sciences—Permanence of Paper for Printed Library Materials. ANSI Z39.48-1992.

Text design by Suzanne Nichols.

RUSSELL SAGE FOUNDATION
112 East 64th Street, New York, New York 10065
10 9 8 7 6 5 4 3 2 1

To Nancy, Adrián, Gabriel
To Maico
—Patricio

To Jessica, Ella Sol, and Isadora Kay
To Ma
—Tim

CONTENTS

ABOUT THE AUTHORS

ROBERTO PATRICIO KORZENIEWICZ is associate professor of sociology at the University of Maryland–College Park, and Professor Titular at the Escuela de Política y Gobierno of the Universidad Nacional de San Martín in Argentina.

TIMOTHY PATRICK MORAN is associate professor of sociology and director of graduate studies at the State University of New York–Stony Brook.

ACKNOWLEDGMENTS

Research and writing for this book were made possible by our Visiting Scholar Fellowships at the Russell Sage Foundation in 2006. Under the leadership of Eric Wanner, the Russell Sage Foundation provides a unique, enriching environment for scholarly inquiry and debate, and our collaborative work thrived during our residence and, in particular, during our luncheon (thanks, Jackie!) interaction with other members of the Visiting Scholars class. In addition, during our stay at Russell Sage, the foundation provided support to hold a small but productive workshop on world-historical patterns of inequality, with the participation of Giovanni Arrighi, Marcelo Cavarozzi, Miguel Centeno, Shelley Feldman, James Galbraith, Jack Goldstone, John Markoff, Luis Reygadas, Rhacel Salazar Parreñas, Beverly Silver, Robert Wade, and Immanuel Wallerstein. Also at the Russell Sage Foundation, Suzanne Nichols has been invaluable as an editor, eliciting extremely helpful comments from three anonymous reviewers and calmly guiding the manuscript to its final production. We would also like to thank April Rondeau, Cynthia Buck, and the rest of the staff at Russell Sage for their help in preparing this book for publication.

The departments of sociology at the University of Maryland and the State University of New York–Stony Brook supported this project and our residence at Russell Sage, and we have greatly benefited from our work with students and colleagues at these institutions. At the University of Maryland, Angela Stach, Vrushali Patil, and David Consiglio collaborated with us on research that contributed to some of the arguments presented here; Jerry Hage and Mike Ryan commented on earlier versions of the manuscript; and Reeve Vanemman generously shared original inequality data for India.

At Stony Brook, the students in Tim's International Studies Program provided engaged, critical commentary on the ideas presented in this book, even if unaware of doing double-duty as book reviewers. Javier Auyero, Ian Roxborough, and Michael Schwartz have supplied, during different times of need, scholarly commentary, professional advice, and friendship—they should note, however, that they will not be relieved of their roles with this book's publication (or even by moving to Austin, Texas).

Many additional friends and colleagues commented on previous versions of the ideas and arguments presented in this book. In particular, we would like to thank Alberto Bártoli, Cathy Bergman and David Dean, María Esperanza Casullo, Miguel Correa, Wally Goldfrank, José Itzigsohn, Alicia Lissidini, Ricardo Nacht, Glenn Perusek, Luis Rosado, Guillermo Rozenwurcel, Alejandro Sehtman, Bill Smith, Jackie Smith, John Torpey, Eliecer Valencia, Pedro Vieira, and Immanuel Wallerstein. Jessica Giovachino helped design and execute several of the figures included in the book. Colleagues and students at the Escuela de Política y Gobierno of the Universidad Nacional de San Martín provided an encouraging sounding board that helped us initially as we developed some of the ideas that we would further pursue in this book. The dean of the Escuela, Marcelo Cavarozzi, has been a constant source of friendship and support.

Our work would have been impossible without the support of our families. Our collaboration was disruptive of domestic life, in part through frequent absences from our families, and in part through intrusive, "scholarly residencies" at each other's home. This meant that Ella frequently had to surrender her bedroom to Patricio, and Adrían and Gabriel the family room to Tim. To them, and to Jessica and Nancy, our thanks for their generosity, patience, and enthusiasm.

INTRODUCTION

It is conceivable that a social system may be unjust even though none of its institutions are unjust taken separately: the injustice is a consequence of how they are combined together into a single system.
—John Rawls, A Theory of Justice

Inequality and stratification have been conceived primarily as processes that occur within national boundaries. Such a focus has produced a number of influential overarching narratives. One such narrative is that the relative well-being of people is shaped most fundamentally by the capacity of home-grown institutions to promote economic growth and equity. Another is that people over time have become more stratified by their relative achievement and effort rather than by the characteristics with which they were born. A third one, a corollary of the other two, is that upward social mobility is fundamentally the outcome of the adoption of better domestic institutions by countries and the acquisition of greater human capital by individuals. This book argues that looking at the unfolding of social inequality in the world as a whole over a long period of time—in other words, from a world-historical perspective—calls these narratives into question.

As we began writing this book two years ago at the Russell Sage Foundation on Manhattan's Upper East Side, we were struck by how frequently portrayals of inequality in the popular media mirrored some fundamental assumptions usually made by the social sciences when approaching this subject. Take a cover story of November 26, 2007, in the *New York Times* on workers in India who make manhole covers for New York City streets (Heather Timmons and J. Adam Huggins, "New York Manhole Covers, Forged Barefoot in India"). The pictures in the article show hot molten iron being poured into molds by shirtless and barefoot workers making a few dollars a day. The manager of the factory, when questioned about the safety of pouring iron in bare feet, responded, "We can't maintain the luxury of Europe and the U.S., with all the boots and all that." Such articles documenting the lives of the world's poor are a regular staple of the newspaper.

Frequently juxtaposed with such articles in the same newspaper are stories that focus on the rich. In one running theme, the newspaper serves as a forum to debate the standards that differentiate the truly wealthy from everyone else.[1] Such stories might focus on children being chauffeured daily to their child care centers in "mostly black luxury-edition sport utility vehicles like the Mercedes GL-Class or the GMC Yukon Denali" ("Once Around the Block, James, and Pick Me Up After My Nap," *New York Times,* January 24, 2007), or they might discuss the relative size of the yachts of the very rich ("As the Yachting Class Grows, So Do Yachts," *New York Times,* October 23, 2007). In an equally common running theme, they focus on individuals and families making high incomes in the United States who are given the opportunity to make their case for why their salaries and assets do not qualify to make them truly rich but merely middle-class.[2] In a recent article, when such respondents "are asked how much money would make them feel secure, they inevitably choose a figure that is double their own net worth," estimating that "you need about $10 million to be considered entry-level rich."[3]

In both running themes, the wealthy individuals who regularly appear in the *New York Times* are constantly scrutinizing themselves, their peers, and wealthier elites to estimate their relative standing in the social hierarchy, and establishing such standards is hard work and a source of anxiety.[4] The articles make it clear that for those in the United States who are concerned about ascertaining their own relative social status, it is their status relative to other elites within their country that seems most relevant to their purposes, and such standards alone provide the appropriate indicators to establish their social standing. From such a standpoint, many in the United States feel that the term "elite" or "rich" can legitimately be applied only to no more than the wealthiest half of 1 percent of the country's population. The rest (except those at the very bottom) are perceived to constitute a great middle class whose members have varying degrees of access to the amenities of life but all of whom face the need "to slog to work every day" (as remarked by the noted economist Edward Wolff; quoted by Joel Achenbach in "That's Rich—But Maybe for Someone Else," *Washington Post,* November 26, 2007, A:2).

Such debates in the United States about what boundaries differentiate the truly rich from everyone else might seem quaint, if not outright ridiculous, to observers in most of the rest of the world. The reference to boots as a "luxury" item by the Indian factory manager might seem outrageous, particularly for those who feel solidarity with people for whom work is considerably more difficult and less rewarding than ours, but the same comment can be read as a powerful statement about the extent to which, when viewed by the vast majority of the world, the amenities enjoyed by most of those living in the United States—even those who "slog" to work—are no less than luxurious wealth by global standards.

The magnitude of *global* disparities can be illustrated by considering the life of dogs in the United States. According to a recent estimate by the American Pet Products Manufacturers Association (an organization that for obvious reasons conducts frequent surveys on the subject), in 2007–2008 the average yearly expenses associated with owning a dog were $1,425 ($749 in health care, $217 in food, and $459 in grooming, boarding, toys, and treats).[5] Of course, these are average figures for the nation as a whole: in some areas, such as the wealthy Upper East Side of Manhattan, the costs of maintaining a dog can be considerably higher.[6]

For the sake of argument, let us pretend that these dogs in the United States constitute their own nation, "Dogland," with their average maintenance costs representing the average income of this nation of dogs. By such a standard, their income would place Dogland squarely as a middle-income nation, above countries such as Paraguay and Egypt. In fact, the income of Dogland, this nation of U.S. dogs, would place its canine inhabitants above more than 40 percent of the world population. (The figure was roughly 60 percent as recently as 2004, before high rates of growth allowed China and its large population to surpass the threshold; at $820, the average national income of India is still merely around 60 percent of the expenditure for U.S. dogs.) And if we were to focus exclusively on health care expenditures, the gap becomes monumental: the average yearly expenditures in Dogland would be higher than health care expenditures in countries that account for over 80 percent of the world population.[7] To such disparities we should add other important dimensions: even from the point of view of protection from violence, the life of urban dogs on the Upper East Side of

Manhattan is considerably more protected than the lives of many of the world's poor.

As we noted, newspapers such as the *New York Times* do acknowledge and report on the existence of these global disparities. But even when recognized, wealth and poverty, in popular perception, tend to be treated as if they are separate from one another. Poverty tends to be seen as an unfortunate characteristic of people who have not yet been exposed to progress. That which constitutes wealth by global standards is perceived as the product of achievement and effort—well rewarded perhaps, but achievement and effort nonetheless. In such a treatment, the world as a whole is perceived as operating according to the rules we see in our immediate surroundings, and the experience of those in other countries is viewed as unrelated to our own.

Likewise, the contemporary social sciences claim to view the world through theoretical perspectives that are purportedly universal but that are constructed by focusing mainly—in some cases even solely—on the experience of a very small fraction of the world's population. Take Émile Durkheim's (1893/1997) influential argument that the development of a more complex division of labor entails a shift from a system of stratification based on ascribed characteristics to one based on achieved characteristics. Observing processes of social inequality and mobility solely or primarily as they take place within the borders of wealthy countries indeed appears to confirm such a shift, and many studies in the social sciences have been dedicated to documenting, over and over again, such a transition. But the vast majority of these studies draw their observations from two dozen or so wealthy nations and deem this a sufficient basis from which to make conclusive statements, with nary a caveat or even acknowledgment that the scope of such inquiries is often limited to little more than the wealthiest 10 percent of the world's population. Such unacknowledged biases are ingrained in the very foundations of much of the social sciences, and they continue to permeate the construction of the social sciences to this day.

But more importantly, since the emergence of the social sciences, and in their subsequent development, inequality and stratification are conceived primarily as processes that occur within national boundaries. As in more popular renditions of the topic, this fundamental assumption is deeply ingrained in academic inquiry, particularly as practiced in the high-income nations of the world.[8] Such an assumption is so fundamental and deeply rooted that the choice of nations as the privileged unit of analysis is often not theoretically informed but driven by a combination of academic custom and the format in which data are most easily available.[9]

By contrast, Max Weber (1905/1996) argues that our choice of the proper unit of analysis should be guided by theoretical criteria, because its boundaries should contain within them all the processes that are relevant for understanding the phenomenon under investigation.[10] This means that even when thinking about individual achievement in wealthy countries, for example, we face crucial decisions in choosing the appropriate unit of analysis, and these choices, Weber argues, should be theoretically informed by the questions we are seeking to address.[11]

This book argues that accounts of inequality and stratification that assume that the nation-state constitutes the fundamental unit of analysis—and moreover, that restrict their observations to wealthy nations, as is most often the case—are bound to miss key processes that shape these phenomena even within the wealthy populations they study. Social inequality and stratification have unfolded globally and over a long period of time, and the study of these phenomena hence requires a world-historical perspective.[12] Such a perspective reveals that the institutional arrangements shaping inequality within and between countries have always been simultaneously national and global; that ascribed criteria continue to play a fundamental role in sustaining inequality at a global level; and that the most significant patterns of social mobility involve challenges to existing patterns of inequality between nations. As we show, our understanding of each of these issues changes dramatically once such *relationships* are taken into account—and this can be done only by broadening the scope of our analysis to the world as a whole.

We suggest that, as in the "blind men and the elephant" metaphor, existing studies of both between- and within-country inequalities can be "partly in the right" in their descriptions of what they perceive. But they are right only within the particular boundaries of the sphere they choose to describe, and with the specific scopes (for example, data, techniques, assumptions) through which they make their observations. Hence, various "parts" are adequately described, but what is missing, we contend, is an account of the whole. The main thrust of this book is to provide an alternative way of theorizing this whole—that is, to account for inequality as a complex set of interactions (for example, interactions that occur simultaneously within and between countries) that have unfolded over space and time as a truly *world-historical* phenomenon.

Some area specialists and historians might find our work to be making very broad and sweeping claims on topics where the evidence might not be sufficiently strong to fully corroborate our arguments. This is somewhat inevitable at the current stage of our formulations. We conceive historical inequality as the type of phenomenon that Weber (1905/1996, 47) refers to as a "historical individual":

> Such an historical concept . . . , since it refers in its content to a phenomenon significant for its unique individuality, cannot be defined according to the formula *genus proximum, differentia specifica,* but it must be gradually put together out of the individual parts which are taken from historical reality to make it up.

In constructing such a "historical individual," however, we have faced important constraints because adequate empirical information often is lacking or yet to be constructed.

For example, in trying to think about trends in world inequality as involving interactions that simultaneously involve different spatial locations—say, by linking the processes through which households are stratified *within* nations to other processes through which the very same households are linked *across* national boundaries—we quickly see that the relevant data (for example, on *world* income distributions) are not easily forthcoming. In fact, national statistical offices collect existing income data in an exercise that necessarily presumes that national boundaries delineate the only possible unit of analysis. And even with national income data, it is generally difficult to ascertain trends over sufficiently long periods of time, for the systematic collection of such data is largely a post–World War II phenomenon (and rather limited to high-income countries at that).

To compensate for such empirical constraints, we have grounded the ambitious claims made in this book on an eclectic range of available quantitative data and historical narratives. We hope that readers will be patient in those areas where our arguments await further empirical corroboration, for the sake of our overall effort to provide a new vantage point from which to advance both the study of inequality and a world-historical perspective.

We should note what this book is not. Some readers might be primarily interested in the following issue: do measures of inequality for the last few decades show "global inequality" going up (as some authors have ascertained; see, for example, Milanovic 2005) or down (see Sala-i-Martin 2006; Firebaugh 2003)? This debate, notably devoid of what most social sciences call "theory," is largely focused on whose econometric techniques and ways of manipulating world-wide income data are more sophisticated, based on more plausible assumptions, or otherwise provide clearer analytical results. Some readers might be looking for a book that provides a dense overview of these methodological and empirical issues, adjudicates between them, considers new evidence, and eventually renders its own judgment on whether "globalization" is associated with rising or falling world inequality.

While the arguments advanced in this book are certainly pertinent to the "convergence-divergence" debate, we seek to move beyond a technical assessment of current empirical trends. Our book constructs an alternative theoretical understanding of how global inequality has unfolded over time and space, unveiling a complex interaction of within- and between-country inequality. We assemble a great deal of empirical information, including one of the most statistically rigorous (in terms of the high degree of comparability) revised samples of cross-national inequality measures compiled to date. Many of our theoretical conclusions—on the interaction between within- and between-country inequalities, or on the role of the nation-state in forming the basis of categorical inequality—provide an alternative standpoint from which to understand the evidence marshaled in debates on global inequality. In this sense, we have greater interest in explaining this phenomenon theoretically rather than forecasting whether world inequality is destined to move up or down in the next few decades.

We hope readers will be forgiving about the areas in which this book treads lightly. For example, readers will find little about the construction of hegemonies, empires, or states—frequent topics in the world-systems and comparative sociology literatures. There is also an extensive literature on race and gender that makes only occasional appearances in our discussion. These are only some examples, and we are sure careful readers will uncover others.

THE OUTLINE OF THE BOOK

While introducing readers to the main arguments and methodological procedures that are pertinent to the study of inequality and stratification, chapter 1 discusses cross-national patterns of within-country inequality. We show that many of the assumptions regarding the extent of change in within-country inequality over the last decades have been derived from studies that focus on narrow groups of countries (such as high-income nations). Using a broader cross-national database (ninety-six countries), we are able to provide very different criteria for assessing the extent of change over time and space. Using these criteria, we identify one cluster of countries characterized by high levels of inequality and another characterized by relatively low levels of inequality, and we argue that these clusters have been characterized by considerable stability over recent decades (with a few noteworthy exceptions).

In chapter 2, we show that these clusters of high and low inequality have shown considerable persistence, not only over recent decades, but over a much longer span of time, sometimes reaching back for centuries. According to a new institutional literature on the topic, the persistence of high inequality is indicative of situations in which, often on the basis of ascribed characteristics, vast sectors of the population early on had restricted access to political and property rights in ways that eventually limited the country's potential for economic growth. In this literature, a more egalitarian pattern of stratification, featuring greater opportunities for upward social mobility and individual achievement and more open access to markets and politics, became conducive to more successful national trajectories of economic growth, as shown by the experience of wealthy countries. Chapter 2 uses such evidence for the historical persistence of high and low levels of within-country inequality to identify what we heuristically define as high-inequality equilibria (HIE) and low-inequality equilibria (LIE): in each of these situations, prevailing institutional arrangements produce considerable stability in the patterns of stratification. (The chapter also examines examples of nations that do not fit neatly and always within one of these equilibria, such as the United States.)

The new institutional literature on inequality and the policy-makers influenced by this perspective tend to see the institutional arrangements underpinning high and low inequality as independent development paths. Chapter 3 argues that HIE and LIE should be understood in relational terms. To make this argument, we draw from Joseph Schumpeter's (1942) insights on "creative destruction": institutional arrangements are themselves part and parcel of the processes of innovation that, unevenly distributed over time and space, generate differential rates of economic growth. In this sense, the institutional arrangements characterizing LIE have indeed been more effective in promoting economic growth since the nineteenth century. But thinking about such outcomes in terms of "creative destruction" requires that we rethink the origins of HIE. Contrary to prevailing assumptions, the institutional arrangements underpinning HIE proved innovative and effective in generating high rates of growth for a long period of time prior to the nineteenth century. Like any other innovation, these arrangements would eventually become comparatively disadvantaged relative to new innovative institutions (such as those characteristic of LIE after the nineteenth century). In this sense, we should assume neither that high levels of inequality act as an impediment to economic growth nor that economic growth inevitably weakens institutional arrangements characterized by high inequality.

Chapter 4 moves on to discuss historical trends and current patterns of between-country inequality. Drawing on the previous chapters, we argue that such inequality can be best understood as entailing a high-inequality equilibrium. Moreover, we indicate that within-country LIE and between-country HIE are related: within-country LIE have been sustained through institutional arrangements that limit competitive pressures within wealthy countries, while simultaneously transferring these competitive pressures abroad. In this sense, what appears to be the product of individual achievement and effort in wealthy countries has entailed simultaneously the construction and reproduction of ascriptive categories as crucial criteria shaping world-historical inequality. We focus on migration policies as an example of these connections and conclude by observing that over the last two centuries nationality has become the crucial ascribed characteristic shaping the status of people within global stratification.

Such an interpretation raises difficult issues. Does it mean that the populations of wealthy nations have attained their privileges by making much of the rest of the world poor? Not exactly. We do not think that the attainment of wealth implies a zero-sum game in which the gain of some requires losses for others—and we barely address long-standing debates about whether and to what an extent the exploitation of colonies served to generate resources to promote the accumulation of wealth in today's high-income nations. Also, we do not try to argue that the character of institutional arrangements and this alone determines the extent of access to income and wealth over time and place; natural resource endowments, historical accidents, and other externalities certainly have played a role as well. Finally, we have no doubts that important path-dependencies are also at work, so that the outcomes discussed in chapter 2 indeed attain a significant measure of self-reinforcement.

On the other hand, it is unlikely that the uneven distribution of income and wealth in the world today would exist in the absence of the institutional arrangements that limit access to markets and political rights on the basis of national borders. In this sense, while it is not the case that the populations of wealthy nations have attained their privileges by making much of the rest of the world poor, we contend that the relative privileges characterizing high-income nations (as we show, constituting no more than 14 percent of the world's population) historically required the existence of institutional arrangements that ensured the exclusion of the vast majority of others from access to opportunity.

Chapter 5 recasts patterns of mobility within global stratification. We show that much of the academic literature on social mobility and inequality (as well as the efforts to draw boundaries distinguishing the very rich from the merely affluent, as discussed earlier in this introduction) is focused on a very small percentage of the world population, all located in the top two deciles of global stratification. We also explore the three principal paths available for social mobility from a global perspective. The first path is engagement in within-country mobility (for example, individuals upgrading their education or occupational attainment, or groups pushing for a political redistribution of resources). This path can bring significant change in status, particularly for poorer populations in highly unequal countries, but is more limited in its overall effects than is generally assumed. The second path entails mobility through national economic growth. This path can be an important means of upward mobility in global stratification, particularly over longer periods of time, but has been restricted until recently to a very small percentage of the world's population. The third path provides the most immediate means of rapid upward social mobility: jumping the national categories that are key to world-historical inequality. As we show in chapter 5, focusing on global patterns of stratification unveils the key advantages that can be gained by engaging in migration as a means of overcoming the persistent role of ascription in limiting social mobility.

Once again, difficult issues are raised. There are important trade-offs in the interaction of within- and between-country inequality: since at least the nineteenth century, and for two hundred years, the key institutional arrangements underpinning LIE within high-income countries simultaneously were key to the persistence of HIE in inequality between nations. The very rise of between-country inequality, however, has generated responses that in recent decades have begun to alter existing patterns of stratification; high rates of economic growth in China and India, we argue, have been one of the expressions of this recent reversal. Insofar as these responses come to be perceived as challenging the continued privilege of high-income nations, as happened in the early twentieth century, they might evoke a strong response by those resentful of the effects of more open borders. Our conclusion explores how these contentious issues might shape various alternative paths for the future of world inequality.

Finally, our work on this manuscript was completed before the full onset of the 2008–2009 economic crisis. While it is hard to foresee the future evolution of events, the patterns we discuss in this book provide a productive standpoint from which to evaluate the direction of trends in world inequality. For example, political responses to the crisis in wealthy countries might aim to reduce within-country inequality, providing further evidence for the type of equilibria we discuss in the first two chapters of the book. Likewise, it remains to be seen whether the crisis will deepen the high level of inequalities between countries we highlight here, or whether it accelerates (most likely through relatively higher rates of growth in China and India) a departure from the high-inequality equilibrium that prevailed for most of the past two centuries.

CHAPTER 1

REINTERPRETING WITHIN-COUNTRY INEQUALITY

The modern study of social inequality and mobility has been built upon the fundamental premise that the nation-state constitutes the key unit of analysis. For much of the twentieth century, somewhat separate literatures on social inequality and on social mobility jointly constructed this fundamental premise, arguing that nations undergo a single overarching transition (shaping equally inequality and mobility) as they move from tradition to modernity. Thus, the twentieth-century social sciences literature focused on theorizing inequality and mobility in terms of a single, overarching process of change.

Over the last twenty years, on the other hand, the literatures on social mobility and inequality have retained a focus on the nation-state as the key unit of analysis but become fragmented in their empirical focus and theoretical conclusions. For example, inquiry on social mobility is focused almost exclusively on wealthy nations. From studies that exhaustively mine survey and census data from these nations, there is a consistent report that the transition to modernity indeed brought high rates of upward social mobility, increasingly based on achievement rather than ascription (findings that would come to be challenged by a more critical body of literature, also centered primarily on wealthy countries, that focuses on the continuing relevance of race, class, and gender). Studies focusing more directly on income inequality, on the other hand, abandoned the previous effort to theorize a single overarching transition to focus instead on the specific patterns of inequality that characterize different areas of the world (such as, again, wealthy nations, but also Latin America and East Asia).

1

Today the study of social inequality and mobility constitutes a highly fragmented area of inquiry, with very little dialogue between the many subfields of specialization. Our purpose in this book is to encourage dialogue between the various parts that constitute the study of inequality and mobility in order to establish a more coherent whole. In our view, this can be accomplished most productively by shifting the relevant unit of analysis away from nation-states to the world as a whole. Once such an analytical step is taken, however, we are led into a reassessment of some of the most deeply entrenched assumptions that have come to characterize the study of social inequality and social mobility.

Theorizing National Transitions

For much of the twentieth century, besides privileging the nation-state as the relevant unit of analysis, somewhat separate literatures on inequality and on mobility developed what came to constitute the "modernization paradigm," which became orthodoxy across the post–World War II social sciences. The modernization paradigm was interdisciplinary and encompassed a broad range of social phenomena; two of its components were an evolutionary theory of large-scale social transformation (used to understand economic development) and a functionalist theory of the working of modern societies (which came to dominate mainstream sociology). Both of these components privileged the nation-state as the site within whose boundaries were contained all the fundamental processes needed to understand the phenomena being studied, be it long-term changes in social inequality or patterns of individual or intergenerational social mobility.

For the understanding of inequality and mobility, three fundamental assumptions of the modernization paradigm are of particular importance: (1) modernization is a long-term process of (ultimately progressive) change; (2) this change represents a singular, overarching transition from traditional to modern; and (3) the transition brings homogeneity, because it ultimately results in growing convergence (of incomes, political institutions, systems of meritocracy, and the like). Likewise, it has generally been assumed, if at times only implicitly, that modernization entailed the interdependent and simultaneous transformation of the economic (through industrialization and/or urbanization), the social (through the growing importance of achievement in shaping stratification), and the political (through democratization). In this sense, the modernization paradigm carried normative connotations: the process was "good" in that it required the virtuous co-development of all three spheres of modern organization.

In economics, the most influential contribution to the modernization paradigm as it relates to inequality can be found in the work of Simon Kuznets (1955). In his classic formulation of what became known as the "inverted U-curve" hypothesis, Kuznets argued that inequality within nations rises in the early stages of economic growth as the population begins to move from rural (less wealthy) to urban (more wealthy) areas, becomes more pronounced at intermediate levels of development, and decreases thereafter as countries become more fully urbanized.

Figure 1.1 provides a rendition of three "moments" in the Kuznets transition, with stylized population deciles representing both the clustering of the population in "traditional" and "modern" arrays and the overall distribution of income between these deciles. The composition effects of the transition from a traditional to a modern array serve to enhance inequality and broaden the gap between the upper and lower bounds of the overall distribution, irrespective of the amount of inequality within each array. Eventually, the very same compositional effects, together with certain institutional transformations, would produce a reversal of the trend, leading ultimately to a reduction in inequality.

Throughout the 1960s and 1970s, in nearly every data set and for nearly every time period, when levels of economic development were plotted against levels of inequality, the resultant shape was a clear inverted U-curve, with fitted regression functions invariably revealing a negative, statistically significant quadratic term.[1] Scholars inferred from such cross-sectional snapshots that modernizing and modernized countries forming the cross-sectional *inverted U-shape* got to their positions by following an *inverted U-trajectory* over time, and they proceeded thereby to assess the relative weight of different independent variables in further shaping these transitions.[2]

Kuznets's hypothesis provides an eloquent and coherent synthesis of the analytical and theoretical assumptions that defined development economics in the 1960s and 1970s. Arguments regarding

Figure 1.1   The Kuznets Transition

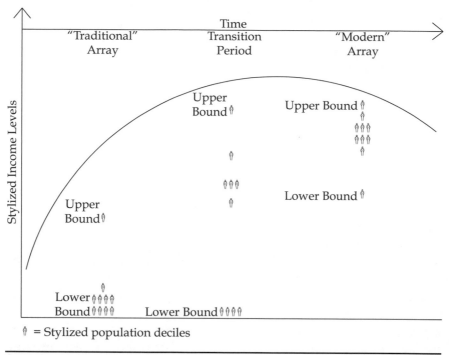

† = Stylized population deciles

Source: Authors' illustration.

the transition from a traditional (mostly but not only agricultural) sector to a modern (industrialized) sector drew on, and further strengthened, the dual-economy models that dominated the field (best exemplified by Lewis 1954, 1955/1960, 1958). The arguments also emphasized what various authors (for example, Kalecki 1942; Lewis 1954; Nurkse 1953) characterized as the "growth-equity trade-off" whereby "development must be inegalitarian" (Lewis 1976, 26).

In this sense, the popularity of the inverted U-curve hypothesis was grounded as well in the politics of the international policy-making arena. For example, the predictions of the hypothesis, the idea that "the dynamism of a growing and free economic society" (Kuznets 1955, 9) would eventually lead to a more egalitarian distribution of resources in countries undergoing modernization,

often helped policymakers implementing contentious development policies to justify rising inequality as a necessary, but short-
term, effect of economic growth. (Although, as Arturo Escobar
[1995, 80] notes, rising inequality was not somehow peripheral
to these development models; indeed, it "belonged to their
inner architecture.") Such uses of the inverted U-curve hypothesis
generally glossed over the careful qualifications Kuznets himself
advanced in his arguments; he explicitly acknowledged constructing the hypothesis on sparse empirical data, combined with much
theoretical speculation. Instead, policymakers coated their own
version of the hypothesis with the optimistic and self-righteous certitude that generally accompanies the construction of developmental
panaceas.

The inverted U-curve hypothesis—with its clear formulation,
broad theoretical fit, and intuitive appeal—became one of the most
significant and influential propositions in the social sciences, linking income inequality to demographic transitions, spurring worldwide research efforts to collect relevant income data, and framing
key issues in economic policymaking. For example, Kuznets's hypothesis shares many similarities with the arguments raised by Ester
Boserup (1970/1989) regarding the changing status of women during economic development: the ability of men to monopolize access
to property and political rights, as well as education, initially leads
to growing gender inequities that are eventually reversed as economic development reaches higher stages.[3] In this and many other
subfields, the inverted U-curve hypothesis became the main paradigm shaping the economic study of inequality during the last half
of the twentieth century, and it remains highly influential today (see
Moran 2005).[4]

Concurrently, sociologists developed their own emphasis on long-
term changes in inequality under the modernization paradigm,
albeit here the focus was social mobility. Early in the development
of the discipline, authors such as Émile Durkheim and Pitirim
Sorokin stressed the interdependence of the institutions of society
and the implications for social order as "primitive" societies underwent the transition to becoming modern, industrial ones. The first
studies of social mobility appeared at the beginning of the twentieth century, and in particular with Sorokin's (1927/1959) influential
work emphasizing the mobility of modern and Western societies

vis-à-vis the "immobile" societies of the past. The field of stratification and mobility became a central topic of sociological inquiry in the 1950s and 1960s with the pioneering work of David Glass (1954) in England, Gösta Carlsson (1958) in Sweden, and Natalie Rogoff (1953) in the United States, followed by the seminal volume by Peter Blau and Otis Dudley Duncan (1967). Over the next fifty years, the field became a prolific centerpiece of the sociological discipline; a bibliography of work on class structures, status attainment, and the intergenerational transmission of socioeconomic advantage would fill half this book.

From the beginning, sociological studies of mobility took the nation-state as the relevant unit of analysis and in particular concentrated on the wealthy, developed countries of North America and Europe. The field was linked to the modernization paradigm through what Robert Erikson and John Goldthorpe (1992) call the "liberal theory of industrialization." In a sense, the study of social mobility became an exercise in attempting to understand the right-hand portion of Kuznets's inverted U-curve where inequality begins to fall after industrialization and urbanization have taken hold. And paralleling the ways in which inequality is theorized in the development version of the modernization paradigm, the focus here was also on how social mobility is simultaneously a function of the long-term transitions to industrialization (driven by dynamic, rational changes in an increasingly differentiated social division of labor) or to political democracy (driven by the need for widely perceived opportunities to protect against class-based collective action). What came to be maintained, more or less factually in mainstream sociology, was that industrial or modern societies, in comparison to pre-industrial or traditional ones, have high rates of (upward) social mobility; that in these modern arrangements social origins do not preordain particular destinations; and that both of these patterns tend to become more predominant over time (Erikson and Goldthorpe 1992). Moreover, high and rising levels of mobility are more than pleasant by-products of the transition to modernity: they are pivotal and functionally necessary to the development of both industrialism and democracy. From a comparative perspective, an empirical consensus quickly formed that such overall patterns of social mobility are much the same across all industrialized countries (Lipset and Bendix 1959).

Crucial to the modernization paradigm, and underlying the literature on social mobility from the midtwentieth century until today, is the claim that modernity transforms the process through which individuals are allocated within the division of labor. In particular, a more complex division of labor (for example, as accompanying industrialization) requires a shift away from ascription and toward achievement as the leading criterion shaping stratification. Indeed, this became the key finding of *The American Occupational Structure* (Blau and Duncan 1967): in the midcentury United States, achievement processes (and most importantly educational attainment) were more important than ascriptive processes (family background) in determining one's station in life. In societies with expanding educational opportunities, the association between one's social origin and eventual destination weakens, and society becomes increasingly "open" as "meritocracy" comes to form the basis for social selection.

Of course, the extent to which such a transition has taken place has always been challenged. Many studies within sociology and other social sciences have argued that social mobility in the United States has been much more rigid than is usually described by scholars in the tradition of Blau and Duncan (see, for example, Bowles and Gintis 1976; Jencks et al. 1972; Kozol 1992; Wright 1979). Others have sought to establish the persistent significance of various forms of categorical inequality—most importantly but not only those involving class, race, and gender (for a useful overview of this literature, see Andersen and Collins 2007). Despite these criticisms, the quantitative study of social mobility and stratification continues to be guided largely by the consensus described here.

The economic development and social mobility literatures converged, in their own way, to construct what we term the modernization paradigm. While barely speaking to one another on some issues—the economic development literature focused on nations undergoing the transition from tradition to modernity, while social mobility studies analyzed almost exclusively nations already characterized by modernity—the two literatures complemented one another and jointly constructed a distinct theoretical and methodological perspective. Within this paradigm, theory and methodology were intricately linked because both were built on the premise that social inequality and social mobility are fundamentally shaped by universal processes of transition that take place within the boundaries of independent nation-states.

FROM A SINGLE PARADIGM TO EMPIRICAL FRAGMENTATION

In the last two decades of the twentieth century, several trends in within-country inequality led to a wave of studies challenging the inevitability of certain transitions assumed within the modernization paradigm. Observers now interpret these trends as suggesting that, instead of following a universal pattern, the impact of economic growth on inequality varies in significant ways across nations and over time. Sharing in common a rejection, for example, of the applicability of the Kuznets hypothesis to particular empirical cases, the current field of cross-national inequality tends to seek explanation of each set of observed within-country inequality trajectories through ad hoc arguments that do not attempt to provide an alternative overall theoretical framework for understanding global patterns of inequality.

Particularly important among these critical studies is a literature that focuses on the relationship between inequality and macro-institutional characteristics; this literature is itself split into various strands, each with its own approach and ad hoc explanations. Of these, two strands are particularly salient: one that focuses on high-income countries and seeks to explain divergent levels of inequality between them; and another that focuses more on economic development and seeks to contrast, for example, the "durable inequality" of Latin America and the "growth with equity" pattern of eastern Asia. We examine each of these two strands in some detail.

The literature focusing on income inequality in high-income countries takes as its point of departure that levels of inequality vary a great deal within this group and that countries with the highest levels of inequality—most notably the United States and the United Kingdom—have experienced a steady, decades-long increase in these levels. After a long period of relative stability, the distribution of income in the United States and the United Kingdom became noticeably more unequal beginning in the 1980s, spawning a subfield of inequality research seeking its explanation. As figure 1.2 illustrates, between 1980 and the early 2000s, the Gini index increased by over 18 percent in the United States and by 36 percent in the United Kingdom

Figure 1.2   Increasing Inequality in the United States and the United Kingdom

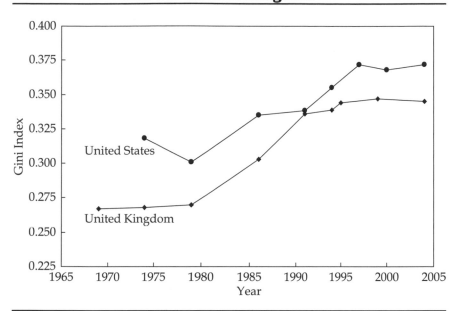

Sources: Authors' calculations based on Luxembourg Income Study (LIS) (2008).

(although, as we note later in this chapter, some caveats should be observed in assessing the relative magnitude of these increases).[5]

There are many ways to measure, or quantify in a single number, the amount of inequality contained in an income distribution (for reviews, see Allison 1978; Atkinson 1970; Jenkins 1991). Throughout the remainder of this book, we rely almost exclusively on the Gini index, the most highly regarded and the best-known summary measure of inequality. The Gini index varies from 1.0 under a condition of complete inequality (one unit has all the income) to 0.0 under a condition of complete equality (every unit has the same income). The highest observed Gini coefficients for countries, as we show later in the chapter, are in the mid-.500 range (Brazil), though they can go as high as the .700 range (South Africa), while the lowest observed coefficients are just above .200 (Sweden, Norway). A practical reason for using the Gini index is that international sources of data—the U.S. Bureau of the Census, the United Nations, the World Bank—usually report Gini coefficients as the only summary measure of inequality. Moreover, it is statistically preferable to other indicators because it is one of only two measures (the Theil coefficient being the other) that satisfies the most desired mathematical properties when the goal is to capture in a single number the degree of inequality present in a distribution (for elaboration, see the statistical appendix).

Bennett Harrison and Barry Bluestone (1988) labeled the rising Gini indices depicted in figure 1.2 "the great U-turn" and argued that increasing levels of inequality in wealthy nations were indicative of a historical shift that called into question the continued relevance of the inverted U-curve hypothesis in this context (see also Bluestone and Harrison 1982; Danziger and Gottschalk 1993).

Although no single "smoking gun" has been found to explain this rise in inequality (Gustafsson and Johansson 1999), debates tend to implicate various forms of economic restructuring that fall under the "globalization" rubric (Alderson and Nielsen 2002). According to these arguments, wealthy countries are experiencing the rise of a "new" economy in which high-value information and technological services have replaced manufacturing as the leading economic sector. In this new economy, changing patterns of trade, deindustrialization, skill-based technological transformations, increasing returns to skill and education, declining unionization, minimum-wage erosion, and increased capital and labor mobility (immigration) all combine to generate a bifurcated distribution of earnings. Shifts in the relative supply of and demand for skilled and unskilled workers result in downward pressures on the wages of the unskilled, while dramatically increasing returns to the skilled (Berman, Bound, and Griliches 1994; Bound and Johnson 1992; Katz and Autor 2000; Katz and Murphy 1992; Murphy and Welch 1992; for a critique of this approach, see Galbraith 1998). Falling (or at least stagnating) wages at the bottom of the distribution combine with rapidly rising wages at the very top, and this bifurcation acts as the driving force behind rising income inequality between households (Bluestone and Harrison 1982; Harrison and Bluestone 1988; Plotnick et al. 2000). The vast majority of inequality research in the United States over the last ten years incorporates this framework, focusing either on changes in the structure of the labor market, and subsequent returns to human capital, or on the institutional mechanisms that may (or may not) ameliorate these changes.

Table 1.1   Inequality Trends Across Europe: Gini Coefficients, 1990 to 2006[a]

	1990	2000	2006	Percentage Change
Austria	0.280	0.257	0.250[b]	−10.7
Belgium	0.232	0.279	0.280[b]	20.7
Denmark	0.236	0.225	0.228	−3.4
Finland	0.210	0.246	0.252	20.0
France	0.287	0.278	0.270[b]	−5.9
Germany	0.257	0.275	0.270[b]	5.1
Greece	—	0.333	0.340[b]	2.1
Ireland	0.328	0.313	0.320[b]	−2.4
Italy	0.303	0.333	0.320[b]	5.6
Luxembourg	0.239	0.260	0.268	12.1
Netherlands	0.266	0.231	0.260[b]	−2.3
Norway	0.231	0.250	0.256	10.8
Portugal	—	0.360[b]	0.380[b]	5.5
Spain	0.303	0.336	0.310[b]	2.3
Sweden	0.229	0.252	0.237	3.5
Switzerland	0.307	0.280	0.274	−10.7
United Kingdom	0.336	0.347	0.345	2.7
European Union (15)[c]	—	.290[b]	0.290[b]	0.0

Source: Authors' calculations based on Luxembourg Income Study (LIS) (2008).
[a]Not every country has data for that precise year. Data under column "1990" could be drawn from 1991 or 1989, for instance.
[b]European Commission (2008).
[c]Excludes Switzerland and Norway.

Given the widespread documentation of the trends in figure 1.2, a tendency developed to extrapolate the experience of the United States as representing a more general trend that all high-income nations have been experiencing economic restructuring and rising inequality over the last twenty years (see, for example, Friedman 2000; Smeeding 2002). But many high-income countries in fact have not experienced the type of upturn in inequality suggested by the U.S. and U.K. trend. Table 1.1 presents inequality levels across Europe over the last fifteen years as measured by the Gini index (for measurement specifications, see statistical appendix). Of the seventeen European countries in the table, nine show an actual decrease in inequality, or relatively no change (less than 5 percent), in the Gini index over the period. In only six countries does the Gini index change by more than 6 percent in either direction, and in each of these cases, changes since 2000 have all been less than 3 percent in either direction. The Gini index across the European Union as a whole fell by nearly 7 percent between 1995 and 2006, from .310 (European Commission 2008; not presented in the table) to .290, and was unchanged between 2000 and 2006. (For comparison, the Gini index for the United States depicted in figure 1.2 was .355 in 1994 and .372 in 2004.)

That the "great U-turn" phenomenon is not characteristic of all, or even most, high-income countries is confirmed as well by statistical analyses of the Luxembourg Income Study (LIS) database. Applying bootstrap resampling techniques, Timothy Patrick Moran (2006a) calculated statistical inference tests on the differences between Gini coefficients in the LIS and found more stability in inequality estimates in these countries (that is, differences in Gini coefficients attributed to sampling error or random chance) than statistically significant directional change. In contrast to a universal tendency toward rising inequality, the prevailing pattern in high-income nations—found in continental Europe and Canada—was characterized by either declining levels of inequality or relatively stable ones over the last twenty-five to thirty years.[6]

Although the data suggest more similarity of inequality experience than difference across wealthy nations, much of the recent social science literature on income inequality still focuses on explaining the relatively small variations that characterize distributional outcomes in these countries.[7] Some of these cross-national studies focus on divergent patterns of technological change: for example, Daron Acemoglu (2002, 1) argues that new technologies have been less skill-based in much of Europe than in the United States and that returns to education and skill increased less sharply in these areas (additionally, because the supply of skilled workers increased faster), leading to "less of an increase, or even no change," in wage inequality in these countries.

For others, drawing on a longer tradition of such comparative studies, the different trajectories of inequality among wealthy countries are the outcome of differences in political and institutional arrangements. Some argue, for example, that European labor policies and wage-setting institutions mitigate the tendency toward increasing earnings inequality (Acemoglu 2002; Blau and Kahn 1996; Freeman and Katz 1995; Nickell and Bell 1996). In particular, many studies find that labor union density significantly reduces inequality (Alderson and Nielsen 2002; Freeman 1993; Gustafsson and Johansson 1999) and that policy liberalism and leftist governments (Bradley et al. 2003; Brady 2003; Kelly 2004), high levels of democratic participation (Mueller and Stratmann 2003), and low public tolerance for inequality (Lambert, Millimet, and Slottje 2003) are all associated with more equal income distributions.[8]

The continued emphasis on comparative differences that prevails in the income inequality literature focusing on high-income countries runs counter to the interpretations advanced within what we characterized earlier as the cross-national literature on social mobility. The analysis of social mobility patterns is one of the longest traditions in the social sciences, and empirical findings from the subfield's seminal scholars became some of the signature contributions to sociology in the twentieth century. This literature is marked by a remarkable consensus—spanning from the first generation of mobility studies in the post–World War II period (Sorokin 1927/1959) to more recent contribution (for example, the collection of papers in Shavit and Blossfeld 1993)—that while cultural arguments focusing on American "exceptionalism" may have some merit in key regards, social mobility regimes show a substantial degree of similarity across wealthy nations and over long periods of time. As Stephen Morgan (2006, 5) states after his review of the historical mobility literature, "sociologists [have] established conclusively that exchange mobility patterns are remarkably similar across most industrial societies."[9]

For the most part, these separate literatures on inequality and social mobility rarely speak to each other. However, a new wave of mobility research was triggered by the "great U-turn" trend in the United States and the United Kingdom; these researchers seek to evaluate whether rising inequality was accompanied by offsetting increases in mobility between economic categories.[10] Illustrating a broader consensus among these recent studies, Stephen Morgan and Young-Mi Kim (2006, 182) conclude that "we have not found any evidence that recent increases in inequality will generate dramatic changes in patterns of social mobility. At best, quite modest changes are unfolding."

In short, these various literatures on inequality and mobility in wealthy countries move in different directions. The literature on social mobility uses ever-changing sources of data and increasingly sophisticated statistical techniques to show that wealthy countries are relatively open societies, with high rates of upward mobility attributed primarily to educational achievement. On the other hand, the literature on social inequality in wealthy countries, while either taking as given or setting aside such patterns of social mobility, has moved away from Kuznets's emphasis on a single transition to modern patterns of inequality to emphasize instead differences across nations and over time.

In the second salient strand of income inequality research that highlights the field's empirical fragmentation, a slightly different shift away from Kuznets has taken place. This is the more development-oriented literature that often contrasts the "growth with equity" pattern of East Asia with the "durable inequality" of Latin America. In what came to be labeled "the East Asian Miracle," rapid economic growth in the second half of the twentieth century was accompanied by rising incomes in the agricultural sector and diminishing urban-rural income gaps, allowing East Asian countries to experience rapid economic growth without significant increases in inequality (Birdsall, Ross, and Sabot 1997; Fei, Ranis, and Kuo 1979; Findlay and Wellisz 1993; Stiglitz and Charlton 2005; World Bank 1993). This "growth with equity" pattern contrasted during the same period with the trajectory of Latin America, where economic growth stayed uneven and high levels of inequality showed considerable persistence (Hoffman and Centeno 2003; Korzeniewicz and Smith 2000; Morley 1995).[11] The relatively high levels of inequality found in Latin America are illustrated in table 1.2.

As is well known, Latin America has some of the highest levels of inequality in the world: for example, Gini indices in 2006 were .528 for Panama, .580 for Jamaica, and .547 for Brazil. The lowest levels of inequality in table 1.2 for 2006—such as .428 for Uruguay and .455 for Venezuela—are still much higher than the highest levels in Europe shown in table 1.1—for example, .380 for Portugal and .345 for the United Kingdom. Moreover, these high rates of inequality have shown considerable persistence in recent decades: as shown in the table, the average Gini coefficient across Latin America and the Caribbean was .495 in 1990 and .502 in 2006—an overall change of less than 2 percent.

Table 1.2   Inequality Trends Across Latin America and the Caribbean: Gini Coefficients 1990 to 2006[a]

	1990	2000	2006	Percentage Change
Argentina	0.430	0.483	0.466	7.7
Bolivia	—	0.600	0.519	−13.5
Brazil	0.583	0.571	0.547	−6.6
Chile	0.537	0.540	0.532	−0.9
Colombia	—	0.554	0.544	−1.8
Costa Rica	0.422	0.439	0.474	11.0
Dominican Republic	—	0.500	0.503	0.6
Ecuador	—	0.542	0.513	−5.4
El Salvador	0.505	0.498	0.464	−8.8
Guatemala	—	0.520	0.467	−10.2
Honduras	0.515	0.548	0.534	3.6
Jamaica	0.551	0.580	0.580	5.0
Mexico	0.507	0.509	0.492	−3.0
Nicaragua	0.543	0.542	0.500	−8.6
Panama	0.538	0.544	0.528	−1.9
Paraguay	—	0.546	0.525	−3.8
Peru	—	0.510	0.466	−8.6
Uruguay	0.404	0.421	0.428	5.6
Venezuela	0.399	0.418	0.455	12.3
Regional Average	0.495	0.519	0.502	1.5

Source: Authors' compilation based on Socioeconomic Database for Latin America and the Caribbean (SEDLAC) (2008).
[a]Not every country has data for that precise year. Data under column "1990" could be drawn from 1991 or 1989, for instance.

By comparison, rates of inequality in East Asia have been significantly lower than in other parts of the world with similar levels of development. Many attributed lower initial inequality in East Asia to regional specificities in the interaction between markets and institutional arrangements. Some studies focused on major reforms following World War II that confiscated and redistributed land and other assets and imposed progressive taxation on wealth. In some countries, these government policies—such as wide adoption of Green Revolution technology, high investments in rural infrastructure, and limited taxation of agriculture—reflected a concerted "shared growth" approach to development that struck a more equal balance between rural and urban public investment and allowed rural incomes and productivity to rise more rapidly in East Asia than in other regions, thereby lessening the distributional impact of rural-urban disparities. For example, the government in Indonesia used rice and fertilizer price policies to raise rural incomes, and Malaysia introduced explicit wealth-sharing programs to improve the lot of ethnic Malays relative to the better-off ethnic Chinese (World Bank 1993). In subsequent decades, inequality remained low not only because of continued investment in rural non-agricultural activities but also because of the East Asian commitment to equitable access to education, which led to a rapid deepening of skills among the working population and widespread increases in human capital. But regardless of the particular explanation they privilege, these various arguments all point to comparative differences in policies and institutional arrangements that prevented a Kuznets-type transition from taking place in East Asia.

These comparative studies, then, join the literature on recent trends in inequality in wealthy countries in abandoning Kuznets's efforts to develop a single, overarching explanation of the relationship between economic growth and inequality. Studies on particular areas of the world continue to portray inequality as susceptible to significant change, but they replace Kuznets's theorizing on a single, overarching process of transition with a more empiricist evaluation of a multiplicity of possible causal variables that are capable of moving inequality in various alternative directions as they unfold in different subsets of countries. Constituting discrete bodies of literature that generally do not speak to one another, studies of inequality have moved toward empirical fragmentation.

Moreover, these studies often fail to acknowledge that each of the discrete groups of countries upon which they focus contains a relatively narrow range of inequality experiences. Across Europe, for example, the Gini index for 2006 ranges from .228 in Denmark to .380 in Portugal, and eleven countries have a Gini index less than .300 (table 1.1). Thus, in studies that use an OECD sample of countries, inequality in the United States is considered "high," but only in comparison to other wealthy countries. Similarly, in Latin America and the Caribbean (table 1.2), the Gini index in 2005 ranges from .428 in Uruguay to .580 in Jamaica, and twelve countries have a Gini index of .500 or above. The outcome of such discrete research frames is a restricted picture of cross-national inequality, since the majority of studies fail to even consider how their particular samples might fit within the broader universe of within-country inequalities.

We should add that in these empirical studies of trends in within-country inequality, a broad concern with the effects of "globalization" has displaced the previous concern with the effects of "modernization." But this is a displacement of terms rather than substance. In fact, debates about globalization often revisit many of the themes of the modernization paradigm, rendering much of the discourse on globalization as the modernization paradigm in a new guise.

Thus, the fundamental changes identified by the modernization paradigm—the decline of ascription and the growing importance of achievement in shaping stratification, the growing opportunities for social mobility—are much the same under theories of globalization. The difference is that now, when flows of people, goods, and money across nations have been growing dramatically relative to the immediate postwar era, there are greater concerns and debates about the uneven effects that these increased flows are likely to have on social inequality within "rich" and "poor" nations. These concerns have contributed further to greater fragmentation in the literature that focuses on trends in within-country inequality.

In short, the rejection of an overarching explanation of changes in inequality has left, on the one hand, a multiplicity of studies focused on developing ad hoc explanations for the divergent trends experienced at the turn of the century, and on the other, a set of unchallenged assumptions regarding the character of the changes that have taken place through modernization and/or globalization (for example, in patterns of social mobility). It is time to reframe these issues by revisiting the available data on inequality from a more world-historical perspective—that is, by considering global rather than discrete patterns of change in inequality.

PATTERNS OF WITHIN-COUNTRY INEQUALITY FROM A GLOBAL PERSPECTIVE

To examine patterns of inequality from a global perspective, a necessary step is to compare inequality measures on a scale that represents the full range of such measures observable in the world. We

Figure 1.3   Income and Inequality, Global Cross-Section, Circa 2000

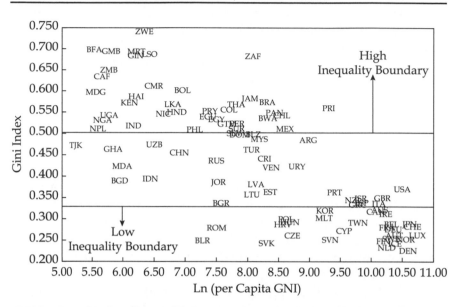

Source: See statistical appendix for data sources and country codes.

conduct such an exercise in figure 1.3, where the scale of Gini coefficients depicted on the *y*-axis ranges from the .200s to the .700s to fully capture the differences in inequality seen around the world. Figure 1.3 presents the Gini index and per capita gross national income (GNI) for ninety-six countries for 2000. Assembling these data is a long and complicated process because the relevant *comparable* information on national income distribution (Gini coefficients calculated using the same methodological specifications) is not readily available. The original sample we constructed is rigorous in its comparability (for specific methodological decisions, as well as the country codes used in the figure, see the statistical appendix). The sample includes data on national income distributions for over 84 percent of the world's population in 2000, providing confidence that the patterns we identify here are indeed relevant for the world as a whole.

Using the sample depicted in figure 1.3, we applied a bivariate cluster analysis to the cross-section, identifying two clear clusters of countries: a cluster of countries characterized by relatively low inequality (centered at a Gini index of .303, roughly at the level of Ireland), and a cluster of countries characterized by relatively high inequality (centered at a Gini index of .543, close to the figures for Ecuador).[12]

Using the results of the cluster analysis, we drew heuristic boundaries (set at plus or minus half a standard deviation from the mean of the two clusters) to establish sets of countries located either in the low- or high-inequality clusters. The resulting upper boundary of the low-inequality cluster is a Gini index of .329, so all countries with a Gini index below this figure constitute the low-inequality cluster of countries. Most high-income nations fall within the low-inequality cluster, including nearly all of western Europe, Japan, Canada, and Australia. Several eastern European countries fall within this cluster as well, as do several of the East Asian nations that have experienced high rates of growth in recent decades, such as Taiwan and South Korea.

The relevant threshold for the high-inequality cluster is a Gini index of .502. Nearly all the sampled countries in Latin America, the Caribbean, and Africa, as well as India, fall within the high-inequality cluster.

Interestingly, the United States falls outside of the heuristic boundary in the 2000 time period, illustrating that not all nations fit neatly into one of the two clusters. Indeed, as we discuss more extensively later in the book, the United States through much of its history has combined some of the features associated with high inequality (for example, a past of racial segregation) with those generally associated with low inequality (for example, a welfare state). In this respect, the United States has often represented a sort of "hybrid"—characterized at times by higher levels of inequality than those prevailing as a whole within the low-inequality cluster. There are several additional hybrid countries—such as Argentina and, more recently, China—as well as countries that have shifted in and out of one particular cluster (although, we should note, there are virtually no examples of countries shifting over time from one cluster into the other).

Figure 1.4 draws on scarcer longitudinal data to illustrate the relative stability in the late twentieth and early twenty-first centuries of inequality levels in several of the countries in each of the two clusters. Considerable stability exists over time within the (more limited) longitudinal data for countries in both clusters. Inequality levels indeed move up and down over time, but always within cluster boundaries. Thus, the most prevalent trend among both subsets of

**Figure 1.4   Trends in High and Low
Within-Nation Inequality**

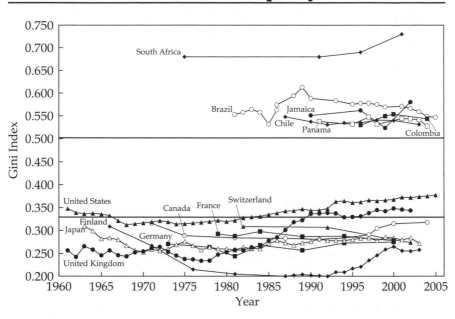

Sources: See statistical appendix.

countries can be interpreted as long-term relative stability of comparatively low, or comparatively high, levels of inequality when the world as a whole is the basis of comparison. The two clusters, then, tend to display within themselves what Sorokin (1927/1959) once denominated "trendless fluctuation."

    In the low-inequality cluster, the trajectories of the United States and the United Kingdom are bold-faced to highlight their uniqueness in moving in and out of the cluster. Furthermore, these countries have experienced a steady rise in inequality for several decades, suggesting a substantive shift in their relative levels of inequality as they move further away from the low-inequality cluster of nations. Yet, even with their rising inequality, these countries are still far from the high-inequality cluster, and in fact they continue to stay relatively closer to (and sometimes back into) the low-inequality cluster. In this sense, a global scale of inequality measurement—here used as a metaphor for the range of observations that are relevant for determining what constitutes high and low inequality—can make a significant difference in how inequality trends are depicted and relative comparisons are understood.

Broadly speaking, for all the current concern about the impact of globalization on inequality in high-income nations, the evidence so far suggests that this impact has not yet been significant. Even the rise of inequality in Belgium, Finland, Luxembourg, and Norway in the last fifteen years (see table 1.1) can be recast as a convergence to the levels of inequality seen in the rest of the low-inequality cluster, and the large increase in inequality still leaves them in 2006 with the lowest Gini coefficients across Europe. Indeed, once we shift the range of observations to recognize the whole range of Gini coefficients recorded worldwide, the inequality levels in these countries remain among the lowest in the world.

We should emphasize that the boundaries of the low- and high-inequality clusters are determined for heuristic purposes: different cluster analysis procedures, as well as changes in the countries included in the sample, can alter the precise position of these boundaries (although the alternative cluster procedures we tested for this exercise returned only slightly different boundary locations and always identified two distinct groups).[13] More importantly, the precise location of the boundaries and thresholds (surely to be addressed by future research) is less important than the extent to which adopting a global perspective identifies two clear inequality patterns, which we build on in subsequent chapters to reformulate key issues in the study of inequality.

In short, the current emphasis on differences and change within narrowly defined areas of the world (OECD, Latin America, East Asia) is largely misplaced. From a world-historical perspective, within-country inequality is characterized more by relatively narrow differences and trendless fluctuation within these areas than substantive, theoretically meaningful difference. Moreover, as we noted earlier, the vast majority of the quantitative studies of inequality are conducted in wealthy areas of the world (using cross-national data available from the EU, OECD, and other such places). As indicated by figure 1.3, this part of the world provides a very narrow range of national income distributions—a relatively small variance when considered within the whole range of within-country income distributions observed in the world. To the extent that practitioners consider these countries representative of a reasonable cross-national sample, their analysis contains only 14 percent of the world's population (as measured by the population of the twenty-two richest countries in the world in 2000). Such a focus on a narrow range of national income distributions tends to lead investigators to overemphasize the impact on inequality of variables that are less relevant worldwide or to overlook the impact of variables that might be significant worldwide, but not in the particular set of nations usually under investigation.

CONCLUSION

Reviewing the existing literature on within-country inequality, this chapter has found that existing studies generally do not consider what the parameters should be to define any given level of inequality as high or low, leading to what we characterize as empirical fragmentation in the inequality literature. We used an original database of measures of within-country inequality for ninety-six countries to explain why it is only by looking at the whole range of observable levels of inequality—that is, those that characterize the world as a whole—that we can identify these parameters. Using cluster analysis with our data, we identified two clearly discrete groups of nations: the low- and high-inequality clusters. We further showed that there has been considerable longitudinal stability in each of these two clusters, and we explained why establishing these clusters allows for greater precision in identifying when a trend should be considered representative of a significant shift from high or low inequality.

As we discuss in the following chapter, we can further build on these clusters as heuristic devices that bring greater clarity into the analysis of within-country inequality worldwide. Eventually, as we show, such an exercise allows us to revisit some of the fundamental premises of the modernization paradigm that we reviewed earlier in this chapter—the paradigm's focus on nation-states as independent paths of transition from tradition to modernity, its arguments regarding the shifting role of ascription and achievement in shaping social inequality, and the assumption that all systems of stratification follow similar paths after undergoing economic growth and urbanization. Paradoxically, as we discuss in the next chapters, this critical evaluation of the modernization paradigm can be carried out by taking advantage of some of the methodological advances made by Simon Kuznets in his studies of inequality.

CHAPTER 2

HIGH AND LOW INEQUALITY
AS HISTORICAL EQUILIBRIA

This chapter argues that the areas identified in the previous chapter as today having low and high levels of inequality are for the most part the very same areas that had relatively low and high levels of inequality during or even before the eighteenth century. This suggests both that contemporary patterns of inequality have an early historical origin and that they might be subject to path-dependencies, a possibility generally overlooked by the various twentieth-century approaches that emphasized a single universal transition from tradition to modernity.

Considerable evidence for the early historical origins of current patterns of inequality, and for subsequent path-dependencies, is advanced in a relatively recent institutional literature on inequality.[1] In this literature, alternative patterns of low and high inequality are used to explain relative success in attaining economic growth: institutions that offered greater protection for private property rights *and* greater access to opportunity for a majority of the population have been more conducive to growth, while more inegalitarian arrangements have been an obstacle to such growth.[2] Within this literature, Daron Acemoglu, Simon Johnson, and James Robinson (2002, 1233) argue that European colonialism led "to the development of institutions of private property" and relatively greater equity in areas that before the eighteenth century were deemed to be poor—such as the New England colonies—"while introducing extractive institutions or maintaining existing extractive institutions" that resulted in greater inequality in areas that at the time were deemed "prosperous"—such parts of Latin America, the Caribbean, and Africa.[3]

In this chapter, we review the evidence for the early origins and continued persistence of these high and low inequality patterns and then argue that such persistence in fact reveals what we characterize as two distinct historical equilibria that have existed at least since the eighteenth century (and possibly somewhat before). We denominate these distinct outcomes as high-inequality equilibria (HIE) and low-inequality equilibria (LIE). We indicate that indeed, as indicated in the relevant literature, HIE have usually entailed entrenched forms of categorical inequality relying on ascribed characteristics (such as race) as a basis for rather rigid patterns of social stratification.

THE HIGH-INEQUALITY PATTERN

Extractive institutions have produced some of the most unequal within-country distributions of income and wealth the world has ever seen. In Latin America, as indicated by Kenneth Sokoloff and Stanley Engerman (2000, 221), "the legally codified inequality intrinsic to slavery [and] greater inequality in wealth contributed to the evolution of institutions that protected the privileges of the elites and restricted opportunities for the broad mass of the population to participate fully in the commercial economy even after the abolition of slavery."[4] High inequality also prevailed in other areas where slavery and similar forms of labor exploitation and control played a crucial role, such as in the South of the United States and the colonized parts of Africa.

Institutional arrangements selectively excluding large sectors of the population from access to wealth and power were endorsed and sustained by the primarily European elites who benefited from such arrangements.[5] "In those societies that began with extreme inequality, elites were better able to establish a legal framework that insured them disproportionate shares of political power, and to use that greater influence to establish rules, laws, and other government policies that advantaged members of the elite relative to nonmembers" (Sokoloff and Engerman 2000, 223). Property rights, as a "set of social and economic relations [that defines] the position of each individual with respect to the use of scarce resources" (Furubotn and Pejovich 1972, 1139), were in place, but a high level of exclusion was constitutive of these arrangements.

Similar features are emphasized by studies that focus on other areas characterized by high inequality. In South Africa, for example, political pressures by employers and trade unions led to the persistence and reinforcement of a formal color bar used to exclude nonwhites from skilled jobs, combined with coercive labor arrangements deployed to secure workers for mining and manufacturing. This produced "a coherent system of racial discrimination and control in the economic realm that . . . provide[d] the linchpin for an entire social order based on segregation or apartheid" (Fredrickson 1981, 237).[6] State-enforced spatial separation of whites and nonwhites was a central pillar of apartheid.[7] The two other pillars were restricted access to education and political power. These inequalities have proven persistent—for some, inequality has become even more pronounced since the end of apartheid (Seekings and Nattrass 2005; Terreblanche 2002).

To be sure, there was considerable heterogeneity in the specific features that coercive labor arrangements assumed in different places and at different times.[8] Even the term "slavery" "does not define a single well-defined labor system any more than 'free labor' usefully describes the full range of non-slave labor relationships in the world" (Wright 2006, 5). In some situations, states played an active role in enforcing segregation within labor markets, while in others exclusionary arrangements were the outcome of more informal arrangements among white employers and/or trade unions; in some instances, territorial segregation was very pronounced and constantly enforced, while in others it was not. The lines of distinction are manifold.

While keeping in mind this heterogeneity, we can highlight what by now should be rather evident. The high level of inequality characterizing extractive institutions was made possible by the construction of between-group hierarchies, or what Charles Tilly (1999) calls "bounded categories" organized around ascribed characteristics.[9] The reliance on categorical inequality or ascribed characteristics is clearly what is behind the institutional arrangements that Eric Olin Wright (2006, 7) describes as "regimes of racial subordination, requiring explicit hierarchies of racial categories and statuses," regimes summarized by Fredrickson (1981) as "white supremacy."[10] In these arrangements, "the degradation of non-whites frequently served to bind together the white population, or some segment of it, to create a sense of community or solidarity that could become a way of life and not simply a cover for economic exploitation" (Fredrickson 1981, 70).

Through the past two centuries, white supremacy, in various forms, has provided a most powerful framework for justifying, maintaining, and defending the institutional arrangements characteristic of high inequality within countries.

High inequality within countries, in these situations, is a marker of the significant role played by *selective exclusion*—most often through white supremacy, but also through other ascriptive mechanisms—of significant sectors of the population from effective access, within their nation of residence, to various forms of opportunity (as embodied in markets, political arrangements, and even civil society association). Under selective exclusion, large sectors of the population are included in some markets and productive arrangements but are simultaneously excluded from others (for example, educational, political, and employment opportunities).[11] Through such arrangements, white elites, *but also* white workers, benefit from restricting competition in markets and political arenas: efforts by nonwhites and others to gain greater access to resources therefore often entailed fighting against selective exclusion.[12]

Of course, this does not indicate an absence of conflict or a lack of institutional interstices through which subordinate groups could find a measure of protection.[13] Even the Spanish colonial system, for example, entailed a legal system that allowed communities to assert the "corporatist property rights of Indian villagers, and such protection eventually came to be seen as a constraint upon property rights" (Garcia Swartz 1993, 78–79). Plantations throughout the Americas witnessed many forms of resistance to slavery, such as sabotage, flight, maronnage, and, occasionally, open rebellion and revolution (Moitt 2004b; Moitt and Henriques 2004; Stampp 1956). These various forms of resistance often generated a "legal recognition of the humanity of slaves" as "a pragmatic response to their ability to resist total domination by being insubordinate or rebellious [rather] than [as] a reflection of a humanitarian concern with their condition" (Fredrickson 1981, 71).

In the prevailing institutional arrangements, then, people with less power and wealth found opportunities to seek a measure of protection from further infringement by elites.[14] In this sense, the institutional arrangements associated with high inequality resulted from the inability of subordinate groups to radically transform the distribution of power and wealth in their favor, but they also derived from the ability of these subordinate groups to resist efforts by elites to further increase inequality.[15] The relevant question, then, sometimes should not be "why so high?" but "why not higher?"

Once established, systems of exclusion proved difficult to overturn. High inequality persisted through the nineteenth century—through the limited access of the majority of the population to public education,[16] the delayed extension of the universal franchise, and land policies favoring elites (Coatsworth 1993; De Ferranti et al. 2004; Hasenbalg 1985; North 2005; Sachs 2005; Silva 1985; Sokoloff and Engerman 2000).[17] In Latin America, for example, authors argue that inequality persistently limited effective access to education and created incentives for clientelism,[18] corporatism,[19] weak state capacities,[20] and Populism.[21] According to such an interpretation,

> the potential for the state to enact pro-equity changes is also constrained by informal political realities, whereby the excessive influence of elites and some well-organized middle-class groups (such as unions) on public discussions often results in the effective "capture" of the state. For public actions to be effective against entrenched interests, the state itself needs to be more or less autonomous from such influence. (De Ferranti et al. 2004, 127)

Moreover, as indicated by Easterly (2006, 267) "polarization because of inequality is a recipe for continuing underdevelopment. Either populist governments will seek to redistribute income to their supporters, or the elites will suppress democracy and mass education."

In colonial Africa through much of the twentieth century, elites continued to restrict and control population flows from rural to urban areas through various legal measures (such as pass laws and vagrancy ordinances). Access to property in urban areas, permanent residence, and formal work were often denied, and the labor force as a whole remained highly segregated. Even after the end of colonialism, African elites have continued to reproduce the economic segregation they inherited. As noted by Mike Davis (2007, 96):

> Despite rhetorics of national liberation and social justice, [elites] have aggressively adapted the racial zoning of the colonial period to defend their own class privileges and spatial exclusivity.

> Sub-Saharan Africa is the extreme case. Even Addis Ababa, one of the relatively few sub-Saharan cities with an autochthonous origin, has preserved the racist imprint of its brief Italian occupation—now in the form of economic segregation.

In short, the high-inequality pattern has been characterized by systematic exclusion, most often articulated through the continued reliance on ascriptive criteria to limit access to economic, social, and political opportunity.

THE LOW-INEQUALITY PATTERN

In contrast to these patterns of high inequality, parts of the world originally characterized by lower inequality and later by high levels of income (leaving aside for now the areas of low inequality that experienced low levels of income for much of the twentieth century) are presented in the literature as having undergone a very different pattern of distribution early in their modern history. According to Sokoloff and Engerman,

> while essentially all the economies established in the New World began with an abundance of land and natural resources relative to labor, and thus high living standards on average, other aspects of their factor endowments varied in ways that meant that the great majority were characterized virtually from the outset by extreme inequality in wealth, human capital, and political power. From this perspective, the colonies that came to compose the United States and Canada stand out as somewhat deviant cases. (2000, 220; see also Engerman and Sokoloff 1997)

Why deviant? One line of interpretation points to endowments: in colonies such as those in New England, "land was cheap and labor was costly. Such circumstances were radically different from those found elsewhere in the hemisphere, and fostered a remarkable degree of equality" (De Ferranti et al. 2004, 110).[22] These circumstances also fostered little interest by Europeans in migrating to North America, since "low returns per land" were perceived to provide "limited prospects for attaining gentlemanly status" (De Ferranti et al. 2004, 111); the region as a whole was perceived by contemporaries to be of marginal interest, at least until "European perceptions of the opportunities available in the region changed."[23]

In addition to the original impact of land and labor endowments, the current literature explains the persistence of low inequality as a consequence of more equitable access to property and political rights.[24] From the very beginning in Australia, for example, early settlers, many of whom were ex-convicts, "demanded jury trials, freedom from arbitrary arrest and electoral representation" (Acemoglu et al. 2001, 8).[25] In colonial North America, in contrast to the Latin American colonies, "the ubiquitous regulatory and fiscal interventions of the Spanish and (to a lesser degree) Portuguese colonies did not exist," "colonies successfully revolted" at efforts by colonial authorities to raise taxes, and "the regulatory acts of local and provincial governments were subject to the constraints of the common law, which protected subjects from arbitrary officials and provided the basis for the relatively untrammeled mobility of both capital and non-slave labor" (Coatsworth 1993, 19).[26]

Along similar lines, Jeffrey Sachs (2005, 33–35) explains that industrial growth after the eighteenth century came to be centered in England because, besides being a "leading center . . . of Europe's scientific revolution, having the adequate natural resources, and enjoying geographical advantages," "British society was relatively open, with more scope for individual initiative and social mobility than most other societies in the world," and "Britain had strengthening institutions of political liberty."

We should note that while portrayed as inclusive in comparison to within-country HIE, the property and political rights characteristic of within-country LIE were generated through (often violent) imposition over other arrangements (including other forms of linking human communities to their environments) that might have been characterized by even lower inequality. The very creation of national states in "nations of recent European settlement" required the subordination or elimination of native populations.[27] Within-country LIE in areas such as the United States and Canada eventually developed as institutional arrangements both alternative to within-country HIE (for example, slavery in the South of the United States) and proscriptive of (and inimical to) arrangements entailing even lower inequality (as in the case of Native Americans in the "open frontiers" of areas of recent settlement, or China and India during the nineteenth century).[28] Just as we previously asked "why not higher?," the relevant question here might be "why not lower?"

We should also note that democracy was not an automatic by-product of economic growth. Agency played a crucial role. In both the "western offshoots" and Europe, according to Acemoglu and Robinson (2000, 1), the extension of political rights and democratization was ultimately a response to the threat of revolution, insofar as "the franchise acted as a commitment to future redistribution and prevented social unrest" (for a similar line of argument for a later period, see Stephens 1989). According to the institutional literature, the extension of the franchise was followed by a more progressive tax system and the use of resources to provide universal access to education (Acemoglu and Robinson 2000, 21). Eventually, by the twentieth century, such arrangements would include the development of a welfare state that further facilitated the type of inclusion absent in situations of high inequality.[29] A considerable literature has developed that distinguishes various patterns of interaction between welfare states and market regulation—exploring, for example, the "three worlds" classification schema developed by Esping-Anderson (1990) (for example, Arts and Gelissen 2002; Gornick and Jacobs 1998; Janoski and Hicks 1994). Much of the literature on economic inequality discussed in the previous chapter, in fact, attempts to assess whether a retrenchment is taking place in the relative importance of the institutional arrangements characteristic of the welfare state and/or to parse the relative impact of various welfare state measures on differences in inequality (for example, Blyth 2002; Campbell 2004; Castles 2004; Huber and Stephens 2001; Korpi 2003; Pierson 2001).

From a more global perspective, however, differences between welfare states in wealthy countries (like differences in their levels of inequality) are strikingly minimal when compared to the institutional arrangements (or levels of inequality) that characterize the high-inequality pattern. As in our discussion of Gini index differences in chapter 1, such comparisons become evident only when the world as a whole is taken as the relevant unit of analysis.

As opposed to situations of high inequality, then, low inequality appears to have entailed the gradual displacement of inequalities based on ascription by those that increasingly result from achieved characteristics (but with important and significant restrictions on the relative extent of inclusion and exclusion, involving what Ira Katznelson (2005, 166) denominates "compounded advantages and disadvantages"). This transition to modernity, with the purportedly growing prevalence of achievement in shaping stratification, has been the focus of the mobility literature discussed in the previous chapter.

High-inequality institutional arrangements can be traced back to colonialism and slavery, but it is less clear how far back we can trace the institutional origins of low inequality (particularly in continental Europe) or how we can assess the *relative* significance of changes in inequality in these latter areas prior to the nineteenth century.[30]

There is considerable confusion, as well, in the discussion of nineteenth-century trends in countries characterized today by relatively low levels of inequality. Some evidence indicates, as Kuznets (1955) argued, that the industrialization of today's wealthy countries in the nineteenth century was accompanied by rising within-country inequality, at least until the First World War. Jeffrey Williamson (1991, 11), for example, indicates that "inequality in Europe and America was at its zenith on the eve of World War One," and he makes the (probably implausible) claim that "the extent of that inequality was very similar to the most inegalitarian NICs of today, like Brazil."[31]

On the other hand, the very same literature indicates that this rise in inequalities was limited to few nations and/or did not last long. Some argue that Britain had begun to experience a leveling in inequality already by the 1860s, when "the income shares at the top fell.., the shares at the bottom rose, the relative pay of the unskilled improved, the premium on skills declined, and the earnings distribution narrowed" (Williamson 1991, 15; see also Kuznets 1955). Similar declines in inequality have been claimed for Australia after the 1850s and for various areas in Scandinavia beginning around 1850 through 1870 (Kaelble and Thomas 1991).

But establishing whether or not these trends represented a significant departure from previous levels of inequality is a topic calling for more comparative future research. The available historical literature, just like the contemporary studies of inequality and stratification we reviewed in the previous chapter, largely does not discuss trends and patterns of income distribution in a global comparative perspective.

Instead, this literature tends to focus exclusively on today's high-income nations, where the extent of variation might be minimal when recast within a more global framework. As in our discussion of contemporary trends in inequality in chapter 1, it is only by adopting a world-historical perspective that we can better determine which trends and patterns are "significantly" distinct, and which represent Pitirim Sorokin's (1927/1959) "trendless fluctuation."

But regardless of whether the nineteenth century was characterized by significant changes in inequality from a global perspective, the evidence does indicate that by World War I the United States and high-income countries in Europe had most definitely experienced a "revolutionary leveling," manifested in a decline along all available measures of income inequality (Williamson 1991, 13–15; see also Fogel 2004).[32] This is what Kuznets (1955, 9–17) identified as the institutional and political changes inherent in "the dynamism of a growing and free economic society," including shifts in the economic and political expectations regarding the "long-term utility of wide income inequalities"; the growth of a "native" urban population "more able to take advantage of the possibilities of city life in preparation for the economic struggle"; the "growing political power of the urban lower-income groups"; and the resulting increase of "protective and supporting legislation" (similar arguments can be found in Stephens 1989). Thereafter, inequality within these particular nations seems to have either remained stable or even declined between the 1930s and the early 1970s.

Our emphasis on equilibria, then, does not mean that no changes have taken place in rates of inequality, nor that the relative distribution of resources among various actors has ceased to be an issue of contention. As in the areas characterized by HIE, agency has mattered, and at various times has led the distribution of income and wealth to move toward greater or less equity. Moreover, from the point of view of the actors involved within LIE countries, these changes in the distribution are certainly experienced as significant, and they mobilize accordingly. But from a world-historical perspective, these changes are less salient.

The group of nations characterized today by low levels of inequality, then, is composed largely of areas that had relatively low levels of inequality in the nineteenth century, and the same is largely true of countries characterized today by high levels of inequality.[33] In contrast to the previous preoccupation with the impact of economic growth and the transition to modernity on levels of inequality, institutional path-dependencies have emerged as the single most important variable predicting current levels of inequality.

THE HIGH AND LOW PATTERNS AS EQUILIBRIA

This historical persistence of two distinct patterns of within-country inequality suggests that we are in the presence of two alternative institutional equilibria—what we characterize in the remainder of this book as high-inequality equilibria and low-inequality equilibria.

According to the *Oxford English Dictionary,* in situations of equilibria, "opposing forces or influences are balanced." In our patterns, efforts by some actors to shift distributions in their favor lead to responses by other actors that tend to return these distributions toward their original state. In this sense, the institutional arrangements characteristic of high and low inequality were the slow product of, but also served to generate anew, particular arrays of social forces.[34] In other words, at both ends of the spectrum of within-country inequality, the arrays of forces manifested in the institutional arrangements associated with the persistence of both high and low inequality seem to be associated with equilibria.

Other authors in the past have emphasized such equilibria in explaining the persistence or resilience of high and low inequality. For example, focusing on low inequality in high-income nations, Gunnar Myrdal (1957/1964, 25) referred to "complex network[s] of systems of regularized public interferences of all sorts which have the common purpose of counteracting the blind law of cumulative social change, and hindering it from causing inequalities between regions, industries and social groups." With a similar focus, Sorokin (1927/1959, 46) underlined the key role of processes that, while operating "permanently and smoothly" to promote growing inequality (or stratification), generate countervailing "forces and interventions which . . . seem to work convulsively and spasmodically, and manifest themselves clearly only from time to time."[35]

In both HIE and LIE, institutional arrangements enhance the access to resources of some sectors of a given population (thereby enhancing inclusion) through measures that simultaneously restrict the relative access to resources (or entail the exclusion) of other sectors within that population.[36] That institutional arrangements regulating inclusion and access have a direct impact on the distribution of resources is a point that has been made throughout the history of the social sciences. In his *Wealth of Nations* (1776/1976), for example, Adam Smith argued that the institutional regulation of competition is what allowed towns to attain greater control over resources than the countryside (or masters to gain relative to workers,[37] or teachers relative to students).[38] For Smith (1776/1976, II, 236), in fact, a fundamental role of institutions (such as civil government and private property) was to provide "for the defense of the rich against the poor, or of those who have some property against those who have none at all."

Broadly, institutional arrangements involve

> a public system of rules which defines offices and positions with their rights and duties, powers and immunities, and the like. These rules specify certain forms of action as permissible, others as forbidden; and they provide for certain penalties and defenses, and so on, when violations occur.... An institution may be thought of in two ways: first as an abstract object, that is, a possible form of conduct expressed by a system of rules; and second, as the realization in the thought and conduct of certain persons at a certain time and place of the actions specified by those rules. (Rawls 1971, 55)[39]

More specifically in relation to inequality, institutional arrangements have "[historically distributed] fundamental rights and duties and [historically determined] the division of advantages from social cooperation" (Rawls 1971, 7).

Douglass North (1981, 1990, 2005) advanced similar arguments in his effort to bring an institutional focus into economic theory. For North (1990, 3), "institutions are the rules of the game in a society or, more formally, are the humanly devised constraints that shape human interaction. In consequence they structure incentives in human exchange, whether political, social, or economic. Institutional change shapes the way societies evolve through time and hence is the key to understanding historical change." Institutional arrangements are persistent: they "give rise to organizations whose survival depends on the perpetuation of those institutions and which hence will devote resources to preventing any alteration that threatens their survival" (North 2005, 51). Most fundamentally, for North, institutions have an impact in shaping property rights, transaction costs, and distributional outcomes (see also Campbell 2004).

Polanyi (1944/1957, 37) suggests that institutions shape distributional outcomes by "altering the rate of change, speeding it up or slowing it down as the case may be." At times, institutional arrangements protect a given population by shielding it from the competitive pressures of markets, in fact *slowing down* the rate at which the relevant parties experience dislocation. In other instances, the role of institutions is precisely the opposite: to provide mechanisms through which to *accelerate* the rate at which innovations are introduced. Historically, the institutional arrangements shaping inequality have combined both sets of strategies, with politically significant actors *accelerating* the introduction of some innovations or dislocations in fields in which they hold various kinds of competitive advantages, while simultaneously *slowing down* and restricting the rate at which innovations or dislocations are introduced in fields in which they have fewer or more limited competitive advantages. The ability to deploy such arrangements is unevenly distributed among actors within and between nations.

Institutional arrangements are key to understanding the LIE and the HIE. But HIE and LIE are not, as much of the new institutional literature would have it, a simple or automatic by-product of the relative availability of different resource endowments. Efforts by elites to gain greater access to specific economic resources have certainly shaped some institutional outcomes, but so have the responses to these efforts—social and political conflict more broadly, then, have been at the core of the arrangements that came to constitute the areas under HIE and LIE. (For example, the extension of frontiers in sixteenth-century Brazil and the nineteenth-century United States involved winners and losers in recurring conflicts over the conditions that would come to characterize the private appropriation of resources.)

Likewise, while emphasizing equilibria, we do not mean to imply that HIE and LIE arrangements have been stable and fixed in time. Even in situations of HIE, the prevailing systems of categorical inequality have not been immutable, but rather, paraphrasing

Fredrickson (1981, xvii), "a changing set of relationships that can only be understood within a broader historical context that is in itself constantly evolving and thus altering the terms under which [the relevant actors] interact." Key to the institutional arrangements that characterize HIE and LIE, then, are multilayered and shifting constructions of solidarities, cleavages, and social identities that *in their overall interaction* generate continuities over time in income distributions.

In this regard, the relative persistence of inequality as measured by a Gini index serves as a metaphor for equilibria. An equilibrium means that mechanisms are at play that transform big inputs, such as large-scale social change, into little output (as measured, in our case, by changes in overall inequality). Within this stability, it is possible and even likely that substantive changes will take place in the relative standing of particular groups or that these groups will experience these changes as real and highly significant (for example, manufacturing workers in the United States). Moreover, it is precisely through the active reaction of people that equilibrium comes into being. As we emphasize throughout this book, whether or not a situation of equilibrium is taking place requires an appropriate unit of analysis.

Of course, as we indicated in the previous chapter on a closely related issue, not every single nation in the world fits neatly and always into an LIE or HIE path. The little evidence we have available suggests that within-country inequality was low in pre-twentieth-century China and India (and perhaps Japan), but that institutional arrangements in these areas differed from those we have identified for today's wealthy countries. Kenneth Pomeranz (2005, 33), for example, compares the few estimates available on the distribution of wealth in late-nineteenth-century China to England and observes that in both countries "there is some indication that disparity between the poor and the very rich was not very large." Boxhong Li (2005, 66) observes that in Jiangnan province in China during the eighteenth and nineteenth centuries "complaints could be heard repeatedly from employers about farm labor becoming more and more expensive." Saito (2005) finds no evidence for rising inequality or wage differentials in eighteenth- and nineteenth-century Japan, a finding he attributes to rising agricultural productivity and the absence of a town-countryside gap. The lack of such a sectoral imbalance appears to have been more crucial in these regions.

HYBRIDITY AND THE UNITED STATES

Moreover, there are nations moving in and out of HIE or LIE, or exhibiting patterns of inequality that do not fall clearly into one path. As we noted in the previous chapter, the United States has for long periods of time been clearly within the LIE but has occasionally moved out of this particular cluster into the intermediate zone; such a mixed pattern can be seen in figure 1.4. More substantially, the historical trajectory of the United States suggests a mix of some of the institutional arrangements characteristic of LIE with some HIE characteristics. (Argentina appears to represent a similarly hybrid case, except that it has moved in between the HIE cluster and the intermediate zone.)

The hybridity of the United States makes sense in relation to the historical literature. Prior to the nineteenth century, the United States included both the region that usually is characterized as the most salient example of LIE (the New England colonies) and the area that embodies the central features of HIE (the slave-owning South). One, as portrayed in the new institutional literature discussed earlier in this chapter, was both a region and a broader pattern of social interaction that from their very origin appeared to embody high social mobility and the prevalence of widespread economic opportunity; the other was an area and a set of practices that embodied the persistent and deep inequalities enmeshed in racial intolerance.[40]

From such a perspective, a history of slavery and the persistence of categorical inequalities after its abolition (not only in the South) brought the United States closer to situations of HIE elsewhere. But simultaneously, other institutional arrangements—for example, the emergence of the New Deal, the redistributive effects of Keynesian economic policies, and the expansion of economic mobility through growing educational and employment opportunities—generated a broader tendency to move levels of inequality closer to a situation of LIE.[41]

Of course, we should be careful in assessing the relative prevalence of inclusion and exclusion on a national scale. True, for many years in the South of the United States "a thoroughgoing program of legally enforced racial segregation" served to maintain "the unyielding inequality mandated by Jim Crow" (Katznelson 2005, 4–5; see also Wright 2006). As in other situations of HIE, "the formal political system [in the South] utilize[d] race to exclude adults from citizenship and full access to civil society. Private terror combined with public law and enforcement to make this political system authentically totalitarian" (Katznelson 2005, 19). These arrangements would come to be targeted by the civil rights movements of the 1950s and 1960s.

But the South was not the only place where categorical inequality prevailed. Exclusion adopted different forms elsewhere but was widely prevalent as well (Fredrickson 1981). In the North, "the linchpin of racial inequality . . . was residential segregation" (Massey 2007, 58), and it remained so well toward the end of the twentieth century. National institutions such as the armed forces remained highly segregated throughout World War II as, in a "military version of white supremacy,"

> the positions, instruction, and final placement that black soldiers did not enjoy were secured by whites, many of whom entered the military with limited experience, weak schooling, poor horizons, and provincial understanding. For most African American individuals, and certainly for the group as a whole, war service ended with a wider gap between whites and blacks, as white access to training and occupational advancement moved ahead at a much more vigorous rate. (Katznelson 2005, 111–12)[42]

Moreover, even the institutional developments that brought the country closer to LIE, such as the development of the New Deal and Fair Deal, were accompanied by significant exclusion and "launched new and potent sources of racial inequality," so that "the federal government, though seemingly race-neutral, functioned as a commanding instrument of racial privilege" (Katznelson 2005, 18).[43] For example, upon the end of the war, the GI Bill, characterized by Katznelson (2005, 113–14) as the "legislation [that] created middle-class America" by enhancing access to housing, education, and jobs, "was deliberatively designed to accommodate Jim Crow [and its] administration widened the country's racial gap." Owing in part to such programs "of affirmative action granting white Americans privileged access to state-sponsored economic mobility" (21), categorical inequality showed considerable persistence.

As noted by Massey (2007, 50), "until the 1960s, rising incomes and declining inequality were confined mainly to households headed by white males and came at the expense of subordinated women and minorities."[44] These patterns of exclusion began to give way with the rise of the civil rights movement in the 1950s and 1960s: a decline in wage disparities between whites and African Americans, for example, "accelerated markedly in the 1960s and 1970s" (85). But over the last twenty years, the decline of the gap has again slowed down. For many, as Massey (2007, 109) explains, "overt racial discrimination largely ended, but discrimination itself did not disappear. Rather, now that naked racism is publicly condemned and discrimination is illegal, discriminatory practices have gone underground, becoming more subtle but remaining quite effective in perpetuating racial stratification."

In short, from the point of view of the interaction between LIE and HIE within the United States, the twentieth century was characterized by two simultaneous stories. First, institutional arrangements characteristic of LIE became more prevalent through the twentieth century and had the general effect of lowering the overall level of inequality. First, institutional arrangements characteristic of LIE became more prevalent through the twentieth century and had the general effect of lowering the overall level of inequality between the 1920s and the 1970s.

On the other hand, this decline did not entail the constant displacement of the exclusionary arrangements characterizing HIE by the more inclusionary arrangements characterizing LIE. Instead, many of the same arrangements that ensured movement toward LIE included features that strengthened or reproduced patterns of exclusion characteristic of HIE during the 1930s and 1940s, particularly in regard to white supremacy and the persistence of categorical inequality. By the 1960s and 1970s, however, and in the face of significant challenges by social movements and organized political forces, many of the institutional arrangements characteristic of HIE began to be dismantled, generating further advances in the reduction of inequality.

But parallel to these processes, and often receiving less attention in the relevant literature, was another type of interaction between

LIE and HIE. In this interaction, the institutional arrangements characteristic of LIE were constructed and consolidated by forcefully imposing such arrangements over alternative institutional arrays characterized by even lower LIE or by strengthening barriers designed to exclude other populations from entry. Both these processes were central to nation-building.

The expansion of the western frontier in the United States often is portrayed as part and parcel of the persistence of LIE: as opposed to other areas of the world where property became more concentrated, white settlers and squatters in the United States mobilized in opposition to the expansion of slavery in the Northwest Territory and held an edge over wealthy landowners and land speculators derived from the difficulty faced by the latter in trying to enforce a more unequal distribution of property over vast distances (Clark 1993, 201; see also Wright 2006). But such private property rights, relatively equitable for white settlers as they might have been, had to be imposed on other peoples (namely, Native Americans) through the systematic deployment of violence.

This violence is often understated in the literature. Daniel Garcia Swartz (1993, 76), for example, notes that "native North Americans were actually pushed westwards and an open-frontier society arose," and Hermann Wellenreuther (1993, 100) observes that "as in colonial times until 1871 Indians remained something of a barrier to territorial expansion." Christopher Clark (1993, 201) avoids such a depersonalized portrayal:

> Republican ideology helped legitimate the process of seizing Native American land for the purposes of settlement, giving the appearance of equity and legality to the treaties and land deeds which transferred millions of acres to white ownership, even when those formalities were merely a screen for theft. By making agrarian society the ideal of "civilization," it legitimated the extirpation of supposedly inferior Native American cultures.

Much of the decline of the Native American population in today's United States occurred over the nineteenth century (Thornton 2000), although the relative impact of depopulation—as driven by disease, expropriation, and violence—differed somewhat depending on the "wide range of responses" of existing (and sometimes new) tribes.[45]

Overall, however, the very same property arrangements that entailed relatively lower inequality for the white population subjected native peoples to much greater inequality than they had experienced ever before. In this regard, recent research reveals that even by the mid-nineteenth century nomadic peoples from the Plains were perhaps the tallest people in the world—the outcome of good nutrition, less exposure to endemic diseases, organizational flexibility in the face of adversity, and, most likely, less inequality and stronger social safety nets than those prevailing among either Europeans or European descendants in the New World (see also Steckel 1995; Steckel and Prince 2001).

In this sense, if one side of the "Janus face" of the legal system as it developed in the United States in the nineteenth century entailed protection of white family farmers and settlers, in response to demands from below, the other side entailed the massive expropriation of non-whites.[46] The establishment of LIE required the forceful elimination of even lower LIE.

The case of the United States illustrates that not all nations fall neatly into a HIE or LIE category, but at the same time it highlights the usefulness of such a distinction for describing the historical trajectory at hand. Moreover, while there are additional examples of hybrid cases, such as Australia or Argentina, it is noteworthy that there appear to have been virtually no recent cases of countries moving from one cluster into the other; historically, the only cases approaching such a pattern might have been some of the transitions in and out of socialism during the twentieth century (although the longitudinal data on these areas restrict our ability to treat this topic in sufficient depth). Moreover, even in the case of these hybrids, the distinction between LIE and HIE provides a useful heuristic tool for moving through the available cross-national data on inequality and highlighting what we deem to be theoretically relevant features of the phenomenon in question.[47] We continue to use this distinction, albeit with important revisions, in the remainder of the book.

CONCLUSION

In this chapter, we have used evidence for the historical persistence of high and low levels of within-country inequality to identify what we heuristically define as high-inequality equilibria (HIE) and low-inequality equilibria (LIE): in each of these conditions, prevailing institutional arrangements produce considerable stability in patterns of stratification. These equilibria tend to invalidate the notion of a single universal transition from tradition to modernity. Instead, empirical research on historical patterns of inequality has revealed contrasting institutional paths that show persistence and little substantive change over time in overall levels of inequality. Moreover, this expanded comparative perspective represents a significant improvement over approaches that focus exclusively on specific subsets of countries (for example, wealthy nations or OECD nations) without situating them within a broader world-historical perspective.

But much of the new institutional literature on inequality tends to retain an emphasis on the nation-state as the crucial unit of analysis. What we have designated as HIE and LIE tend to be explored in this literature as contrasting patterns of inequality, but in a sense they evoke the tradition-modernity duality ascertained in the modernization paradigm—now high inequality is represented as more of a persistent trap preventing economic growth over the long run, but low-inequality arrangements continue to embody much of what was virtuous in the older paradigm. As in the modernization paradigm we discussed in chapter 1, such an approach again tends to portray situations of high and low inequality as relatively independent paths of institutional development and fails to explore the historical interaction between both sets of arrangements. The remainder of our book turns to a critical exploration of such interactions, as well as of the broader impact that HIE and LIE arrangements have had on historical inequality.

CHAPTER 3

HIGH INEQUALITY, LOW INEQUALITY, AND CREATIVE DESTRUCTION

Having established the importance of thinking about patterns of within-country inequality in terms of high-inequality equilibria (HIE) and low-inequality equilibria (LIE), as well as the need to understand the considerable historical persistence of these equilibria, this chapter turns to expanding on the relationship between HIE and LIE. For, while much of the new institutional literature approaches situations of high and low inequality as representing independent institutional paths, our effort to rethink historical inequality calls for reconceptualizing HIE and LIE as eminently relational and interacting over time.

The new institutional literature on the legacy of inequality portrays "extractive institutions" as associated with forms of organization of production and markets that by the nineteenth century had become outdated. Thereafter, national institutional arrangements characterized by high inequality—where property and political rights remain restricted, and "the concentration of political and social power in the hands of a small elite implies that the majority of the population risks being held up by the powerful elite" (Acemoglu, Johnson, and Robinson 2002, 17)—became less suited for attaining sustained growth. According to this interpretation, national institutional arrangements characterized by relatively lower inequality and greater protection for property rights followed the opposite path, thus extending opportunities in ways that generated greater economic growth. These divergent paths of high and low within-country inequality purportedly explain, then, differential rates of economic growth and the persistence of an income gap between wealthy and poor nations.

Although the new institutional literature makes an important empirical contribution to the study of inequality, such an approach tends to portray paths of low or high inequality as if they emerged independently from one another. In this regard, the new institutional literature replicates some fundamental assumptions that prevailed earlier in the modernization approaches, whereby processes of economic growth and income distribution within individual nations are understood to be largely independent from those that characterize other nations. By contrast, a world-historical perspective allows us to rethink the eventual competitive advantages of the institutions involved in LIE since the nineteenth century as having emerged precisely in response to certain rigidities that came to characterize the coercive institutions characteristic of HIE. That analysis is the purpose of this chapter.

RETHINKING HIGH-INEQUALITY EQUILIBRIA AS INNOVATION

To begin, we must abandon the preconception that the institutional arrangements of HIE have always been intractably tied to inefficient forms of organization of production and markets. In fact, after European colonization and well into the eighteenth century, the areas characterized by HIE (for example, Latin America and the Caribbean), where coercive labor arrangements (such as slavery or the forced recruitment of indigenous populations) were used in high-yielding activities (commercial agriculture, mining), constituted in their time a world epicenter for the creation and accumulation of wealth.[1]

Plantations, for example, provided a very effective and innovative basis for the organization of large-scale production in commercial agriculture.[2] Key among these innovations was the ability of owners to impose unprecedented levels of labor discipline in what Sidney Mintz (1985, 47) characterizes as "a synthesis of field and factory" and Robert Fogel (1989, 162) as a "gang system [that] played a role comparable to the factory system or, at a later date, the assembly line, in regulating the pace of labor."[3]

Sugar, whose transformation into a cheap mass commodity itself constituted a key substantive innovation of the eighteenth century (Mintz 1985), was the principal staple associated with slavery:

"Between 60 and 70 percent of all Africans who survived the Atlantic voyages ended up in one or another of Europe's sugar colonies" (Fogel 1989, 18).[4] The slave sugar plantation system established in Barbados in the midseventeenth century "became a model not only for other Caribbean slave societies but also for American mainland colonies such as the Carolinas" (Moitt 2004a, 2). Similarly, in Brazil, "with the 'technology' of gang labor, sugar could be produced at a very low cost on large slave plantations," and so the country "rather quickly developed a vibrant agricultural sector" around such arrangements (De Ferranti et al. 2004, 110). Sugar plantations also served as the basis for the "vast fortunes that were realized in a relatively short period of time" in Cuba in the late eighteenth and early nineteenth centuries, when revolution disrupted supplies from Saint-Domingue (Allahar 2004). Later, in the 1790s and until the Civil War, cotton, which "generated extraordinary profit opportunities" (Wright 2006, 85), came to play this role in the South of the United States.

The imposition of extractive institutions was not limited to agricultural plantation systems. Mining played a key role as well, in Latin America and elsewhere.[5] Before the nineteenth century, for example, gold and diamond mining in South Africa relied on a combination of the selective recruitment of skilled white Europeans with coercive indenture and territorial segregation for nonwhites (rather than formal slavery), a system that produced "the same dual society characteristic of plantation regions" (Frieden 2006, 103; Fredrickson 1981).[6] Moreover, the wealth generated by plantations and mines was not limited to their commodity exports. The slave trade itself was a source of considerable profits.[7] Agricultural plantations and mines generated demand for goods such as foodstuffs and basic manufactures and hence were viewed by observers at the time as stimulating the growth of production in surrounding areas and elsewhere.[8] This is why Gavin Wright (2006, 14) concludes that "slavery was at the heart of the Commercial Revolution, which set the stage for the modern era of economic growth."

The interests built around such arrangements gained access to extraordinary levels of wealth. Fogel (1989, 24) notes that "throughout the eighteenth century, the great slave plantations of the sugar colonies, with profits averaging about 10 percent on invested capital, were the largest privately owned enterprises of the age and their owners were among the richest of all men."[9] Kenneth Sokoloff and

Stanley Engerman (2000, 221, 217) observe that "the economies that specialized in the production of sugar and other highly valued crops associated with extensive use of slaves had the highest per capita (including slaves) incomes in the New World":

> In 1700, there seems to have been virtual parity in per capita income between Mexico and the British colonies that were to become the United States, and the most prosperous economies of the New World were in the Caribbean. Barbados and Cuba, for example, had per capita incomes that have been estimated as 50 and 67 percent higher, respectively, than that of (what was later to be) the United States. . . . Haiti was likely the richest society in the world on a per capita basis in 1790, on the eve of its revolution.[10]

More broadly, comparing the West Indies and three areas of settlement in North America (New England, the Middle Colonies, and the South of today's United States), Daniel Garcia Swartz (1993, 54) argues that around 1774 "the West Indies evidenced the highest level of per capita wealth and income" ("and also the greatest degree of inequality," he adds).[11]

Similar patterns prevailed in the United States.[12] Wright (2006, 57) observes that while in the late eighteenth century the economies of the South and the North were similar in overall levels of wealth, the "nonhuman wealth per member of the free population" was about 40 percent higher in the South, suggesting "that slave labor made possible an accumulation of wealth for the free population of the South that put them considerably ahead of their northern counterparts."[13] Even by the 1860s, by a measure of wealth per free capita, the South outperformed the North, giving rise to the belief among slave-owners of the South that they were "justified in feeling that they were fully as successful as their northern counterparts in the game of wealth accumulation, if not more so; but they held their wealth mainly in the form of human property rather than land values" (Wright 2006, 61).[14] Thus, "the southern plutocrats were considerably richer on average than their northern counterparts, by a factor of roughly two to one. Indeed, nearly two of every three males in the United States with wealth of $100,000 or more (the super rich of the era) lived in the South in 1860" (Fogel 2003, 62).

As these examples indicate, coercive strategies of labor control, including but not limited to plantations, represented *in their own time* what Joseph Schumpeter (1942) would characterize as *innovative* activities that yielded extraordinary levels of wealth. The extractive institutions associated with HIE, as it is usually acknowledged, provided crucial competitive advantages to the elites benefiting from such arrangements, but in addition, these institutions did so by simultaneously providing a very effective basis from which to promote wealth maximization (and economic growth) for several hundred years. As synthesized by Fogel (1989, 10), "it was virtually uninterrupted economic success for more than 200 years that made [modern slavery] thrive and grow to monstrous proportions."[15]

LOW-INEQUALITY EQUILIBRIA
AS RELATIVE COMPARATIVE ADVANTAGE

By contrast to the economic success of HIE, at least until the nineteenth century, many of the areas that contained the type of arrangements we would today characterize as LIE, particularly those in the "New World," were somewhat marginal and perceived for a long time as being far from wealthy. For the most part, the entrepreneurial activities developed in these areas were limited to exploiting the interstices left open by the mercantilist colonial arrangements (smuggling, filling commercial needs not easily met by colonial empires, and so forth).

The new institutional literature advances a certain narrative about how these areas eventually came to gain greater access to wealth. In this narrative, relatively more egalitarian arrangements promoted greater access by the majority of the relevant populations to property and political rights, thus eventually providing a more efficient basis for the expansion of markets and economic growth. In time, according to this narrative, democracy, equity, and property rights came to reinforce one another in virtuous interaction.

Douglass C. North provides a good example of this type of account as used to describe pre-nineteenth-century developments. For North (2005, 134–35), the discouragement of "monopoly privileges" and the "favorable incentives embodied in the rules and property rights" promoted by Burgundian and Habsburg rulers explain why "it was in the Netherlands and Amsterdam specifically that modern economic growth had its genesis." Spain, by contrast, under the fiscal pressures resulting from "maintaining and expanding the empire," followed an opposite trajectory by strengthening monopolies, restricting markets, and increasing taxation (North 2005, 134). Thus, these contrasting trajectories corroborate that "growth has been generated when the economy has provided institutional incentives to undertake productivity-raising activities such as the Dutch undertook. Decline has resulted from disincentives to engage in productive activity as a consequence of centralized political control of the economy and monopoly privileges" (134). In this account, the plantations and mines in Latin America, for example, were not conducive to the generation of true wealth because "the objective of the Spanish mercantilist structure was to implement the movement of precious metals to Spain, not to promote the development of Latin America" (112).[16]

In significant ways, such narratives replicate many aspects of the arguments advanced in modernization approaches. In both, today's wealthy countries are scrutinized to establish various features that appear to be correlated: wealth, the prevalence of achievement in shaping stratification, democracy, the expansion of private property rights. The specific causal interactions emphasized in these perspectives might vary slightly: in one, the growing complexity of the division of labor eventually leads to more reliance on achievement and greater upward social mobility; in the other, more equitable access to property and political rights strengthens democracy and markets. In both, however, any one of these dimensions is then traced back in time to identify its origins and is subsequently followed forward in time to show how it came to interact eventually with the other dimensions, culminating in a virtuous equilibrium.[17]

The new institutional literature on inequality ultimately remains embedded in a modernization type of framework. The institutions characterizing situations of high and low inequality are portrayed as having developed largely independent from one another, and the eventual path of each is assessed in terms of the extent to which the two sets of institutions (and the interest groups that shape them) acted to promote or constrain and distort market forces and when they began to diverge.[18] Eventually, the emphasis shifts away from the relationship between institutional arrangements and inequality to focus instead on the extent to which markets and private property are regulated (assuming that markets are in and of themselves a more efficient mechanism for generating the morally desirable goals of economic growth and progress). In short, authors such as Acemoglu, Johnson, and Robinson (2001) make an effort to acknowledge the role of institutional arrangements in underpinning markets, but in a way that eventually returns to treating institutions as being exogenous to markets, and "markets" as having an existence independent from institutional arrangements.[19]

The emphasis on property rights and reliance on markets helps us understand why the approach adopted by the new institutional literature on inequality has come to be enthusiastically adopted even by multilateral circles in Washington.[20] As formulated, the new institutional interpretation serves to reconcile sensitivity to the negative legacies of inequality with a normative approach that emphasizes the need to strengthen property rights for the sake of greater economic efficiency and social welfare. From such a normative perspective, appropriate institutions are the main force allowing for effective industrialization, and the adoption of such institutions is facilitated by "globalization."[21] Moreover, the new institutional literature on the legacy of inequality often draws on a longer tradition that portrays extractive institutions as associated with outdated forms of organizing production that have had little to do with the fundamental logic of the more contemporary world-economy (or, in the modernization variant of such an interpretation, as associated with a more traditional "agricultural" stage that eventually gave way to a more modern "industrial" stage).

Such an approach has important methodological consequences for historical research. Often, in taking such an approach, the tendency is to assume retrospectively that if a virtuous equilibrium is to be found in recent times, similar virtuous interactions must have existed back in time. Moreover, if democracy, markets, and equity seem to go hand in hand today, the presence of any single one of these variables in the past is assumed to signal the presence or immanent presence of the others.

Paradoxically, some of the perspectives that have been most critical of modernization approaches, such as studies in the world-systems tradition, frequently fall into the same methodological trap. For example, world-systems studies in the 1970s often assumed that if wealthy nations were at the time characterized by the prevalence of manufacturing and wage labor, the relative presence of these variables could be used to classify retrospectively where wealth tended to be generated in the past.[22]

The previous section showed why such a methodological assumption is problematic: prior to the nineteenth century: it was precisely the areas that were characterized by coercive labor arrangements and that were the most unequal at the time that were epicenters of wealth generation at the time. In this regard, rather than assume the historical persistence of a virtuous interaction between equity and wealth generation, so that the presence of one becomes indicative of the presence the other, we should critically evaluate the possibility that the relationship between equity and wealth generation has changed over time.

Let's consider a basic tenet of the new institutional literature on inequality: its argument that equity explains the relative success of LIE in promoting economic growth. This was not evident to contemporaries. The relative advantages of wage labor as compared to slavery were initially defended on moral grounds rather than according to any notion of economic efficiency. In fact, as Fogel (1989, 203) reminds us, "the greatest obstacle to the rise of an antislavery ideology was the belief that slavery promoted material improvement"—so much so that in the original stages of the abolitionist movement "religious radicals of the late seventeenth and early eighteenth centuries denounced slavery as 'a filthy sin' not because it was an economic failure but because its economic successes were abhorrent to them."[23] The eventual efficiency of LIE in generating economic growth, then, might have been for the most part an unintended effect of the pursuit of other goals (the pursuit of profits, to be sure, but social, political, and moral objectives as well).[24]

To some extent, the more elegant versions of the new institutional literature on inequality acknowledge that "institutions of private property . . . should matter more during the age of industry," when these institutions yielded results that thereafter "provided a significant competitive edge" (Acemoglu, Johnson, and Robinson 2002, 25). But the point is that "the age of industry" and the particular shape that markets adopted in this period were precisely evidence of the competitive advantages demonstrated by the institutional arrangements of LIE. Once these arrangements gained such an edge, and for a considerable period of time, the advantages they conferred continued to mount, as explained by Wallerstein (1974, 98, emphasis added):

> If, at a given moment in time, because of a series of factors at a previous time, one region has a *slight* edge over another in terms of one key factor, *and* there is a *conjuncture* of events which makes this *slight* edge of central importance in terms of determining social action, then the slight edge is converted into a large disparity and the advantage holds even after the conjuncture has passed.

Of course, the story of how LIE gained such an edge, and of how this edge became more pronounced over time, does not involve merely (or even primarily) competitive economic advantages. The institutional arrangements that came to characterize LIE offered forms of categorical identity (such as citizenship) that people embraced as they sought to challenge, with uneven success, existing forms of inequality (including those entailed in HIE).[25] From this perspective, as we indicated earlier, HIE and LIE always have been eminently political—but still fundamentally relational—constructions.

From a comparative perspective, then, it is important not to extrapolate from the logic of economic arrangements that became subsequently successful; these criteria of rationality for evaluating HIE and LIE were simply not in operation at the time. Rather than retrospectively evaluating "design" according to some standard that emerged hundreds of years later, we seem to be on firmer ground when we understand different institutional paths as the outcome of processes of conflict and negotiation between social forces that enjoyed different degrees of relative bargaining power, and where the consequences of specific institutional paths changed over time *precisely because of their interaction*. This is precisely the point made by North (2005, 22) when he notes that "institutions adopted for a particular time, even if optimal (that is, correct perception) at that time, may be far from optimal as the human environment changes over time."

Such a perspective reframes some of the crucial arguments made in the new institutional literature on inequality, which often makes the argument that the prevalence of extractive institutions reduced incentives for continuing technological innovation. For some, this is because the arrangements characteristic of HIE continued to ensure high margins of profit for elites (see, for example, Mandle 1981). For others, the ruling elites in such arrangements were likely to fear the potentially disruptive *political* impact of technological change.[26]

We should weigh such arguments with caution. To begin with, there is some empirical evidence (some of which we presented earlier in this chapter) suggesting that the institutions associated with HIE were not as impermeable to technological innovation as they often are made out to have been.[27] But even more important, HIE institutions initially developed because they proved effective in delivering extraordinary gains (in the form of profit and power but also specific forms of solidarity), and to the extent that they continued to deliver these gains, elites and other actors had few incentives to seek—but often a strong motivation to prevent—more fundamental changes in institutional arrangements that could threaten the existing distribution of power and wealth.[28]

Of course, HIE institutions delivered these gains in association with particular ways of organizing production, distribution, consumption, and solidarity (concentration in a few crops destined for export markets, restricted purchasing power among the poor, ostentatious consumption of imports among the wealthy) that eventually generated the type of rigidities that would come to provide competitive opportunities for LIE.[29]

But the competitive advantages eventually displayed by the institutional arrangements of LIE were possibly not part of the original intent in the design of these arrangements. In a situation in which the shifting interaction between HIE and LIE generated considerable uncertainty, it was probably not easily predictable which institutional features would be better suited to take advantage of future opportunity.

As we shift our unit of analysis to consider the relationship between LIE and HIE over a longer span of time (and a broader space), we are simultaneously led to revisit the assumption that there is a clearly established causal relationship between the institutional arrangements characteristic of LIE and economic growth. The relationship indeed holds to some extent for a specific period, beginning sometime in the nineteenth century and running until the late twentieth century. But there is considerable evidence that for a few centuries before this period, and probably longer, it was the arrangements associated with HIE that were considered most conducive to growth and the accumulation of wealth. From a broader historical perspective, we can paraphrase Mintz (1985, 44) to argue that HIE and LIE developed "in two ecologically different settings and were critically different in form. Yet they served the same overarching economic goals, and were created—albeit in such different form—by the evolution of a single economic and political system."

RECASTING THE INTERACTION BETWEEN HIGH- AND LOW-INEQUALITY EQUILIBRIA AS CREATIVE DESTRUCTION

We now want to formulate some of the empirical arguments made earlier within a more theoretical framework.

In Kuznets's hypothesis on the relationship between economic growth and inequality, development is assumed to be concomitant with industrialization, and industrialization to be the highest stage of such development. Moreover, as explained in chapter 1, a fundamental premise of the inverted U-curve hypothesis was that different levels of within-nation inequality were an outcome of the uneven pace at which *individual nations* underwent a universal transition (from the production of raw materials to the production of manufactures, or from rural to urban societies, or from traditional to modern arrangements). Kuznets assumed that both the demographic transition and the institutional transformations that were predicted to follow were embedded in this universal process of national transitions to modernity. Modernization, then, entailed a nationally based transformation (that is, nations constituted the appropriate unit of analysis), along the path of a singular, universal transition between two distinct distributional arrays (rural and urban).

To reformulate inequality as a world-historical process, we need to shift the fundamental theoretical premises of how to understand economic growth. Joseph Schumpeter (1942) suggests that instead of a single transition from one state of equilibrium to another, as usually posited by modernization approaches, we should conceive of capitalism as entailing continuous transformation.[30] For Schumpeter (1942, 82–83),

> capitalism . . . is by nature a form or method of economic change and not only never is but never can be stationary. . . . The opening

up of new markets, foreign or domestic, and the organizational development from the craft shop and factory to such concerns as U.S. Steel illustrate the same process of industrial mutation—if I may use that biological term—that incessantly revolutionizes the economic structure from within, incessantly destroying the old one, incessantly creating a new one. This process of Creative Destruction is the essential fact about capitalism. It is what capitalism consists in and what every capitalist concern has got to live in.[31]

In the Schumpeterian model, the introduction and clustering of innovations constantly transform existing economic and social arrangements and drive cycles of prosperity (characterized by intense investment in new productive opportunities) and depression (characterized by the broader absorption of innovative practices and the elimination of older activities).[32]

The notion of creative destruction fundamentally challenges many of the prevailing assumptions of the modernization paradigm. Rather than a universal pattern drawn from repeated national transitions to modernity, Schumpeter's notion of creative destruction highlights a single process, incessantly rendered anew, through which *both* wealth and scarcity, inseparable from one another, are created.[33] This formulation has two implications. First, the extent to which particular arrays of institutional/productive arrangements (such as "agriculture" or "industry," LIE or HIE) secure relatively greater access to wealth is subject to constant change over time. Second, understood in this way, the study of the relationship between inequality and the processes of economic growth, qua creative destruction, requires a specific unit of analysis—one that includes not only the arenas in which creation prevails but those in which destruction prevails, in the incessant mutation of creation and destruction over time.

We can interpret the institutional arrangements that have shaped inequality (the LIE and the HIE) within countries themselves as having constituted a crucial arena of innovation that yielded changing competitive advantages. As we indicated early in this chapter, extractive institutions and within-country HIE prior to the nineteenth century were not a set of peculiar social arrangements that were associated with relatively inefficient forms of agricultural exploitation and by their very nature were incompatible with the development of the modern world-economy.[34] Instead, avoiding the types of dichotomies favored by modernization approaches (agricultural-industrial, traditional-modern), the construction of the institutional arrangements entailed in within-country HIE (the subordination of indigenous and slave populations to use their labor in commercial agriculture by means of force) represented in its own time a significant Schumpeterian innovation that provided competitive advantages to colonial and settler elites in their search for greater wealth and power and allowed for an extraordinary accumulation of wealth and power.[35]

As we have seen, this argument runs counter to the common depiction of slavery as a largely inefficient form of organizing production. Moreover, there is an all too prevalent assumption that more-advanced technologies and forms of organization of the labor process are generally characterized by greater skill requirements and therefore higher relative wages. Even the early Wallerstein (1974, 103), for example, tended to differentiate between the activities of the core and the periphery by using criteria that emphasized "the complexity of economic institutions, the degree of economic reward (both in terms of average level and range), and most of all in the form of labor control," and in this sense, "slavery" was considered to be "inferior" to wage labor as a mode of labor control.[36] But as discussed earlier, there is no such necessary correspondence.

Instead, thinking of slavery as Schumpeterian innovation emphasizes the importance of focusing on institutional arrangements (such as the origins of within-country HIE) as linked to the processes of creative destruction. The task then becomes one of assessing empirically how the relevant wealth-generating activities have changed over time and how they interact with dimensions such as "institutions," "forms of labor control," or patterns of within-country stratification. From this point of view, it was the very success of within-country HIE that created the conditions for the competitive advantages eventually gained by the very different institutional arrangements entailed in within-country LIE. We expand these arguments in chapter 4.

To make the trajectories of pre-nineteenth-century HIE and LIE more evident, we can combine some demographic elements of Kuznets's original inverted U-curve hypothesis with a Schumpeterian emphasis on creative destruction. Rather than conceptualizing economic growth as proceeding from a homogenous "traditional" pattern toward a *single* equilibrium, the homogenous "modernization" end-

Figure 3.1   Stylized Historical Trends in HIE and LIE, 1600s to 1800s

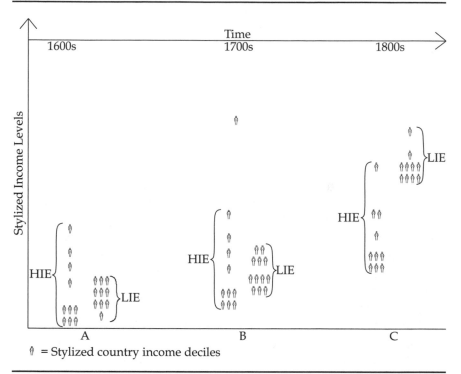

⇑ = Stylized country income deciles

Source: Authors' illustration.

point emphasized by so many, we can recast both the modern and traditional as having been constituted, in very different ways, by both HIE and LIE.[37]

We make a stylized representation of these arguments in figure 3.1. Of course, it is very difficult to attain comparable estimates of trends in within-country inequality for the period we are considering here. For this reason, all the usual caveats apply: as Kuznets stated in regard to his own hypothesis, the stylized representation in figure 3.1 is based on 95 percent speculation and 5 percent fact. In our case, the facts are drawn from the empirical estimates cited earlier in this chapter. According to these estimates, for much of the period before the nineteenth century the incomes of elites in a HIE country were probably around 50 percent higher than those of elites in a LIE country. Thus, in time A, we locate the upper boundary of HIE as being considerably higher than that of LIE, and the access to resources of the lower strata in each set of equilibria to be only a little bit different.

In time B, which for our purposes we can specify as somewhere in the eighteenth or nineteenth century, the institutional arrangements of LIE begin to generate higher and more sustained rates of growth, generating the shift in the observed comparative advantages of HIE and LIE.[38] By time C, which would correspond to the initial stages of growth in Kuznets's formulation, the modern and the traditional in fact entail two very different equilibria, a LIE characterized by relatively less inequality and with more opportunities for mobility, and a HIE characterized by much greater inequality and segregation. In this manner, the institutional arrangements entailed in HIE and LIE can be recast as involving a historically specific relationship to the production of wealth, rather than constantly entailing either a virtuous (LIE) or vicious (HIE) interaction with the growth of markets and wealth-creating processes.

The competitive advantages of LIE were not easy to replicate all over. The LIE entailed institutional strategies that effectively exploited the rigidities of the economic and institutional arrangements characteristic of HIE. Efforts at diffusion were invariably less successful because they ended up diluting precisely the innovative character of the original strategies themselves. Moreover, elites tended to become invested in maintaining existing patterns of inequality. As noted by Acemoglu and Robinson (2006a), "political elites will block beneficial economic and institutional change when they are afraid that these changes will destabilize the existing system and make it more likely that they will lose political power and future rents."[39]

Economic success always entails the construction of institutional rigidities that will both constrain further growth and provide new opportunities for effective competition *through innovation*. Thus, the arrangements that brought greater access to wealth at one point in time (such as HIE) became, over time, a source of competitive disadvantages or a locus of dislocation.[40] Innovation is thereby eminently relational. Innovation makes sense only within a spatial and temporal field in which the adoption of new forms of action by some actors provides greater access to the opportunities available within that field than the access attained by other actors who do not deploy similar strategies—and who generally experience through the very same process a relative (and sometimes absolute) decline in their access to opportunity.[41]

The arguments advanced here are different from explanations of between-country inequality that focus on exploitative relations between poor and wealthy nations. More broadly, some readers of our work have expressed consternation at the absence of any substantive engagement with Karl Marx and the notions of exploitation, economic surplus, and profits as crucial to the processes shaping inequality.

Many aspects of the work of Marx are certainly relevant to several of the issues explored here. His effort to understand capitalism as the outcome of specific social relations characterized by exploitation and conflict, in ways that led to the "constant revolutionizing of production, uninterrupted disturbance of all social conditions [and] everlasting uncertainty and agitation"—as well as to the inevitable geographical expansion of markets to eventually encompass all areas in the world (Marx and Engels 1848)—has had a profound impact on the study of social inequality and stratification across the social sciences. This effort was influential as well in various critical perspectives (such as the dependency critique of the modernization approach) that extrapolated Marxist notions of exploitation to explain inequality between nations as an outcome of the transfer of economic surplus from poor to wealthy nations.

Although the Marxist perspective on inequality and stratification certainly influenced the interpretations we advance in this book, we have chosen not to make arguments about exploitation a central component of our framework. One reason for this decision is that adequate data are lacking to appropriately assess the extent to which transfers of economic surplus were central to the processes of innovation and exclusion described in this book. For example, we might suspect that in the seventeenth and eighteenth centuries the wealth generated through colonial sugar production in the Americas and the slave trade in Africa provided resources for investment by merchants and manufacturers in the countries that would attain high incomes in the nineteenth century, but such arguments need further research and are not necessary for the interpretations developed here.

There are additional reasons why we pay less attention to issues of exploitation. To a considerable extent, Marx, writing critically against Adam Smith, was less concerned with focusing on exclusion and restrictions on markets as crucial forces shaping inequality and instead more or less assumed the existence of open markets and endeavored to find in them, and in wage labor, the roots of contemporary inequality. In fact, many subsequent readers of Marx relied on such an emphasis to argue that inequality and stratification under capitalism are shaped foremost by the specific way in which bourgeoisies and working classes interact within any given set of national borders. From the point of view of the arguments made in this book, such an interpretation, while critical in its own terms, has been constitutive of the institutional arrangements underpinning world inequality—that is, the nation-state itself.

CONCLUSION

This chapter argues that HIE and LIE should be understood in relational terms. Drawing from Schumpeter's insights on creative destruction, we have described the ways in which institutional arrangements are themselves part and parcel of the processes of innovation that, unevenly distributed over time and space, generate differential rates of economic growth. Contrary to some prevailing assumptions in the literature, the institutional arrangements underpinning HIE proved innovative and effective in generating high rates of growth for a long period of time prior to the nineteenth century. Like any other innovation, these arrangements eventually became comparatively disadvantaged relative to new innovative institutions (such as those characteristic of LIE after the nineteenth century). But this was a relational outcome.

This chapter calls into question the assumption—dear and crucial to the new institutional literature on inequality—that the future is destined to bring us an inevitable virtuous interaction leading to the simultaneous growth of equity, democracy, and markets. But before explaining more fully why such a virtuous interaction is more difficult (and perhaps has been more fleeting) than usually expected, we must develop further the relationship linking within-country LIE and HIE to trends in between-country inequality. In the next chapter, we argue that such inequality can be best understood as entailing a high-inequality equilibrium.

CHAPTER 4

THE DISTRIBUTION OF INCOME BETWEEN
NATIONS AS A HIGH-INEQUALITY EQUILIBRIUM

Drawing on our discussion of the within-country patterns of high- and low-inequality equilibria (HIE and LIE) developed in the previous chapters, we now turn to patterns of between-country inequality. In this chapter, we argue that between-country inequality can be understood best as involving over the last two centuries a high-inequality equilibrium (HIE). The overall level of inequality between nations—as expressed by a Gini coefficient that measures the dispersion of gross national income (GNI) between the nations of the world—has been both extremely high and historically persistent. Once again, as in the previous chapter, we draw on Schumpeter's notion of creative destruction to explain the persistence of such a HIE, but conclude by linking the notion to the causal relations characterizing the interaction of between-country HIE and within-country LIE.

THE DISTRIBUTION OF INCOME
BETWEEN NATIONS

As we discussed in the previous chapter, within-country HIE and LIE constituted alternative modes of organizing institutional arrangements that over time differed in the extent to which they were compatible with relatively greater or lesser command over wealth. In this sense, the institutional arrangements entailed in within-country HIE and LIE themselves have constituted a key source of *comparative and shifting advantages and disadvantages,* manifested historically in differential rates of economic growth among nations. Over time, such Schumpeterian processes of creative destruction have resulted in the persistence of high inequality between nations.

The measurement of inequality between nations is an issue of contention, and before reviewing some data on the relevant trends, we should make some observations on one particular topic: whether national income data should be adjusted by exchange rates (FXs) or purchasing power parities (PPPs) for the purpose of cross-national comparisons. When adjusted by FXs, national income data, measuring the output of a nation according to globally standardized procedures, are converted from national currencies to a common international denominator (generally, the U.S. dollar). Critics of FX adjustments argue that such conversions fail to adequately value the actual command that households have over resources (particularly in poor nations) because many of these resources tend to be undervalued or undercounted. For example, China might not be valuing its medical resources correctly because doctors and nurses are paid at much lower rates than what medical labor commands in high-income countries. Moreover, advocates of PPP adjustments argue, such measures tend to suffer less from the volatility of exchange rate fluctuations.

But PPP adjustments have their own problems, issues that are either not addressed or (more frequently) ignored by those who are unfamiliar with the actual procedures used to generate these adjustments. We have detailed several of these problems elsewhere (Korzeniewicz et al. 2004), so here we highlight only a few.

To start, it is very difficult to figure out how to estimate accurately the value of resources that are not counted or are deemed by observers to be undervalued. This is why, since the PPP data collection efforts began in the 1950s, the relevant procedures have changed, often significantly, between each round of data collection; this difficulty also helps us understand why the publication of these data has been very irregular and marked by major delays (for example, no new data on PPPs were made available between 1993 and 2008). Further contributing to these difficulties, the participation of some major countries in these surveys has been very restricted: India, for example, did not participate between the 1985 and 2005 surveys, and China had never been surveyed before the last round.[1] Illustrating all these difficulties, actual PPP estimates have varied greatly from round to round, so that each set of PPP adjustments is not comparable over time: for example, the data published in 2008 were found to have overestimated or underestimated the income of 60 percent of the world's population by more than 25 percent in the 1993 PPP adjustments. (We discuss these differences more fully in the statistical appendix.) The suggestion that there is a vast amount of measurement error in PPP data makes such data unreliable.

Another major issue is that no over-time PPP data have ever been collected. When advocates insist that PPP data can be used to describe change over time, they reveal a fundamental misunderstanding of how these data are collected and should be used. We do not mean that *some* over-time PPP data were collected, or *a little* were collected—we mean *none.* Historical GNP-GDP data adjusted by PPPs are simply an index derived from existing GNP-GDP data series, which use the latest round of PPP estimates to adjust national incomes to a new baseline, constant through time. Thus, PPP-adjusted data are simply inappropriate for an analysis that seeks to understand long-term changes in the interaction of within- and between-country inequalities.

Finally, even if PPP data did not have all these problems (which are further detailed in the statistical appendix), the choice of the appropriate indicator should be guided by the theoretical concerns being addressed. To advocates of PPP data, the most fundamental issues regarding income distribution involve the relative access that national populations have to goods and services within their borders. But in thinking about world inequality, we are concerned as well with the relative command that different populations across the world have over the goods and services of one another. To illustrate the perceived importance of such command we note that people around the world often mobilize in response to a dramatic devaluation, but are unlikely to even notice any major readjustment of PPP estimates. The choice of the appropriate indicator, from this point of view, should be guided by our theoretical concerns. In this regard, we have long maintained that FX-adjusted measures of income are the most appropriate in analyzing global inequality (Korzeniewicz and Moran 2000), even if all the additional problems discussed here were not a concern.

However, because PPP-based data are often used in studies of between-country inequality, and because PPP advocates can be surprisingly insular when it comes to measurement questions, we anticipate that persuasion would be difficult and therefore proceed in

Figure 4.1   Trends in Between-Country Inequality, 1820 to 2007

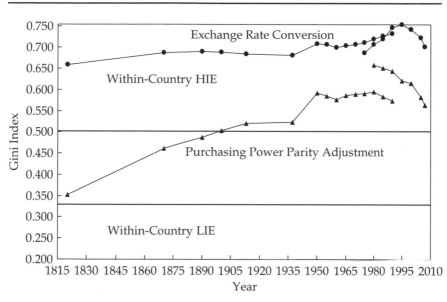

Sources: Authors' calculations based on two samples: 1820 to 1990, Maddison (1995); 1975 to 2004, World Bank (2008).

this chapter to report simultaneously on both FX- and PPP-based indicators.

Figure 4.1 shows two different estimates of between-country inequality over the last two centuries, using GNI (adjusted alternatively by purchasing power parities and exchange rates, both population-weighted; see statistical appendix).[2] According to one estimate, the PPP-adjusted data used by authors such as Lant Pritchett (1997) and Jeffrey Sachs (2005)—the gap between poor and wealthy countries—constitute a relatively newer phenomenon, traceable to the nineteenth century. The FX-adjusted data, on the other hand, suggest that inequality might already have been pronounced in the early nineteenth century. The difference arises because PPP-based data tend to raise the income of poor nations relative to FX-based data for the recent period, accentuating the impact of the low growth experienced by those same nations before the last two or three decades. According to both estimates, however, between-country inequality has increased since the late nineteenth century and remains today above the boundary demarcating the cluster of within-country HIE we discuss in this book.

Exchange-based data on national incomes unequivocally show that inequality between countries throughout the twentieth century was as high as the highest inequality exhibited within any single nation-state.[3] For example, as we noted in chapter 1, the countries with the highest contemporary levels of inequality (by most accounts, Zimbabwe, South Africa, and Brazil) have Gini coefficients in the range of .571 to .746. These extremely high rates of inequality are nonetheless comparable to equivalent contemporary measures of inequality between nations: a Gini coefficient ranging from .702 to .755 in 1980 to 2007 using FX-based data, and from .564 to .659 using PPP-based data.

The HIE between nations has been historically persistent. Over the 1820 to 2004 period, there have been major shifts in the organization of production and consumption, the rise and fall of very different patterns of state-market interaction, two world wars, and revolutionary change among large swaths of the world's population. Despite the turbulence implied in these transformations, overall inequality between countries, as an output of global interaction, retained a remarkable stability—at high levels when the indicator used is FX-based, showing a steady rise when the indicator is PPP-based. This stability is indicative of a high-inequality equilibrium similar to the kind we established regarding patterns of within-country inequalities.

Of course, to say that interactions between countries have constituted a system that reached equilibrium through most of the nineteenth and twentieth centuries is not to say that the trajectories of all individual countries showed rigidity and stability. We know that during the same period individual nations experienced considerable mobility. In the nineteenth century, what are often ethnocentrically labeled as "countries of recent settlement" (for example, Argentina, Australia, Canada, New Zealand, and the United States) were characterized by very high rates of economic growth. In the late nineteenth and early twentieth centuries, much of Scandinavia likewise experienced growth in national incomes and standards of living. Japan stood out in terms of its rapid economic ascendancy after World War II and was joined—particularly in the last quarter of the twentieth century—by the so-called East Asian Tigers (Taiwan,

Figure 4.2   Economic Growth for Selected Countries Relative to the United States, 1900 to 2006

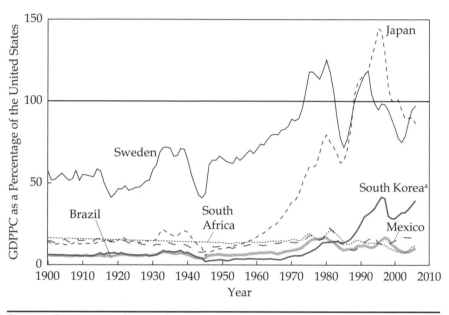

Sources: See statistical appendix.
[a]Until 1913, contains North and South Korea.

Hong Kong, South Korea, and Singapore). More recently, China and India have been characterized by extraordinary rates of growth (although the benefits of this growth have not been equally distributed among all country income deciles), and this has been driving the decline in between-country inequality observed in figure 4.1. (The decline begins earlier and is more pronounced when using PPP-based data.)

We provide some salient examples of upward mobility in figure 4.2, where relative levels of gross national product per capita (GNPPC) are calculated as a percentage of the gross domestic product per capita (GDPPC) of the United States between 1900 and 2006. Since the United States is always one of the principal high-income countries for the overall period being considered here, such a measure allows us to capture the relative extent of the mobility experienced by different nations. As indicated by figure 4.2, countries such as Sweden, Japan, and South Korea, at different points in the twentieth century, serve as clear examples of successful upward mobility.

But since the early nineteenth century, and until the late twentieth century, such individual cases of "successful" upward mobility were accompanied by the stable persistence of high inequality between nations (as indicated by the groups of countries that have remained "poor" or "wealthy" over the entire two centuries), in a pattern resembling the HIE of divergent patterns of within-country inequality. In other words, for most of the twentieth century the mobility of individual countries has gone hand in hand with a persistent HIE between nations.[4] In figure 4.2, this is illustrated by the examples of Brazil, Mexico, and South Africa, where different styles of development—many of which were perceived as models of success in their own time—allowed these nations, in relative terms, to merely run very fast to simply stay in the same place.

There are debates over the trends in between-nation inequality during the last twenty years. Many argue that globalization has brought an impressive degree of convergence. Along these lines, Rati Ram (1989) notes, albeit without discussing in detail the mechanisms at hand beyond highlighting the dualism at work within the world-economy, that

> the basic postulate of Kuznets' U-hypothesis is . . . likely to be applicable to the course of intercountry ("world") inequality in a growing world system. Therefore, in a world system that is experiencing more or less secular economic growth of the kind observed since World War II, intercountry income inequality may at first be expected to increase and then, after some "turning point," may be predicted to decline.

More recently, Glenn Firebaugh (2003; see also Firebaugh and Goesling 2004), focusing solely on the PPP-based indicators presented in figure 4.1, has advanced a similar interpretation. After noting that income inequalities between nations declined after the midtwentieth century (following their long-term rise over the two prior centuries), Firebaugh (2003, 190) seeks to explain the apparent inverted U-curve by drawing on Kuznets and thus attributes much

Figure 4.3   Xavier Sala-i-Martin's "Convergence Period!"

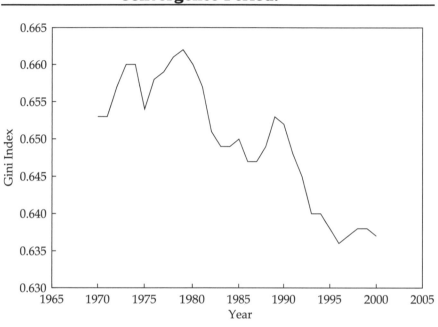

Source: Authors' compilation based on Sala-i-Martin (2006), 384, table III.

of the rise in between-country inequality to the differential rates of industrialization in wealthy and poor nations:

> As industrialization took root first in the initially richer nations, the rich became richer and inequality shot up across nations. Now, as industrialization is spreading to poorer nations, poor regions are reaping the benefits of industrial growth, and inequality is declining across nations. In other words, the trajectory of between-nation income inequality over the course of global industrialization is tracing a Kuznets curve.

Many other scholars, as well as advocates of globalization, have advanced similar interpretations. A good example is provided by Xavier Sala-i-Martin (2006), who, in a play on the title of a previous article by Lant Pritchett (1997), simply labels current trends as "Convergence, Big Time" (see figure 4.3).

Such arguments draw on the longer tradition of the modernization paradigm. Various "modernization" approaches (including
those now cloaked in the guise of a "globalization" discourse) argue
that in the same way nations undergo a transition from rural (or
agricultural-traditional) to urban (or industrial-modern) arrangements, inequality between countries is caused by some nations taking the lead in becoming industrialized while others lag behind.[5] As
in Simon Kuznets's inverted U-curve hypothesis, this rise in inequality is merely transitional and will last only as long as it takes for
lagging nations to catch up with the leaders.[6] In this line of interpretation, nations tend to be perceived as independent and autonomous
entities that embark, albeit with differences in timing, on a universal
process of transformation from tradition into modernity. Wealth is a
consequence of modernization, and the achievement of wealth by
nations is indicative of their relative success in embracing key elements of modernization. Over time, as all nations converge toward
universal practices and modes of thought, convergence ensues and
inequality between nations declines.[7]

The convergence argument rests on shaky empirical foundations. To begin, the extent of convergence over the last ten or twenty
years has not been very pronounced. For example, figure 4.4
depicts the same Gini coefficients used by Sala-i-Martin in figure 4.3,
but rather than presenting the trend on a limited metric of the Gini
measure, as he does, we use the fuller range of this metric (as we
have done in the rest of the book).[8] As indicated by figure 4.4, when
showing the trends on this fuller scale, the extent of convergence
of the recent period appears much less pronounced than suggested
by figure 4.3. Of course, the extent of convergence becomes much
more pronounced when using PPP-adjusted data. (As noted earlier, while intuitively appealing because of their promise of better
capturing differences between nations in access to welfare, such
data have serious problems that are not usually acknowledged by
their users.[9])

Finally, the meaning of the current decline in between-country
inequality is often overstated. As indicated by figure 4.5, the trend
depends heavily on the trajectory of China. Although it is true that
China has a major impact on world inequality, we should be more
careful about not overreaching in assuming that the Chinese experience synthesizes what is going on in the rest of the world.

Figure 4.4   Xavier Sala-i-Martin's Convergence . . . Not So Much!

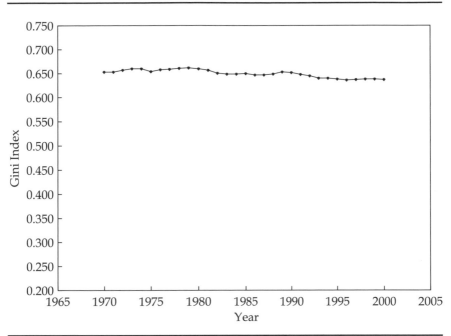

Source: Authors' compilation based on Sala-i-Martin (2006), 384, table III.

Thus, in an earlier study (Korzeniewicz and Moran 1997), we emphasized the continuing increase in between-country inequality in the late 1980s and early 1990s.[10] In a more recent contribution, Milanovic (2005) concludes that while *global* inequality (combining data on between- and within-country inequality) has remained rather stable, inequality *between* countries declined slightly over the last two decades of the twentieth century, but that this decline is smaller if we take into consideration growing regional disparities within China, and it disappears altogether if China is excluded from the sample. Similarly, Robert Hunter Wade (2004, 581; see also Wade 2008) argues that by several measures world inequality has been increasing over the last two decades; by one measure—average incomes per capita adjusted by purchasing power parities—between country inequality has declined, "but take out China and even this measure shows widening inequality." And in their review of studies on trends in world inequality over the last decade, Sudir Anand

Figure 4.5   Recent Trends in Between-Country Inequality, With and Without China

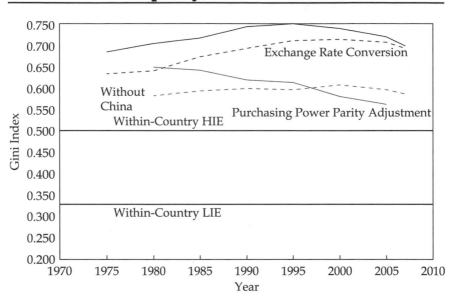

Source: Authors' calculations based on World Bank (2008).

and Paul Segal (2008, 83) conclude that "there is insufficient evidence to determine the direction of change in global interpersonal inequality."

This does not mean that we argue that no convergence is taking place. Instead, the perspective we have been advancing in this book calls for paying attention to institutional equilibria that show considerable persistence, and trends so far have not been sufficiently extended or persistent enough to make a substantive claim that the equilibria of the past few centuries has been left behind. For example, today as in the past, relative national trajectories are heterogeneous: some countries (for example, South Korea, more recently China, and to a lesser extent India, and all with different rates of mobility for various deciles of the population) are undergoing considerable upward mobility, but others remain more stable or even show some economic decline relative to the United States (for example, Mexico) (see figure 4.6). Moreover, as in the Schumpeterian processes of creative destruction, these divergent outcomes may be

**Figure 4.6   National Trajectories of Growth Relative
to the United States, 1980 to 2007**

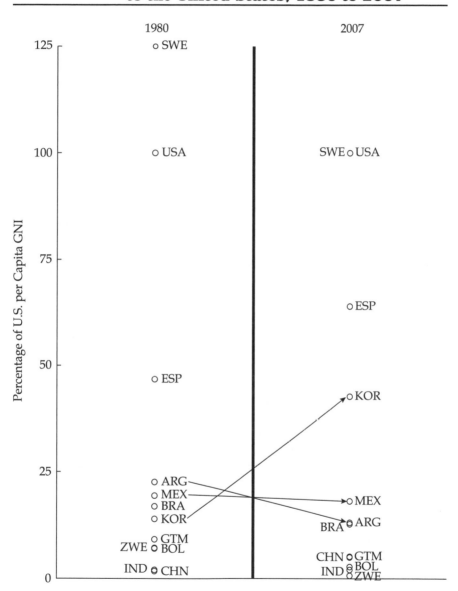

Source: Authors' calculations based on World Bank (2008).

related: the success of some nations may be resulting in the growth of economic constraints elsewhere.

To assess more substantively the extent to which existing equilibria are being transcended, we must return to the question of the appropriate unit of analysis, an issue that has always been present in the discussion of between-country inequality. At different points in the latter half of the twentieth century, Raúl Prebisch and Arghiri Emmanuel argued that the gap in wealth separating rich and poor nations was maintained or deepened by international patterns of trade, because wage differentials between core and periphery persisted in interaction with a deterioration in the terms of trade between peripheral and center products (Prebisch 1950) or unequal exchange (Emmanuel 1972). For Andre Gunder Frank (1967, 9), "one and the same historical process of the expansion and development of capitalism throughout the world has simultaneously generated—and continues to generate—both economic development and structural underdevelopment."[11] Immanuel Wallerstein (1974, 1980) and other scholars drew from these and other critical approaches to launch a "world-systems" perspective, positing that the development of a single world-economy, characterized by multiple nation-states, has entailed since about the fifteenth century the uneven growth of core, semiperipheral, and peripheral nations.[12]

Such relational claims have been attacked from many fronts. Many historical empirical studies have set out to demonstrate that the surplus appropriated by core nations from peripheral areas through colonial arrangements in the eighteenth and nineteenth centuries was not of sufficient importance to explain the rapid accumulation of wealth that accompanied the industrial revolution.[13] Others, usually focusing on the twentieth century, have argued that there is no evidence of persistent unequal exchange between core and peripheral nations, nor evidence, in particular, of any observable tendency toward a deterioration of the terms of trade between raw materials and manufactured products. Additionally, a plethora of cross-national studies have set out to test (or dismiss) "dependency–world-system" theories by quantitatively assessing whether certain variables (such as the relative weight of raw materials in exports or rates of foreign investment) prove statistically significant in regression models seeking to explain some measure of contemporary development (such as rates of economic growth or level of national income).

These criticisms often belie oversimplified versions of the issues at hand. Critics collapse dependency and world-systems approaches together, arguing that both explain the gap between rich and poor countries as an outcome of exploitation—either direct (for example, the appropriation by the core of surplus in the periphery through colonial arrangements or foreign control of key areas of production) or indirect (such as through unequal exchange, most often involving the production of raw materials in the periphery and manufactured products in the core).

Indeed, some who claim to use either a dependency or world-systems approach have themselves advanced such oversimplified versions of the argument at hand. For some, not only is the wealth of core nations a result of the direct appropriation of some economic surplus in the periphery, but the relevance of this interaction can be demonstrated merely by assessing the significance of variables (such as rates of foreign investment or the weight of raw materials in a country's exports) in cross-national regression models. Even worse, others treat conceptual distinctions such as those of core-semiperiphery-periphery as mere "classification schemes" (Hopkins 1982b, 151), and they provide categories that can be simply "tested" by assessing the significance of some dummy variable in equations that explain differential rates of economic growth or industrialization.

But in their more serious versions, modernization and world-systems approaches do posit important theoretical and methodological disagreements over how to approach the study of world inequality. These disagreements, as we have been discussing throughout the book, revolve around the relevant *unit of analysis*. For modernization and globalization approaches, the relevant units of analysis are individual nation-states, since nation-states are assumed to contain within their borders all the processes (such as patterns of saving and investment, technological innovation, and shifts in institutional arrangements) that are relevant for understanding long-term patterns of uneven economic growth. For world-systems perspectives, the relevant unit of analysis is the world-economy as a whole, and nation-states represent sites in which we can observe broader relational processes playing out. These relational processes might include at some historical moments and in some places the particular patterns of direct or indirect exploitation of peripheral nations by core nations that are often emphasized in the simplified depiction of relational approaches; these broader relational processes are not limited, however, to these particular interactions and are considerably more complex.

We can illustrate this point with an example. Even in the initial arguments regarding the deterioration of terms of trade or unequal exchange, differences in the relative prices commanded by the products of peripheral and core nations were not supposed to be merely the outcome of some intrinsic characteristics of manufacturing or raw materials as such. In fact, authors such as Prebisch and Emmanuel most often emphasized that the specific processes or commodities that yield greater or lesser wealth are changing constantly over time: mechanized textile or shoe production, for example, resided in core nations at one point in time (say, the third quarter of the nineteenth century), but one hundred years later came to be characteristic of peripheral nations.[14] Instead of simplifying the issue to some intrinsic characteristics of manufacturing or raw material production, then, even early formulations of a more relational approach sought to explain the high level of inequality between nations by linking patterns of competition between nations to the institutional arrangements prevailing within poor and wealthy nations.[15]

So what does this mean? As we discussed in the previous chapter, Schumpeter's notion of creative destruction addresses directly the issue of the unit of analysis in its call for focusing on the relational aspects of growth that have important consequences for between-country inequality. Adopting such an approach, between-country inequality is an outcome of the comparative advantages that some nations gain over others *in their interaction*. The relevant unit of analysis shifts from individual nations to a single process of creative destruction, and inequality between nations becomes an expression of the inextricable links between the "creation" that characterizes some places (or nations) and the "destruction" that prevails in others.

An example of this alternative approach is provided by the work of Mike Davis (2001, 9), who focuses on the role of famines in the "making of the Third World" over the late nineteenth century.

> We are not dealing . . . with "lands of famine" becalmed in stagnant backwaters of world history, but with the fate of tropical humanity at the precise moment (1870–1914) when its labor and products were being dynamically conscripted into a London-

centered world economy. Millions died, not outside the "modern world system," but in the very process of being forcibly incorporated into its economic and political structures.

For Davis, "the forcible incorporation of smallholder production into commodity and financial circuits controlled from overseas tended to undermine traditional food security," while "the integration of millions of tropical cultivators into the world market during the late nineteenth century was accompanied by a dramatic deterioration in their terms of trade," and "formal and informal Victorian imperialism, backed up by the supernational automatism of the Gold Standard, confiscated local fiscal autonomy and impeded state-level developmental responses—especially investments in water conservancy and irrigation—that might have reduced vulnerability to climate shocks" (289–90). In contrast to the modernization approach, then, the emphasis here is on how the expansion of wealth-generating activities went hand in hand with the destruction of existing patterns of production and institutional arrangements.

When we replace a Schumpeterian notion of creative destruction with the dualistic assumptions of the modernization paradigm, capitalism and economic growth are redefined as "incessantly revolutioniz[ing] the economic structure from within, incessantly destroying the old one, incessantly creating a new one" (Schumpeter 1942, 83), but generating, in the process, an overall system in relative equilibrium—such as the HIE that has prevailed between countries since at least the nineteenth century.

Economic success, in this formulation, always entails the construction of institutional rigidities that simultaneously constrain further growth over time and provide new opportunities for effective competition *through innovation.* Arrangements that bring greater access to wealth at one point in time (for example, the plantation systems in the eighteenth century or assembly-line automobile production in the 1950s) eventually become a source of competitive disadvantages or a locus of dislocation.

Historically, policymakers and business entrepreneurs in some nations have been able to design innovative growth strategies that exploit the rigidities of the prevailing economic and institutional arrangements (along similar lines, see Arrighi and Drangel 1986). As discussed earlier in this chapter, such innovative strategies have occasionally generated sufficient momentum to allow for significant upward mobility in the world-economy of some individual nations. In the wake of all such successful transitions, policymakers in international agencies and in poorer countries have striven to follow the track of innovators and catch up with wealthy nations by adopting panaceas that claim to distill the key ingredients of the success story of the moment.[16]

But these efforts at diffusion have invariably been less successful because efforts to generalize such strategies end up diluting precisely the innovative character of the original strategies. Also, elites in situations of HIE often have discarded opportunities for escaping between-country polarization (through innovation) for the sake of maintaining the privileges derived from the standing they enjoy through within-country inequality. Moreover, as we showed in the previous chapter, not only are innovative production strategies generally embedded in distinct institutional arrangements, but just as investments "sink" capital in physical infrastructure in ways that often diminish the capacity of entrepreneurs to adapt rapidly to new strategies of production, institutional arrangements help create rigidities that often become difficult to leave behind.[17] To some extent, the whole logic of innovation revolves precisely around this characteristic: if it were costless to shift from one productive strategy to another or from one set of institutional arrangements to another, diffusion would not be constrained and the life span of innovations would be extremely short. Historically, the opposite pattern has ensued: as we discuss in this book, the type of institutional arrangements in which innovations are embedded have tended to result in uneven rates of national economic growth.

Such a perspective provides us with a vantage point from which to assess whether we are in the midst of a qualitative transformation in the type of equilibria that characterize inequality between nations. Inequality between nations has been characterized by a single process of creative destruction whose uneven effects were distributed unequally between nations, resulting in a persistent gap between wealthy and poor countries. From this point of view, a shift in the existing equilibrium would imply that creative destruction (its relatively "creative" and "destructive" components) is no longer unevenly distributed principally along national borders. Such a shift, as we discuss later, would have far-reaching consequences, as between-country HIE are closely linked to the within-country LIE we have been discussing in the preceding chapters of this book.

Between-Country HIE and Within-Country LIE

Indeed, the institutional arrangements that came to characterize LIE in some wealthy nations *simultaneously established or deepened* the HIE between countries. This argument highlights the importance of adopting the whole world as the relevant unit of analysis to understand the processes shaping inequality between nations and simultaneously serves to reframe our understanding of alternative patterns of inequality within countries, as well as of current trends in between-country inequality.

Earlier we established that within-country HIE, originally linked to the exploitation of coerced labor and the restricted access of large segments of the population to property and political rights, entail the persistence of what we call *selective exclusion.* Such exclusion generally is justified by categorical criteria. By comparison, LIE, where free workers and small property owners have considerable access to property and political rights, involve relatively greater inclusion—through redistributive state policies, the ability of labor to use trade organizations to enhance its bargaining power, and the effective use of education to enhance skills and thus wages.

In fact, while institutional arrangements centered on selective exclusion and categorical inequality appear to be the most salient distinguishing characteristic of within-country HIE, selective exclusion and the deployment of categorical inequality are just as central to the development and persistence of within-country LIE.

In within-country HIE, institutional arrangements enhance economic opportunities for some while simultaneously restricting the access of large sectors of the population to various forms of opportunity, such as educational, political, or economic opportunity. Enhanced opportunities for some and the restricted access of the majority are related: selective exclusion serves to reduce competition among elites through institutional arrangements that simultaneously enhance competitive pressures among excluded populations (in the arenas or markets to which these populations are restricted). In within-country HIE, this selective exclusion operates fundamentally *within national borders.*

The role of selective exclusion is less evident in situations of within-country LIE. In fact, the institutional arrangements characteristic of within-country LIE appear to differ from those of within-country HIE precisely by the extent to which they enhance for their overall population a broader access to educational, political, or economic opportunity. Whereas within-country HIE are most manifestly characterized by exclusion, ascription, and categorical inequality, within-country LIE appear as the very embodiment of universal opportunity, facilitating the possibility of success through individual achievement and providing the altar at which the vast majority of the social sciences kneel in adoration.

But the institutional arrangements characteristic of within-country LIE *do* restrict access to opportunity for large sectors of the population, except that excluded populations now are located primarily *outside national borders.* Selective exclusion, in the case of within-country LIE, operates fundamentally through the very existence of national borders, reducing competitive pressures within those borders, while simultaneously enhancing competitive pressures among the excluded population outside the very same borders (again, in the arenas or markets to which *those* populations are restricted). Hence, the establishment of within-country LIE and the persistence of between-country HIE are not two separate processes: rather, they are the outcome of the fundamental institutional arrangements undergirding world inequality.

We represent these patterns in figure 4.7, which takes up where figure 3.1 left off. By the 1800s, the arrangements characteristic of within-country LIE had developed considerable advantages in ensuring a greater relative command over income than the institutional arrangements contained in the nations characterized by within-country HIE.

Around the late nineteenth and early twentieth centuries, wealthier nations characterized by LIE were undergoing the type of transition envisioned by Kuznets in his inverted U-curve hypothesis. (In fact, the overall pattern of transition characterizing within-country LIE in figure 4.7 is the same as in figure 1.1.) Note, however, that this transition was accompanied by relatively more open flows of people (represented by the arrows in the figure) from poorer areas of

Figure 4.7   Stylized Trends of HIE and LIE, 1800s to 2000s

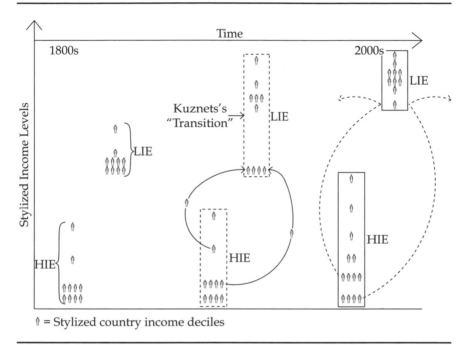

⇑ = Stylized country income deciles

Source: Authors' illustration.

the world (represented in the figure by LIE) into richer ones (represented in the figure by LIE). National barriers to entry were relatively less pronounced (as suggested by the dotted boundaries surrounding each stylized cluster of country deciles).

By the twentieth century, national barriers to entry had become more pronounced as part of an effort to restrict competitive pressures or reduce inequality within the LIE cluster. (To represent the strengthening of such national barriers to entry, we use a solid line to represent the boundaries surrounding the HIE and LIE clusters at the end of the transition indicated in figure 4.7.) As these barriers to entry became more pronounced, flows between the two clusters (HIE and LIE, poorer and richer) diminished (as represented by changes in the arrows indicating mobility across national borders).

Such patterns of interaction bear a striking resemblance to how Adam Smith (1776/1976) described the relationship between town and country in the emergence of capitalism. As in wealthy LIE countries today, town inhabitants in Smith's account found it easier than those in the country to associate, and indeed they used corporate association to regulate production and trade in their towns to restrict outside competition.[18] Although such arrangements tended to raise the wages that town employers had to pay, "in recompense, they were enabled to sell their own just as much dearer; so that so far it was as broad as long, as they say; and in the dealings of the different classes within the town with one another, none of them were losers by these regulations" (Smith 1776/1976, I, 139). Moreover, as a result of such arrangements, in their dealings with the country ("and in these latter dealings consists the whole trade which supports and enriches every town") town dwellers were "great gainers" able to "purchase, with a smaller quantity of their labor, the produce of a greater quantity of the labor of the country" (139–40). What Smith thereby describes is a process of selective exclusion: through institutional arrangements establishing a social compact that restricted entry to markets, town dwellers attained a virtuous combination of growth, political autonomy, and relative equity that simultaneously transferred competitive pressures to the countryside.

Of course, we do not mean to imply that the uneven global distribution of competitive advantages and disadvantages resulted solely from the way in which within-country LIE transferred competitive pressures from one location to another. Surely, the story is much more complicated. To the extent that within-country LIE strengthened and protected property rights, areas under such arrangements did provide phenomenal incentives to potential producers that were absent elsewhere. Here, as in Adam Smith's (1776/1976, I, 426) towns, "order and good government, and along with them the liberty and security of individuals, were, in this manner, established . . . , at a time when the occupiers of land [elsewhere] were exposed to every sort of violence."[19] Moreover, once having gained a certain competitive edge, areas characterized by LIE tended to have at their disposal much greater resources to maintain and extend this edge (for example, through technological innovation and a more constant upgrading of the labor force).

But when focusing only on wealthy nations, as is the practice of most of the social sciences, these institutional arrangements indeed appear, like those of Adam Smith's towns, to be characterized primarily by inclusion; likewise, economic growth and markets seem to constitute virtuous spheres where gain is fundamentally an outcome of effort. From such a perspective, success appears to be the outcome of individual achievement, as measured by universal criteria, in spheres characterized by relatively unrestricted access (such as education and labor markets).

As in Smith's town and country, the interaction of such virtuosity with processes of selective exclusion can only be observed when we shift our unit of analysis to encompass the world as a whole (producing the type of patterns suggested by figure 4.7).[20] Such a shift reveals that the prevalence of what appear to be "achieved" characteristics in today's wealthy nations is predicated on processes operating between nations that hide how the institutional arrangements characteristic of within-country LIE entail privileges based on both exclusion and "ascribed" characteristics.[21]

BETWEEN-COUNTRY HIE, WITHIN-COUNTRY LIE, AND MIGRATION

The exclusionary features of the development of within-country LIE can be identified best by focusing on migration around the late nineteenth and early twentieth centuries. In the late nineteenth century, there was a staggering increase of free migration across national borders, driven primarily by the promise of high wages in receiving countries.[22] Indeed, in relative terms, annual immigration was more significant than that in recent times.[23] These high rates of global migration were facilitated by the weak capacity of states to enforce tight controls over their boundaries, but they were also indicative of a prevailing consensus regarding the right of individuals to move across borders, a right that "had become so generally accepted that formal guarantees [such as the use of a passport system] were considered unnecessary" (Dowty 1987, 54).[24]

This mass migration had a major impact on within- and between-country inequality. Movement across national borders led to considerable convergence among the wealthier nations of the world-economy in the late nineteenth century (primarily Europe, North America, Australia, and New Zealand)—a convergence explained for the most part "by the collapse of the wage gap between Europe and the New World" (O'Rourke and Williamson 1999, 15).[25] Global migration flows shifted population from countries of relatively lower income and slower growth (sending countries) to countries of relatively higher income and rapid growth (receiving nations) and tended to even out wage rates between core countries and between core and semiperipheral areas. Furthermore, insofar as mass migration was accompanied by large return flows of migrants to their areas of origin, it also provided an *indirect* mechanism for reducing world income inequalities through the circulation of investment capital, innovations in the organization of production and consumption, and so forth.[26]

Although mass migration generated some convergence in between-country inequality (at least among the relatively wealthier nations of the world-economy), its impact on within-country inequality was more mixed. By promoting higher overall wages and a decline in inequality between skilled and unskilled workers, mass migration resulted in declining within-country inequality among the principal sending countries (Dowty 1987; Williamson 1991). On the other hand, by providing a large supply of unskilled workers who experienced growing wage differentials relative to skilled workers, mass migration resulted in the rise of inequality within receiving, higher-income nations (Dowty 1987; Williamson 1991).[27]

The perceived rise of inequality in receiving nations generated a backlash against open migration.[28] The case of the United States is illustrative. Here the shift toward the exclusion of foreign populations was gradual: "attitudes changed slowly and over a number of decades rather than all at once" (O'Rourke and Williamson 1999, 185). Although nativism and opposition to immigration (mixed with anti-Catholicism) had been present since colonial times, and the Naturalization Act of 1790 restricted citizenship to "free white person[s]," the first significant drive to restrict migration in the United States came in the 1870s, led by "Californians [who] envisaged themselves as guardians of the imperiled frontier of white civilization" (Higham 1956, 216).[29] The drive to restrict migration, which "accus[ed] the Chinese of taking jobs away from white laborers and call[ed] for violent action against them," drew heavily upon support from blue-collar European migrant workers (employed and unemployed) but included broader forces that came to portray such restrictions as a necessary deterrent to vice (namely prostitution and opium smoking) (Ahmad 2007, 14; Shumsky 1991).[30] The considerable political strength wielded by these constituents led to "the act of 1882, 'suspending' the entry of Chinese labor for ten years. . . . At the turn of the century, suspension became permanent exclusion" (Higham 1956, 216).[31]

In the last decades of the nineteenth century, concerns over growing inequality led anti-immigration forces to move beyond targeting Chinese labor to focus on European migrants as well.[32] Labor unrest was a contributing issue, as "nonunionized workers and white collar people began to suspect that the whole wave of industrial discontent was somewhat foreign-inspired" (Higham 1956, 219). Italians, as part of the new migration from southern and eastern Europe, were a major target of this anti-foreign drive: "By Western European standards, the new immigrant masses were socially backward and bizarre in appearance. . . . Moreover, a number of eastern intellectuals began to argue that the southern and eastern Europeans were not only socially dangerous but also racially unassimilable" (219).[33]

For the moment, however, formal restrictions on European migration remained limited: Higham (1956, 220) attributes this to a persistent faith in assimilation, the reluctance of Republicans to engage in protectionism, and the ambivalence of Democrats in the Northeast due to their reliance on immigrant votes. Moreover, after 1896 "a dazzling resurgence of prosperity inaugurated a long period of good times and quieted the fierce industrial unrest of the preceding years" (221).

Despite this truce, the underlying restrictionist drive continued to grow, linked with eugenics and anthropological studies that differentiated European races: with these scientific justifications, "nationalism was naturalized" (Higham 1956, 224). The drive against migration, drawing on three forces—"patrician race-thinkers," trade unions, and "the common people of the South and West" (225–26)—strengthened after 1914. For Higham, the new role of the last group represented a major shift:

> The Deep South and the Far West, where the new regional lineup started, had long been the areas of most intense race-feelings. The instincts of white supremacy had not seemed widely relevant to European immigration, however, until after the imperial adventures of 1898. Imperialism popularized the Anglo-Saxon idea of nationality and linked it with primitive

race-feelings. Even without the sophisticated rationale of the new racial science, southerners and westerners could now regard the unfamiliar nationalities of southeastern Europe as somewhat less than completely white. (236)

Moreover, after the 1906 outbreak on the West Coast of an anti-Japanese movement (which also drew on fears that nations such as Japan would become increasingly competitive with the United States), "Asiatic and European migration were now, and would henceforth be, treated as different phases of a single question, not as entirely separate from one another" (226).

World War I finished off the strong belief in assimilation, whose demise culminated in the 1917 immigration law, which included restrictions on migration based on literacy, restrictions on most Asian migration, and provisions for the deportation of undesirables. Quotas followed in 1921, and "henceforth, ethnic affiliation would be the main determinant for admission to the United States" (Higham 1956, 229). That these restrictive immigration policies were given legal sanction indicated that "for many federal judges, doctrines of human liberties, even economic liberties, were confined within an ascriptive frame that granted full rights only to superior races and nations" (Smith 1997, 368).

Following the 1921 quotas, immigration would steadily decline for several decades, reaching a trough during the 1970s. Unionization and the reduction of wage differentials between the skilled and unskilled, the protection extended by the New Deal and the Fair Deal to less well-off (but politically mobilized) segments of the white population, and even the institutional transformations eventually attained by the civil rights movement (and by the women's move-ment)—all would mobilize and give substance to notions of citizen-ship as a basis of entitlement. Only in more recent decades has immigration begun to regain importance, although even today it does not have the relative magnitude it achieved during the 1910s.

Moving back from the United States to elsewhere in the world, the political backlash was not only against migration but against open markets in general. In various areas of the world, agricultural and manufacturing producers reacted to the competition of exports, with each sector, as O'Rourke and Williamson (1999) remind us, divided within itself along various criteria rather than operating as a single, unified force.[34] Of course, the particular shape and consequences of this backlash varied from country to country.[35] But throughout, in the words of Karl Polanyi (1944/1957, 217), nations and peoples "shielded themselves from unemployment and instability with the help of central banks and custom tariffs, supplemented by migration laws."[36]

Protectionism and restrictions on immigration had their intended effect: reversing the rise in within-country inequality across much of the core.[37] According to O'Rourke and Williamson (1999, 183), "the rising inequality in the rich countries ceased exactly when labor migration was choked off by quotas, global capital markets collapsed, and the international community retreated behind high trade barriers. Are these interwar correlations spurious? The pre–World War I experience suggests not."

The "backlash" against global markets in the early twentieth century and the moderating responses to within-country inequality among wealthier countries in the following decades revolved around strengthening the nation-state as a basis upon which to organize categorical differences. Constraints on migration and the rise of the welfare state involved the consolidation of identities constructed around the nation-state and citizenship; to extrapolate from Wright's (2006) discussion of opposition to slavery, these strategies both universalized and simultaneously excluded on the basis of national identity (and the latter became the key basis of categorical inequality from a global perspective).

Similarly to the situation described by Adam Smith, the institutional arrangements of within-country LIE and the national regulation of international migration in the twentieth century reduced competitive pressures among workers within wealthy nations and thereby contributed to the declining income inequality in wealthier nations at the time. But the institutional arrangements and market mechanisms that served to reduce inequality within high-income nations simultaneously generated or strengthened constraints that accentuated inequalities between nations. Constraints on international migration, for example, accentuated competitive pressures in labor markets elsewhere in the world and in the process eliminated for much of the twentieth century one possible mechanism for reducing the income gap between countries—the transfer of populations from poor to wealthy nations.[38]

The crucial importance of restricted migration flows to patterns of between-country inequality was well understood by observers who critically assessed theories of economic growth in the 1950s. Prebisch (1950) argued that between-country differences in income were ultimately linked to the uneven bargaining power of workers in center (or wealthy) and peripheral (or poorer) nations: in the center

> during the upswing, part of the profits are absorbed by an increase in wages occasioned by competition between entrepreneurs and by the pressure of trade unions. When profits have to be reduced during the downswing, the part that had been absorbed by wage increases loses its fluidity, at the center, by reason of the well-known resistance to a lowering of wages. The pressure then moves toward the periphery, with greater force than would be the case if, *by reason of the limitation of competition,* wages and profits in the center were not rigid. The less that income can contract at the center, the more it must do so at the periphery.[39] (Prebisch 1950, 13, emphasis added)

For Prebisch, a smooth transfer of productivity gains did not take place across the world precisely because of restrictions on the mobility of labor. Thus, such transfers, either through prices or the raising of incomes,

> would have required, throughout the world, the same mobility of factors of production as that which characterized the broad field of the internal economy of the United States. That mobility is one of the essential assumptions of the theory. In fact, however, a series of obstacles hampered the easy movement of productive factors. Doubtless the high wages paid in the United States, as compared with those in the rest of the world, would have attracted large masses to that country, with a very adverse effect upon wages, tending to reduce the difference between them and those in the rest of the world. (16)

Likewise, Arthur Lewis (1954, 177) noted that

> if there were free immigration from India and China to the U.S.A., the wage level of the U.S.A. would certainly be pulled

down towards the Indian and Chinese levels. . . . This is one of the reasons why, in every country where the wage level is relatively high, the trade unions are bitterly hostile to immigration, except of people in special categories, and take steps to have it restricted. The result is that real wages are higher than they would otherwise be, while profits, capital resources, and total output are smaller than they would otherwise be.[40]

Just as race becomes a crucial ascriptive criterion sustaining within-country HIE, national identity and citizenship constitute the central ascriptive criteria shaping between-country HIE. John Rawls (1971, 102) argues that "aristocratic and caste societies are unjust because they make [natural] contingencies the ascriptive basis for belonging to more or less enclosed and privileged social classes." This is precisely the logic that has prevailed in interactions between the populations of nation-states in the world-system as the within-country LIE pattern came to entail selective exclusion on the basis of citizenship. In this sense, the problem with the types of representation of within-country inequality reviewed in chapter 1 is not that they distort the transitions that accompanied within-country LIE, but that they omit the significant role played by exclusion and the reconstitution of ascription in reducing competitive pressures within the social arrays at hand.

In short, the very same discourse through which HIE were challenged within nations—a discourse focusing on citizenship and a community of national interests—transferred much of the inequality that prevailed within nations to the arena of between-nations distribution, where HIE today is most prevalent. Since the nineteenth century, such arrangements have led to an incredible increase in wealth and welfare (see, for example, Fogel 2004), accompanied by inequality so extreme that it is comparable to the highest within-country levels of inequality that have ever been experienced.

Conclusion

Inequality must be understood as it unfolds within world-historical institutions. Rather than being nationally bounded, as in the modernization perspective that frames the arguments of Simon Kuznets, institutional arrangements constitute *relational* mechanisms of regulation that operate *within* countries while simultaneously shaping interactions and flows *between* them.[41] Shifting the relevant unit of analysis in this way, from the nation-state to the world-system, changes our understanding of what Rawls (1971, 99–100) calls the "relevant positions" from which to assess justice. From a world-systems perspective, the same institutional mechanisms through which inequality historically has been reduced *within* nations often have accentuated the selective exclusion of populations from poorer countries, thereby enhancing inequality *between* nations. Shifting the unit of analysis to the world-system thus reveals that ascriptive criteria remain the fundamental basis of stratification and inequality and that national identity has been the most salient of these criteria in the contemporary world.

As we explore in greater detail in the following chapter, if we were to construct a global map of inequality, showing where each household or individual stands vis-à-vis everyone else in the world (that is, combining information on within- and between-country inequality), the relative standing of all households and individuals would continue to be shaped most heavily by whether they inhabited a poor or wealthy nation (that is, by inequality between nations).[42] This is a consequence of, as well as evidence for, the crucial impact of the high level of inequality between nations on global patterns of stratification.

Thus, we have reason to be a bit skeptical that we have already left behind the HIE that characterized the distribution of income between nations over the past few centuries—and not only because of the rarity of upward mobility of nations over the past two centuries. We might be entering such a transition, but the various trade-offs entailed in such a change are likely to lead to many political conflicts that are still to be played out (as was the case in the previous great period of increased global flows in the late nineteenth and early twentieth centuries). On the other hand, the perspective advanced in this book highlights the area that is likely to serve as the epicenter of these conflicts: the meaning of national borders in the face of globalization.

CHAPTER 5

GLOBAL STRATIFICATION AND
THE THREE PATHS OF SOCIAL MOBILITY

*If the slopsellers and others of their class have lowered the wages of tai-
lors and some other artizans, by making them an affair of competition
instead of custom, so much the better in the end. What is now required is
not to bolster up old customs, whereby limited classes of laboring people
obtain partial gains which interest them in keeping up the present
organization of society, but to introduce new general practices beneficial
to all; and there is reason to rejoice at whatever makes the privileged
classes of skilled artizans feel that they have the same interests, and
depend on their remuneration on the same general causes, and must
resort for the improvement in their condition to the same remedies, as the
less fortunately circumstanced and comparatively helpless multitude.*
    —John Stuart Mill, Principles of Political Economy

Throughout this book, we have emphasized the importance of taking the world as a whole as the proper unit of analysis in order to understand inequality. Such a step allows us to discern that patterns of inequality today entail a complex global interplay of trends in between- and within-country inequality, particularly through the interaction of the institutional arrangements character-istic of high-inequality and low-inequality equilibria (HIE and LIE) through the last two centuries. Understanding inequality as a global historical phenomenon allows us to render visible what is otherwise veiled by mainstream social science: since the nineteenth century, the nation-state itself has come to constitute the primary criterion for the reconstitution of ascriptive exclusion as the principal basis of social stratification.

Yet, as we discussed in chapter 1, most of the social science literature operates under the (sometimes) explicit (or, most often, implicit)
assumption that inequality, stratification, and social mobility result
from economic, social and political interactions that take place primarily or even exclusively *within nations*. Under such an assumption,
the relevant units of analysis to understand inequality are discrete,
bounded "national" territories. (We should note that this assumption
is generally made by default, since much of the contemporary social
sciences do not seriously engage in theoretically establishing the relevant unit of analysis for a given phenomenon.) Within such nationally bounded territories, inequality is shaped by the interaction of
groups or classes of people "who by virtue of what they possess are
compelled to engage in the same activities if they want to make the
best use of their endowments" (Huber and Stephens 2001, 17). With
such a focus, much of the existing social science literature then pro-
ceeds to establish as universal the trends and patterns characteristic
of the particular sample of nations in which within-country inequality or economic growth are being observed—more often than not the
wealthy countries (as discussed in chapter 1).

Taking a similar definition of the forces shaping inequality as the
definition that prevails in much of the social sciences, but adopting a
global perspective, we argue that nationhood and citizenship have
been as much a part of the constitution of the identity of social forces,
and of the demarcation of their interest, as class.[1] From a global perspective, the constitution of class interests often had the (intended or
unintended) consequence of constructing nation-states as the crucial
criterion of stratification—that is, "the unequal distribution of people across social categories that are characterized by differential
access to scarce resources" (Massey 2007, 1).

When we choose the historical development of the world-economy
as the relevant unit of analysis, our attention is redirected to the
changing processes of institutionalized social interaction that
result in inequality or mobility. The social attributes used in the
mainstream social sciences (as reviewed in chapter 1) to "explain"
inequality—attributes such as education, skill, gender, race and
ethnicity, and so forth—become instead the changing expression
of processes of differentiation that entail both within- and between-
country inequality. In this chapter, we explore how a shift in the
unit of analysis to the world as a whole can generate new and pro-

ductive insights into the changing face of inequality. What do stratification and inequality look like from a global perspective? What constitutes social mobility when seen from the world as whole?

Answering these questions requires more than a slight shift in emphasis aimed at considering some between-country dimensions of inequality that simply coexist with some more fundamental within-country processes. In both its social-scientific and more popular versions, the prevalent mode of understanding the forces that shape inequality and stratification (and hence, the main way to delineate the relevant boundaries of a unit of analysis) is itself part and parcel of the process by which citizenship and nationhood were constructed and are constantly reconstituted as a justifiable basis for categorical differentiation. To question such a mode of understanding requires challenging the natural categories through which high levels of global inequality are legitimated.

GLOBAL STRATIFICATION

Social stratification is drastically reformulated once we adopt the world as a whole as the proper unit of analysis. To illustrate how to move toward such a global perspective on social stratification, we combine the within-country distributional information presented in chapter 1 with the between-country measures of economic performance used in chapter 4.[2] Thus, information about the shares of income accruing to national population deciles (beginning with the richest 10 percent and moving through each decile until we reach the poorest 10 percent) is combined with each nation's per capita gross national income (GNI) in 2007 to produce an estimate of the per capita income of each country decile (for a fuller explanation of the procedure, see the statistical appendix). Hence, for every country in the data set, the procedure yields ten "country deciles," each representing one-tenth of the country's population, from the richest to the poorest, and each with an estimated per capita GNI. USA10, for example, represents the wealthiest 10 percent of the population of the United States, and USA1 the poorest 10 percent. The data set includes country decile information for 85 nations, which we used to calculate the distribution of income for 850 country deciles. The results of the exercise are presented in figure 5.1.

Figure 5.1   Global Stratification: 850 Country Deciles Ranked from Rich to Poor

Global Deciles and Estimated per Capita GNI, in U.S. Dollars, 2007

164,700

10

NOR10 LUX10 CHE10 USA10 IRE10 GBR10 LUX9 DEN10 NOR9 SWE10 CAN10 BEL10 FIN10 LUX8 AUT10 NOR8 NLD10 CHE9 DEU10 FRA10 ITA10 AUS10 LUX7 NOR7 DEN9 ESP10 NOR6 CHE8 GRC10 LUX6 IRE9 USA9 NOR5 GBR9 DEN8 SWE9 NLD9 LUX5 CHE7 IRE8 FIN9 NOR4 DEN7 AUT9 CAN9 BEL9 USA8 LUX4 FRA9 CHE6 ISR10 DEU9 NLD8 SWE8 AUS9 DEN6 GBR8 NOR3 FIN8 IRE7 AUT8 ERT10 ITA9 DEN5 CHE5 LUX3 NLD7 CAN8 SWE7 BEL8 USA7 FIN7 DEU8 FRA8 IRE6 AUS8 AUT7 GRC9 KOR10 ESP9 GBR7 NLD6 NOR2 DEN4 CHE4 SWE6 FIN6 BEL7 CAN7 LUX2 SVN10 TWN10 ITA8 USA6 AUT6 DUE7 NLD5 FRA7 SWE5 IRE5 AUS7 BEL6 CHE3 FIN5 DEN3 GBR6 GRC8 CHL10 AUT5 ESP8 CAN6 DEU6 NLD4 EST10 SWE4 ITA7 FRA6 USA5 ISR9 BEL5 FIN4 IRE4 AUS6 MEX10 DEU5 AUT4 GBR5 DEN2 CHE2 GRC7 CAN5 NLD3 FRA5 SWE3 CZE10 ESP7 LUX1 HRV10 ITA6 BEL4 KOR9 FIN3 NOR1 SVN9 USA4 DEU4 AUS5 LVA10 AUT3 PRT9 FRA4

27,894

9

NLD2 CAN4 HUN10 GRC6 GBR4 IRE3 BRA10 ESP6 TWN9 SWE2 ITA5 LTU10 FIN2 BEL3 MYS10 DEU3 SVN8 KOR8 FRA3 AUS4 AUT2 RUS10 DEN1 ISR7 USA3 SVK10 GRC5 CAN3 POL10 ESP5 SVN7 VEN10 PRT8 PAN10 GVR3 ITA4 TWN8 ARG10 BEL2 KOR7 DEU2 IRE2 EST9 CHE1 FRA2 SVN6 CZE9 URY10 AUS3 GRC4 ISR6 ESP4 NLD1 PRT7 TWN7 FIN1 ITA3 CAN2 SVN5 KOR6 CRI10 GBR2 SUR10 USA2 SWE1 CZE8 PRT6 HUN9 ISR5 KOR5 TWN6 SVN4 AUS2 GRC3 ESP3 EST8 SVK9 JAM10 HRV9 AUT1 ITA2 PRT5 CZE7 LTU9 LVA9 BEL1 THA10 BLZ10 POL9 KOR4 TWN5 IRE1 SVN3 COL10 FRA1 SVK8 ROM10 ISR4 DOM10 ECU10 HUN8 PER10 EST7 CZE6 DEU1 PRT4 MEX9 GRC2 ESP2 TWN4 RUS9 SVK7 CHL9 HRV8 POL8 LTU8 KOR3 CZE5 HUN7 VEN9 SVN2 GBR1 SVK6 LVA8 ISR3 EST6 TWN3 BGR10 CAN1 CZE4 POL7 SLV10 MYS9 HRV7 AUS1 HUN6 URY9 SVK5 LTU7 ARG9 GTM10 USA1 EST5 CZE3 BRA9 PRT3 LVA7 SVK4 POL6 HUN5 RUS8 PAN9 MEX8 TWN2 VEN8 CRI9 ISR2 LTU6 HRV6 BLR10 ROM9 ITA1 KOR2 CHL8 CZE2 SVK3 EST4 LKA10 POL5 SUR9 LVA6 HUN4

7,898

8

ESP1

LTU5 URY8 RUS7 HRV5 PRT2 SVN1 CHN10 MYS8 GRC1 ROM8 VEN7 ARG8 MEX7 LVA5 POL4 HUN3 PRY10 EGY10 SVK2 EST3 CRI8 BGR9 LTU4 HND10 LVA4 HRV4 PHL10 ROM7 PAN8 CHL7 JAM9 HUN2 URY7 BRA8 RUS6 THA9 TWN1 VEN6 CZE1 POL3 ISR1 BOL10 MEX6 BLR9 BLZ9 ROM6 LVA3 DOM9 MYS7 PRT1 LTU3 EST2 ARG7 BGR8 LSO10 PER9 SUR8 CRI7 HRV3 IDN10 ROM5 CHL6 URY6 CMR10 COL9 MRT10 VEN5 RUS5 BLR8 PAN7 BGR7 SLV9 MEX5 POL2 ROM4 BRA7 ZMB10 MYS6 ECU9 LVA2 ARG6 CRI6 BLR7 JAM8 LTU2 SVK1 HUN1 NIC10 URY5 BLZ8 CHN9 BGR6 CHL5

4,179

7

KOR1

VEN4 RUS4 HRV2 DOM8 SUR7 BLR6 ROM3 THA8 PER8 NGA10 MDA10 PAN6 MEX4 BGR5 IND10 GTN9 CRI5 MYS5 BLR5 ARG5 URY4 BRA6 COL8 CHL4 SLV8 BLZ7 EST1 ROM2 BGR4 VEN3 SUR6 JAM7 BLR4 RUS3 ECU8 CHN8 DOM7 PER7 CRI4 MEX3 BLR3 PAN5 MYS4 KEN10 BFA10 ARG4 URY3 BGR3 THA7 BRA5 SUR5 CHL3 HND9 BLZ6 HAI10 PRY9 SLV7 COL7 UZB10 GTM8 PHL9 BLR2 IDN9 JAM6 HRV1 LVA1 DOM6 ECU7 VEN2 PER6 CRI3

2,377

6

CHN1

RUS2 GIN10 EGY9 MYS3 PAN4 GHA10 POL1 BGR2 ROM1 BLZ5 ARG3 SUR4 BRA4 URY2 CHL2 MEX2 SLV6 ZWE10 COL6 THA6 BOL9 MDA9 GTM7 CAP10 DOM5 ECU6 GMB10 LTU1 PER5 JAM5 IDN8 HND8 BLR1 PRY8 CHN6 PHL8 BLZ4 LKA9 CRI2 MYS2 SLV5 LSO9 COL5 GTM6 BRA3 IND9 ECU5 CMR9 DOM4 PAN3 EGY8 ARG2 SUR3 MDA8 PER4 MDG10

1,547

5

IDN7

THA5 UGA10 BGD10 BLZ3 NIC9 NGA9 PRY7 NPL10 CHN5 HND7 PHL7 BOL8 JAM4 SLV4 GTM5 COL4 LKA8 BGR1 IDN6 ECU4 VEN1 URY1 DOM3 MDA7 EGY7 UZB9 CHL1 MRT9 PER3 BRA2 PRY6 THA4 SUR2 KEN9 IDN5 CHN4

1,104

4

IND8

CMR8 ZMB9 RUS1 GTM4 PHL6 LKA7 MDA6 HND6 BOL7 MYS1 BLZ2 NIC8 COL3 SLV3 ECU3 MEX1 NGA8 EGY6 GHA9 LSO8 PAN2 IDN4 DOM2 ETH10 UZB8 PRY5 CHN3 LKA6 MDA5 PHL5 CRI1 HAI9 GTM3 JAM3 PER2 EGY5 IND7 IDN3 ARG1 THA3 BOL6 HND5 CMR7 KEN8 NIC7 NGA7 MRT8 BGD9 ECU2 MDA4 LKA5 ZMB8 UZB7 PHL4 GHA8 PRY4 COL2 EGY4

666

3

CHN2

IDN2 SLV2 GIN9 IND6 GTM2 BOL5 NIC6 LSO7 CMR6 CAP9 HND4 NGA6 BRA1 MDA3 BFA9 KEN7 LKA4 HAI8 PHL3 UZB6 NPL9 BGD8 MDG9 GHA7 EGY3 THA2 MRT7 PRY3 ZMB7 UGA9 SUR1 IND5 NIC5 DOM1 NGA5 ZWE9 CMR5 GMB9 MDA2 UZB5 KEN6 HND3 IDN1

443

2

BGD7

BOL4 PHL2 LKA3 BLZ1 PER1 HAI7 GHA6 LSO6 CHN1 NIC4 IND4 NPL8 NGA4 JAM2 CAP8 EGY2 ZMB6 BGD6 PAN1 CMR4 MDG8 ECU1 UZB4 MRT6 GIN8 UGA8 KEN5 GHA5 HAI6 IND3 PRY2 NIC3 BGD5 NGA3 ETH9 BFA8 NPL7 GTM1 HND2 PHL1 ZMB5 LKA2 BOL3 LSO5 ZWE8 BGD4

266

1

UZB3

COL1 GHA4 HAI5 UGA7 CAP7 CMR3 KEN4 GMB8 MDG7 MDA1 IND2 NGA2 NPL6 MRT5 NIC2 SLV1 ETH8 BGD3 ZMB4 UGA6 HAI4 GIN7 GHA3 LSO4 ZWE7 EGY1 KEN3 CAP6 NPL5 BFA7 THA1 UZB2 MDG6 ETH7 BGD2 UGA5 GMB7 CMR2 HAI3 MRT4 ZMB3 ETH6 HND1 NPL4 UGA4 GIN6 GHA2 NGA1 ZWE6 LSO3 CAP5 PRY1 MDG5 IND1 ETH5 BFA6 GMB6 NIC1 KEN2 BOL2 UGA3 HAI2 GIN5 ETH4 CAP4 MRT3 NPL3 BGD1 ZMB2 JAM1 MDG4 ZWE5 LKA1 BFA5 LSO2 GMB5 ETH3 UGA2 UZB1 GIN4 CMR1 CAP3 ETH2 BFA4 MDG3 ZWE4 NPL2 GHA1 GMB4 MRT2 GIN3 KEN1 CAP2 UGA1 BFA3 LSO1 GMB3 GIN2 HAI1 MDG2 ZWE3 ETH1 ZMB1 BOL1 GMB2 BFA2 NPL1 CAP1 MRT1 GIN1 ZWE2 MDG1 GMB1 BFA1 ZWE1

5

Source: Authors' calculations; see statistical appendix.

Figure 5.1 ranks the 850 country deciles in our sample from rich to poor. Having ranked these country deciles, we calculated a global distribution of income for our sample (accounting for roughly 80 percent of the actual world population) and sorted the country deciles into *global* population deciles. In other words, the figure shows how the income of a country decile locates the decile within global stratification (the global population deciles identified on the left side of the figure). Here again, global population decile 10 represents the wealthiest 10 percent of the world population, and global population 1 the poorest 10 percent (as represented by our sample). The left side of the figure also indicates the income levels that constitute the boundaries for each global population decile: the wealthiest global decile, for example, has an average per capita income of $28,570 or higher, while the same average for the poorest global decile is $265 or lower. Nine country deciles split their population between two adjoining global population deciles: for example, the fourth decile of the United States is divided between the two wealthiest global deciles. Of course, while each global decile has an equal population, some global deciles (such as global decile 4) have fewer country deciles than others (such as global decile 9): this is because the population size of specific country deciles varies a great deal—say, from 47,999 in the Luxembourg country deciles to over 100 million in the China or India country deciles. The wealthiest country decile in our sample is the richest 470,915 people of Norway—in fact, the whole country of Norway is included in the top global income decile. The poorest country decile is the bottom 1,340,266 people in Zimbabwe.

We should note that the reported incomes for each decile are average incomes. The wealthiest and poorest deciles can vary significantly in the extent of their respective tails. The top decile of the United States in figure 5.1, for example, has an average income of $127,517. But there are over 30 million in the top decile of the United States, and some of these will have considerably higher incomes than the average—for example, USA10 goes roughly from the salary of a tenured professor at a research university to the income of Bill Gates. Likewise, the average income of the poorest 10 percent in the United States is $9,837, but some will have considerably lower incomes. The wealthiest and poorest deciles of each country can have long tails (very wealthy people in country deciles 10 or very poor people in country deciles 1) that are far from the average.

Figure 5.2 selects the twelve countries discussed in chapter 4 to provide a clearer visual representation of what global stratification looks like. The figure uses the same global decile boundaries used in figure 5.1 to locate the precise relative position of each of the country deciles of these twelve nations. (The circles used to represent each country decile are drawn to scale to convey the relative population contained in the different country deciles.)

The populations of most wealthy countries are contained wholly within the two top global income deciles: in the case of the United States, for example, USA10 through USA4 are contained in the top global decile, while USA3 through USA1 are contained in the second-wealthiest global decile (and similar characteristics are shared in figure 5.2 by Sweden and Spain). At the opposite end of the spectrum, the population of a country like Zimbabwe is almost wholly contained within the poorest global deciles, but high within-country inequality in Zimbabwe allows the wealthiest deciles to occupy a significantly higher position in the global hierarchy. The figure conveys the effects of some of the economic success stories of the last thirty years that we reviewed in chapter 4, with most of the population of South Korea (except for the poorest 10 percent) having moved across the threshold separating the two wealthiest global deciles from the rest, and China showing some advantages relative to India in every single country decile (and particularly those closest to the bottom). Finally, the figure conveys the effect of the high inequality levels that characterize many Latin American countries (a pattern that might or might not come to characterize the future trajectory of China and India): the populations of the five Latin American countries included in figure 5.2 are spread much more widely among wealthier and poorer global deciles.

This type of exercise helps reformulate social stratification from a global perspective—who constitutes the rich and the poor, who makes up a world's economic elite or its middle class. Social categories such as "elite," "middle class," and "the poor" are usually conceived as being nationally bounded—a national distribution of income dictates which people fall under each of the relevant categories. But from a global perspective, middle classes and even working classes in rich countries are located within the world's wealthiest deciles, often surpassing the status achieved by relatively wealthy sectors in poorer countries; for example, the poorest country decile

Figure 5.2   Country and Global Income Deciles for Twelve Nations

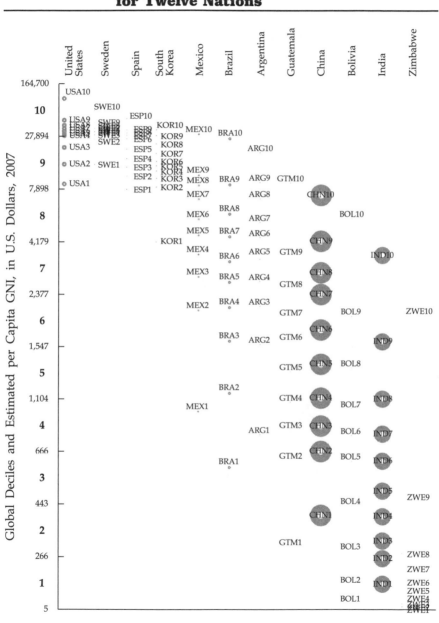

Source: Authors' calculations; see statistical appendix.

in the United States still has a higher average income than the wealthiest country decile in China. In this sense, scholars and observers often use terms such as "elite," "middle class," and "the poor" without considering that such categories might be referring to very different income levels on a world scale. At a national level, comparative levels of income or relative social position look very different when assessed within global stratification.

Such a portrayal of global stratification tends to generate some common critiques. First, people in wealthy countries, when hearing these findings, often challenge the notion that they should be considered rich. University professors in the United States are particularly likely to deny that they should be considered part of a "global elite" and argue that their incomes place them, at most, among an upper middle class. Of course, as we noted in the introduction to the book, in the United States many people in households with yearly incomes above $250,000 consider themselves part of the working middle class and virtually none are likely to consider themselves rich, even though their incomes would place them in the wealthiest 5 percent of U.S. households—and off the chart in figures 5.1 and 5.2. This tendency to define one's social position by "looking up" rather than down is not limited to the United States: a similar tendency can be found in most countries in the world. Who is "elite," "middle class," or "poor" is drastically redefined when such relative social positions are established using global criteria.

But, some might object, are we to assume that it is preferable to be in USA1 than in the richest decile in Bolivia (as indicated by the relative position of each of the two deciles in figure 5.2)? This question brings us back to the issue of the long tails of the distribution within the poorest and wealthiest country deciles. Although the average income of the wealthiest Bolivian decile in figure 5.2 is situated below the average income of the poorest U.S. decile, some Bolivians might have incomes that far exceed not just the poorest U.S. decile but some of the wealthiest U.S. deciles as well. But while some extremely rich Bolivians in BOL10 might have second homes in Manhattan or Miami, there are relatively few of them, *so on average* the richest 10 percent of Bolivians have incomes that are much lower than those of USA1. Thus, a professor in Bolivia might have an income that places him or her among the wealthiest 10 percent of Bolivians, but on a global scale this income might be much lower than the income received by a secretary in the United States. The point is that while Bolivians might have a select few whose income places them in the top global decile, a country like the United States has roughly 70 percent of its population in the same decile.

Similar points apply to comparisons involving the poorest of a country's deciles. Here again, the poorest country decile has a pronounced lower tail composed of relatively few people with very small incomes. For example, USA1 includes chronically unemployed people with extremely limited incomes, but these individuals are relatively few compared to the number of, say, full-time service workers earning the minimum wage. The point remains, however, that the average income of a food service worker in USA1 can be considerably higher than the earnings of the professional middle class in many poor countries.

The second line of criticism of such global comparisons focuses on differences in the cost of living: while incomes may be higher in wealthy countries, the argument goes, so are living expenses. There are many variations to such arguments, such as: "It costs more to live here in the United States," "You don't need as much money to 'live well' in poorer country X," and "It's better to be rich in a poor country than middle-class here." In a more academic version of this criticism, many argue that only purchasing power parity (PPP)–adjusted data should be used to make meaningful comparisons of incomes across the globe.

In chapter 4, we addressed some of these challenges, particularly in relation to the use of PPP data. We noted that the choice of appropriate indicators should be theoretically informed and that for the purposes of assessing differences in the relative command that people around the world have over the labor of others, foreign exchange (FX)–adjusted data provides a more appropriate indicator. We also noted, here and elsewhere, that the collection of PPP data is fraught with technical problems and contentious methodological assumptions; for example, China has never fully participated in a price survey, and many price estimates fail to demonstrate the appropriate adjustment for differences in the productivity of factors of production across the world.

All the exercises on global stratification reported in this chapter have been carried out using FX-based data. But despite all our reservations regarding the quality of PPP adjustments, as well as the theoretical reasons why FX-based data are more appropriate to understanding global inequality and stratification, we replicated our exercises reported with PPP-adjusted data. The ranking of country deciles reported in figures 5.1 and 5.2 is virtually unchanged (the correlation between PPP- and FX-adjusted data is .99), as is the global decile to which country deciles are allocated (here the correlation is .98): only 8 country deciles (out of 850) move by more than one global decile. Although the overall effect of using PPP-adjusted data is to increase slightly the relative ranking of the wealthiest country deciles of poor nations, while slightly reducing the relative ranking of the poorest deciles of the wealthier nations, the patterns of global stratification reported in this chapter (for example, the results represented in figures 5.1 through 5.4) are much the same.

We should add a few more points regarding standards of living. It is true that people in the upper strata of poorer countries can appear to "live better": because of the prevailing levels of inequality and extreme rates of poverty, such upper strata usually have access within their country to large quantities of the labor of others, since a small fraction of upper-strata income easily pays for the services of the poor. But at the same time, there are major quality-of-life issues in poorer countries that are neither effectively captured in PPP data nor taken into account by those who argue that the ability to pay cheaply for the labor of others provides many in poor countries with higher standards of living than their relative incomes would suggest. For example, access to basic services (and some transactable goods) is often very irregular or riddled with difficulties. The quality of life is also affected by environmental pollution and contamination to an extent that is not fully appreciated by those not exposed to such conditions. And perhaps the single biggest quality-of-life issue is the prevalence of widespread and severe violence, which can make personal safety an ever-present concern (and often drives the hiring of security personnel, property caretakers, and drivers). A university professor in a poorer country might have somewhat greater command over local personal services than his or her counterparts in a wealthier country, but this individual often faces significantly less command over personal safety than those counterparts. These differences are not trivial, and they remain unacknowledged by PPP data or in statements such as "It's better to be rich in a poor country than middle-class here."

Differences in the cost of personal services, on the other hand, are certainly relevant for illustrating some of the complexities of the interaction of within-country and between-country patterns of social stratification. A university professor in India might have an income that places him or her in the wealthiest 10 percent of the Indian distribution, but that income might translate into very little command over the labor of others when visiting the United States. On the other hand, a professor from the United States on a Fulbright Fellowship to India might have a domestic staff during his or her year abroad, services that he or she might not be able to afford back home. This is also the reason why some people from wealthy countries often choose to retire in a poorer country abroad, where their resources can stretch much further, and why the largest sending country of migrants to Mexico is the United States. This type of command is better captured by the FX-based data we are using here.

Finally, figures 5.1 and 5.2 show the relative distribution of global income. We are modest in our claims about the impact of different locations within such an income-based distribution in terms of more subjective assessments of relative welfare (such as happiness or discontent, alienation or belonging, achievement or frustration). It is also important to acknowledge that average levels of income tell us little about how people perceive their relative social position and the justice or injustice of their condition: ultimately, moreover, such subjectivity is key in the everyday construction and understanding of social categories such as "elites," "middle class," "working class," and "poor."

Global stratification, we argue, does not equal adding up the "elites," "middle classes," and "working class" or "poor" from different countries, as if they all occupied the same objective position in terms of interests. This has been the predominant tendency in much of the social sciences since the nineteenth century and throughout the twentieth century; from the point of view of the processes emphasized in this book, such a perspective was in fact a fundamental aspect of the very institutional creation of national states and interests organized around such "social classes." Global stratification involves instead intersecting processes in which national identity itself becomes the crucial axis of inequality. Social locations in global stratification are determined, not primarily by the relative position attained *within* a given country, but by the position occupied by such a country relative to others.[3]

In the twentieth century, national citizenship became constituted as the principal basis of categorical inequality. Today it remains the single most important variable that can be used to predict the eventual position of a person within global stratification—in spite of frequent claims that in our globalized world national boundaries have ceased to matter—and it is often ignored even in studies that explicitly undertake to explain the interaction between categorical inequality and stratification.[4] Here as elsewhere, the processes and categories that are relevant for understanding stratification depend on the criteria we use to define the relevant unit of analysis.

In this respect, the persistence of categorical inequality is justified today, as it was in the past, by appealing to images and forms of constructing identity that appear as natural rather than as the social artifacts they are. In this sense, the idea of nationhood as a "natural" category has become as deeply embedded in common sense (and unchallenged) as the idea of divine rights or white or male supremacy were in their own day.[5] But although categorical inequality and ascription are built into the very organization of markets and social stratification, they are simultaneously naturalized, rendering the categories with which we perceive the social world.[6] Categorical inequality and ascription are perhaps more fundamental than ever to the workings of global inequality: nevertheless (but this is not coincidental), such inequality coexists with a system of beliefs that asserts the primacy of individual achievement and opportunity, as pursued within nations, as the engine of everything.

RETHINKING SOCIAL MOBILITY

Thinking in such a manner about global stratification has implications as well for understanding social mobility. Although studies of socioeconomic mobility in wealthy nations (such as those we reviewed in chapter 1) generally assume that their conclusions are universally relevant, such studies actually are focusing on interactions among and within relatively wealthy strata in the world (mainly, the two top world income deciles shown in figures 5.1 and 5.2). Such a narrow focus provides a very partial perspective on mobility patterns. To make a historical parallel, it would be as if we were to assume that a study of individual trajectories in the French or British nobility in the fifteenth century represented the overall character of social stratification and mobility at the time.

Taking the world as the relevant unit of analysis allows us to reassess the character of different strategies of social mobility. From a global perspective, there are three main paths to social mobility: (1) a change (up or down) in the relative position of individuals or groups within national income distributions; (2) a change in the relative position of nations within the international income distribution; or (3) a shift in the relative location of individuals or groups within the global distribution of income attained through categorical mobility.

Path 1: Within-Country Mobility

Within nations, path 1 is the most apparent path of mobility. Through this path, for example, individuals or groups change their relative standing in national income distributions through the upgrading or devaluation of human capital (most importantly, skills and education). Cast more broadly as evidence for the gradual displacement of ascription by achievement as the primary criterion shaping social stratification, the pursuit of this strategy at an individual level has been the principal focus in the study of mobility by much of social science over the twentieth century.

Studies focusing on intergenerational mobility in wealthy countries end up measuring movement at the very top of the global income distribution, the ninth and tenth deciles of figures 5.1 and 5.2. In 2005 median earnings for a high school graduate in the United States were over $31,500, while the same figure for someone with a bachelor's degree or higher was over $56,000 (U.S. Bureau of the Census 2006). Shifting from one income to the other certainly represents a major attainment for the individuals or groups who make such a transition: within the United States this educational attainment would imply a move from USA4 to USA8. But even such a major within-country transition represents, in figures 5.1 or 5.2, a more limited movement in global stratification, as earnings of both $31,500 and $56,000 are contained within global income decile 10.

On the other hand, global mobility through educational attainment is more significant the higher the level of within-country inequality, particularly in middle-income nations. As we discussed in chapters 2 and 3, restricted access to education is precisely one of the principal mechanisms through which high levels of inequality were reproduced in HIE nations throughout the twentieth century. In a country such as Brazil, where levels of inequality are extremely high, and less than 10 percent of the population has a college degree, a shift for an individual or group similar to the one described for the United States would probably entail a movement from BRA5 or BRA6 to BRA10, translating into a shift from global decile 7 to global decile 9. From the point of view of relative standing in global stratification, the returns to education in such high-inequality, middle-income nations are even more considerable than in wealthy nations.

Complicating this path to mobility, however, are significant obstacles. Most importantly, the relative returns to any given level of human capital or educational attainment undergo significant change over time. For example, attaining a primary school education was a standard of high educational achievement in the late nineteenth century but is not considered a high marker of human capital attainment today. Computer literacy virtually did not exist forty years ago but is certainly a crucial skill today. More broadly, as Andrew Abbott (2006, 143) notes, "occupations change, absorb, and lose tasks, they merge and redivide, all within a time-scale commensurate with the length of an average career." Particularly in poorer nations, efforts at capturing the returns associated with enhanced human capital and greater educational attainment often involve engaging in a race whose finishing posts are constantly being moved forward.

In much of the prevailing mainstream literature, changes in the differential returns to skilled and unskilled labor and in who has access to such opportunities are fundamental in understanding social stratification and mobility. Indeed, these changing returns are one of the fundamental axes around which inequality has been constituted historically. But what is often missing in the mainstream literature, and what a world-historical perspective leads us to focus on, are the changing ways in which "skill" has been constructed over time as a criterion through which to differentially distribute returns to various populations.[7]

Such a perspective helps us understand, for example, why certain criteria (such as literacy, elementary education, secondary education, or computer skills) serve to claim (or justify) higher returns in one period but not later on in time; why some jobs are perceived as unskilled in some countries but skilled in others; or why new production processes might be read as deskilling in some countries but as upgrading in others. A world-historical perspective, in other words, highlights that the human capital criteria that underpin inequality are themselves an outcome of institutional arrangements linked to Schumpeterian processes of creative destruction.

Rather than reflecting an objective capacity to meet certain technical requirements (or anything related to actual tasks performed in production), the assortment of relevant populations across the world into the skilled and unskilled categories is linked to processes of creative destruction. For the most part, the skilled within any particular distributional array are those who are involved in the more creative end of the processes of creative destruction described by Schumpeter. Deskilling and the creation of the unskilled is precisely the outcome of constant destruction, and processes of construction of categorical inequality are linked precisely to the criteria used at any given historical moment to assort populations into the skilled and unskilled categories. (For example, "unskilled" today refers for the most part to those activities, once considered skilled, that are now carried out by populations in or from outside the top two global income deciles of figures 5.1 and 5.2.) Historically, entry into skilled positions has been constrained by the regulation of competition (such as in Adam Smith's towns). The use of ascriptive criteria to sort populations and thereby construct what is skilled or unskilled (for example, town and country, but also women and men, blacks and whites, and poor nations and rich nations) has been constitutive of the very creation and reproduction of inequality.

While the strategies reviewed here focus on mobility at an individual level, within-country mobility has included the various forms of collective action (for example, social movements, corporate organization) and political mobilization (from electoral participation to lobbying to revolutions) through which various actors have sought to enhance their command over resources within national boundaries. From a world-historical perspective, as illustrated in chapter 4, the impact of these strategies has always been complicated: the success of claims by one actor (for example, organized labor in wealthy countries) might go hand in hand with the exclusion of others (immigrants from poorer countries). Thus, as noted throughout this book, one and the same process—such as the pursuit of a more equitable distribution of resources by welfare states in wealthy countries—can have very different outcomes depending on whether we examine its impact solely within the boundaries of individual nation-states or in the world as a whole.

So how should advocates for greater equity assess the outcome of struggles that simultaneously enhance wealth and well-being for some (for example, male urban workers in post–World War II higher-income countries) while strengthening institutional arrangements that lead to the exclusion of others (immigrants from poorer countries)? Many answers are possible. Some argue that all countries have their respective disadvantaged populations who can only be expected to define themselves and their aims primarily in relation to their national surroundings, and that the struggle of poorer populations in wealthy countries is not only meaningful in and of itself but also helps raise the bar for standards of well-being across the world. Others, focusing on the effects of exclusion in enhancing relative inequality and facilitating the reproduction of absolute deprivation in poorer countries, would argue that the gains made by disadvantaged populations in wealthy countries are trivial relative to the needs of the majority of the world's population. And of course, most advocates of greater equity would probably reject approaching the question as a dilemma and instead would seek to recognize as valuable all efforts to advance the interests of the underprivileged relative to wealthier populations—no matter whether these efforts take place within national or global boundaries. Choosing among these standpoints is, of course, up to our readers: the purpose of this book is not to provide a ready solution but to expose the range of choices that emerge in a world-historical system of inequality and stratification.

Path 2: Between-Country Mobility

The second path to mobility in global social stratification, entailing national economic growth, is represented in figure 5.3, which shows the trajectory of the various national deciles of South Korea and Mexico relative to the per capita GNI of the United States in 1980 and in 2007. (Ideally, we would represent such trajectories by situating them within the overall global stratification that characterized

Figure 5.3   **Path 2: Economic Growth as Social Mobility, 1980 and 2007**

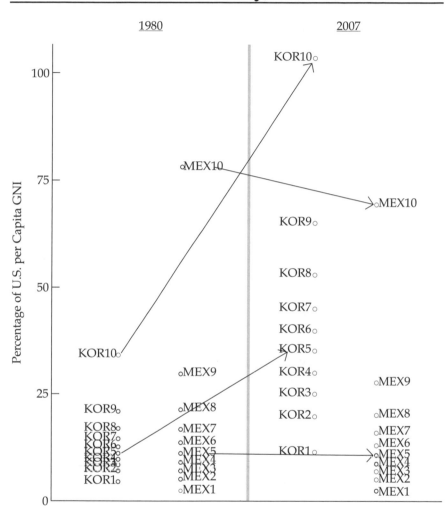

Source: Authors' calculations; see statistical appendix.

each of the two periods, but the exercise we conducted to construct figures 5.1 and 5.2 cannot be easily reconstructed for 1980.) In contrast to figure 4.6, which focused on relative rankings and data in the relative resources accruing to whole nations, figure 5.3 provides a more disaggregated approach, showing how the various country deciles are actually affected differently by gains and losses in national income. In the figure, South Korea illustrates the attractive promise of economic growth: all its national deciles rose during the period, albeit some at a faster rate than others. (The top deciles experienced the greatest convergence relative to the United States.) As with education, upgrading (as represented by high *relative* rates of economic growth) provides a promising route to global social mobility.

China and India today embody much of the optimism about the potential rewards of such a path. As we noted earlier, if the current growth rates of these two countries remain as high as they are today, they will eventually change the face of global stratification. Historically, there has always been mobility of individual nations, such as Sweden in the late nineteenth century, Japan in the immediate post–World War II era, and South Korea in the 1970s and 1980s. But in the past, as shown in chapter 4, the upward mobility of individual nations took place within a setting in which systemic inequality continued or became even more pronounced. The larger size of China and India makes the story different than before, because their effective mobility, even if limited to the two countries, would imply a shift in the logic that has prevailed until now in the world-economy.

As discussed in chapter 4, over the last two centuries the development of a HIE between countries was closely linked to the institutional arrangements that came to characterize within-country LIE. In a sense, such institutional arrangements—a particular way of distributing the relative gains and losses arising from the more day-to-day processes of creative destruction—have constituted a historical Schumpeterian innovation. But eventually the very institutional arrangements created through innovation themselves become characterized by rigidities, creating new competitive opportunities for global mobility, as in Adam Smith's town-and-country example. The very effectiveness of barriers to entry generates new niches of opportunity, as in the cheap labor mobilized in China and India during their first decades of sustained high growth.

We should note here that the pursuit of national economic growth is often portrayed in terms of a willingness of people to allow for greater inequality in their own country in exchange for the growth of the overall wealth available for distribution. Leaving aside the fact that not all strategies of economic growth entail rising within-country inequality (as demonstrated by the "growth with equity" literature reviewed in chapter 1), even the existence of such a trade-off would not indicate a lack of concern with inequality. The pursuit of economic growth involves a recognition of the crucial role of *between*-country inequality in shaping world stratification. When people in South Korea and China endorse policies designed to generate economic growth, rather than abandoning their concern for inequality, they are recognizing the potential significance of such a path for engaging in upward social mobility within a *global* system of stratification.

But such a road of national economic growth has not been easily accessible to vast parts of the world, and success stories have been the exception rather than the rule for most of the world's population. For most of the past two centuries, the path of social mobility through national economic growth has failed to deliver its promise. As shown in figure 5.3, even in Mexico, tied as it has been for the past fifteen years to a free trade agreement with Canada and the United States, economic growth has not been high enough to allow a single country decile to catch up relative to the United States.

As with educational attainment, this is again a situation in which the goalposts are constantly being moved forward. It is, at bottom, what Schumpeter's notion of creative destruction is all about. Constant processes of innovation historically have ensured the eventual obsolescence of whatever prevailing standards characterized a particular moment in time, such as standards of education or productive technologies. In a country such as Mexico, such processes might mean running very fast to simply stand still—if not fall further behind. For the past two centuries, this has been the most prevalent story for most countries in the world. The development and implementation of growth panaceas (Japan in the 1970s, South Korea in the 1980s, or China today) seldom have provided a replicable model for success and in fact have been part and parcel of the constant creation of obsolescence.

Path 3: Jumping Categorical Inequality

We thus arrive at the single most immediate and effective means of global social mobility for populations in most countries of the world: migration. Given the crucial role of nationality in shaping global stratification, "jumping" categories by moving from a poorer country to a wealthier one is a highly effective strategy of mobility.

Figure 5.4 returns to our global stratification sample to highlight certain patterns of international migration. The figure takes the relative global standing of the country deciles of six nations from figure 5.2 that have considerable migration flows between them: Guatemala, Mexico, and the United States on one side of the figure; Bolivia, Argentina, and Spain on the other. Mexico is a receiving country for migrants from Guatemala and a sending country to the United States, just as Argentina is a receiving country for migrants from Bolivia and a sending country of migrants to Spain. The main point of the figure is to illustrate how global stratification produces strong incentives for migration for individuals and groups of people in relatively poorer countries. In Guatemala, for example, anyone belonging to the poorest seven deciles would be engaging in upward mobility by gaining access to the average income of the second-poorest decile in Mexico. In Mexico, the incentives are even more striking, as all but the wealthiest decile would find upward mobility in gaining access to the average income of the second-poorest U.S. decile.

Like the other example, in Bolivia anyone belonging to the poorest eight deciles would be engaging in upward mobility by gaining access to the average income of the second-poorest decile in Argentina. In Argentina, relative to a wealthier country (Spain), the incentives again are even more striking, as all but the wealthiest decile of Argentina would find upward mobility in gaining access to the average income of the second-poorest decile in Spain.[8] Such disparities help explain why economic migrants often are willing to abandon a professional status in their country of origin to work in relatively more menial positions in their country of destination— once again underlining the contingent meaning of "skill" and "human capital."

Of course, migration is not merely the product of differentials in income incentives. Engaging in migration requires access to manifold resources—from those needed to meet the costs of transportation and entry into a foreign country to those involving social networks that can facilitate access to housing and jobs—and these resources are not equally available to all populations within a given country. Even in the presence (or absence) of strong income incentives,

Figure 5.4   Path 3: Migration As Social Mobility

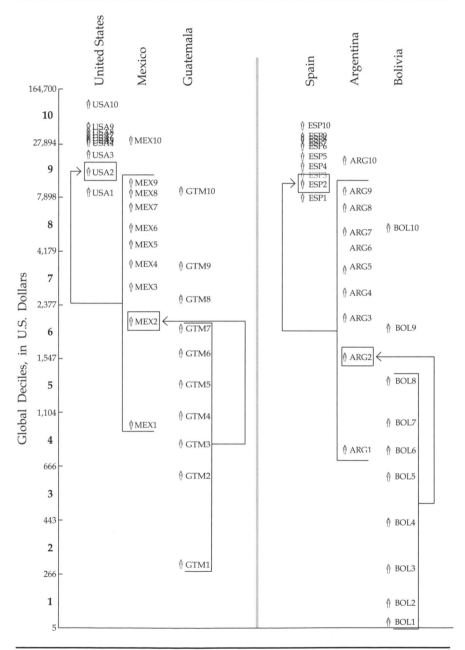

decisions to migrate are also based on broader considerations regarding security, safety, well-being, and personal attachments.

Both of the first two paths of mobility, the upgrading of human capital and the pursuit of national economic growth, take a long time to generate their intended returns, and both are fraught with a high degree of uncertainty as to whether such returns will be available as expected. By contrast, the third path of mobility in global stratification, migration, though it often requires a high level of courageous determination, tends to offer much more immediate and certain returns (even if a different type of uncertainty is precisely what calls for high doses of courageous determination, particularly for undocumented migrants). Thus, while academics might remain convinced that national borders provide the appropriate boundaries for understanding social mobility, migrants, in their crossing of such borders, reveal the boundaries of stratification to be global.

As seen in chapter 4, mechanisms of institutionalized selective exclusion have had a direct impact on trends in inequality by helping to reduce inequality within countries, while restricting migration and thereby enhancing inequality between countries.[9] Thus, the decline in inequality experienced in several wealthy countries earlier in the twentieth century was to a large extent the consequence of the introduction of wage-setting institutions across those countries that in effect limited competition in their labor markets.[10] True, much of the literature emphasizes the importance of the macroeconomic trends that enhanced the demand for unskilled labor (thereby reducing wage differentials), unionization, or favorable state policies, but the introduction of restrictive international migration policies was the sine qua non for the operation of each of these variables (see, for example, Williamson 1991).[11]

On the other hand, growing income disparities between nations over time themselves have generated strong incentives (such as drastically lower wages in poor countries) for outsourcing skilled and unskilled jobs to peripheral countries in a "market bypass" that in effect overcomes twentieth-century constraints on labor flows. Rising world inequality becomes a driving force as well for migration, and the latter holds the promise of providing a quick path for overcoming the gap between wealth and poverty. In this sense, migration embodies social mobility. A truly free flow of people across the world, in fact, would provide the fastest means for thoroughly transforming the equilibria that have characterized global stratification for the past two hundred years.

CONCLUSION

Tilly (1999, 7) argues that "at a scale larger than a single organization completely bounded categories are rare and difficult to maintain." This is not quite true. The development of the world-economy has been characterized by considerable mobility across the relevant bounded categories—for example, by the migration of labor and capital across national borders—and there is much hybridity in the cultural and institutional arrangements that prevail across the world. However, despite mobility and hybridity, the discussion in this chapter indicates that nation-states—the bounded categories that have accompanied the development of a world-economy—became the main axis for the articulation of inequality and social stratification over the past several centuries and continue to constitute such an axis today. This is why national citizenship provides the single most important characteristic that predicts the social standing of a person or group of persons within global stratification.

Current trends involving the three global paths to social mobility are generating a sense that we are in the midst of change. For some, this is cause for celebration: economic growth in countries such as China and India shows that previously poor populations have been able to upgrade their human capital and take advantage of the opportunities afforded by globalization to reduce the gap separating them from wealthy nations. Globalization works, and convergence is finally at hand. For others, there is little to celebrate: for workers facing unemployment in declining industrial towns, globalization has brought hardship, growing competition from cheap manufactures, and the growing presence of migrants. Globalization only brings vulnerability and must be constrained.

Globalization, then, has been accompanied by a restructuring of labor markets and welfare states, increasing a sense of vulnerability among many who in the past benefited from these arrangements (for example, the deskilled manufacturing workers in both high- and middle-income nations). This same restructuring, however, has provided a sense of opportunity for others: the "newly skilled" in middle- and high-income nations that are doing better and those in low-income nations that in the past were excluded from markets. This is the inequality that generates the popular concerns in question.

We are thus facing a dilemma similar to those that characterized the expansion of world markets in the late nineteenth century—another period of uncertainty, when the growth of markets generated both a constituency for globalization and a protective reaction. Current patterns of social stratification, mobility, and inequality might be transformed in the future as a consequence of the very opportunities generated by the growth of between-country inequalities through much of the twentieth century—just as the unequal development of Adam Smith's town and country generated the very market forces that would eventually bring such inequality to an end. On the other hand, the interests challenged by such a transformation might engage in the type of protective reaction experienced in the early part of the twentieth century—although the size of India and China, together with their linkages to other countries in Asia and elsewhere, might contribute to producing very different outcomes than those of the twentieth century. Which forces become more significant, and at which rates, is yet undeterminable.

CHAPTER 6

CONCLUSION

Hitherto [1848] it is questionable if all the mechanical inventions yet made have lightened the day's toil of any human being. They have enabled a greater population to live the same life of drudgery and imprisonment, and an increased number of manufacturers and others to make fortunes. They have increased the comforts of the middle classes. But they have not yet begun to effect those great changes in human destiny, which it is in their nature and in their futurity to accomplish. —John Stuart Mill, Principles of Political Economy

And all this life and love and strife and failure,—is it the twilight of nightfall or the flush of some faint-dawning day?
—W. E. B. Du Bois, The Souls of Black Folk

Drawing on what has become virtually a commonsense account of the historical trajectory of today's wealthy countries, the social sciences have usually portrayed development as the attainment of a virtuous combination of economic growth, equity, and democracy, all of which come to reinforce one another over time. Countries that are poor today have not yet undertaken the institutional transformations needed to embark on the righteous path, but eventually they will—all they need is the political will to make the hard choices required to embrace opportunity.

In this book, we have advanced an alternative account of inequality. Inequality needs to be studied as a world-historical, highly complex phenomenon rather than as a universal and inevitable transition. At any given moment, and often as an outcome of the very same processes, it rises in some places and falls elsewhere, and the very same characteristics associated with declining inequality at one point

113

in time often lead to an increase in another. In addition, one important lesson we have sought to emphasize is that in the very effort of actors to enhance their position within existing forms of inequality, they often create new forms of inequality, sometimes willingly, sometimes not; thus, trends in inequality are profoundly shaped by both the actions taken by people to enhance their relative social standing and the unintended consequences of those actions.

As we have recognized throughout this book, data constraints make the mapping of world-historical inequality a difficult task. Over thirty years ago, Wallerstein (1974, 14) noted that, "at this point, all we can do is analyze scattered data, sketch out what seems more and less solid, review explanatory models that encompass the data, suggest a theoretical view, and arrive at some notion of our empirical lacunae and theoretical conundrums." As Simon Kuznets acknowledged regarding his own work on inequality in the 1950s, we want to recognize that the arguments advanced in this book—constituting our effort to map out inequality as what Weber would call a "historical individual"—are in some respects incomplete. In this regard, the very creation of nationality as a central axis of categorical inequality has simultaneously entailed ways of understanding the world, collecting information, and constructing data that limit the availability of appropriate measures and indicators for units of analysis that move beyond the boundaries of the nation-state. Despite these data constraints, we hope to have attained sufficient empirical rigor in advancing a world-historical account of inequality.

Economic growth, equity, and democracy have not always existed in virtuous combination. As we discussed in chapters 2 through 4, for several centuries economic growth went hand in hand with slavery and other coercive labor arrangements in the areas that were an epicenter of such growth (such as Latin America and the Caribbean). Moreover, we described what is most often ignored in accounts of the development of wealthy countries: that since the nineteenth century the institutional development of low-inequality equilibria (LIE) within higher-income nations has gone hand in hand with global constraints that accentuate and entrench a high-inequality equilibrium (HIE) between countries.

In other words, the very existence of the virtuous trinity in some countries has been itself premised on severe forms of inequality.

This relationship is not readily apparent to accounts of inequality, stratification, and mobility that privilege national borders as marking the appropriate units of analysis. In these accounts, our past, present, and future are marked by the growing triumph of individual achievement over ascription as the crucial criteria shaping growing opportunity. Such might indeed be the patterns revealed when the field of vision is limited to discrete, "nationally bounded" "societies": the actual patterns of inequality, stratification, and mobility experienced by most people, as well as the persistence of ascriptive criteria as a basis of stratification, only become unveiled when the world as a whole is taken as the proper unit of analysis.

Others have made similar points. North (2005, 77), for example, notes that

> the long run economic success of western economies has induced a widespread belief that economic growth now is built into the system, in contrast to the experience of the previous ten millennia when growth was episodic and frequently non-existent. Since much of the world either still does not share in the growth experience or has only recently experienced growth, it is still an open question whether in fact that supposition is correct.

North's is certainly a sober assessment when contrasted with the optimistic panaceas advanced most often by those who wittingly—or what is worse, unwittingly—adopt the type of narrative advanced within the modernization paradigm. An even more explicit criticism of such a paradigm has been long advanced within the world-systems perspective, for at the core of such a perspective is the notion that inequality constitutes a world-historical phenomenon.

We indicated in chapter 5 that we indeed live in a world characterized by a single stratification system in which nation-states have played in the past, and continue to play today, a crucial role as an institutional mechanism mediating inequality. Within this global system of stratification over the last two centuries, nationality became the crucial ascribed criterion shaping the relative social standing of people. The relative level of wealth of the country of an individual's birth is the key determinant of the relative position that individual will occupy within a global system of stratification. As much as markets have become "globalized" over recent decades, social stratification and mobility continue to revolve around institutional arrangements that unequally distribute resources on the basis of ascriptive categorical differences.

Such insights are not apparent when the focus is on inequality and stratification using nation-states as the unit of analysis. From such a standpoint, each nation is perceived to have wealthier and poorer populations that are engaged in negotiation or conflict with one another over the distribution of resources, and institutions and political actions have the effect of *either* enhancing or reducing overall levels of inequality and social mobility. Outcomes, limited to the national spaces within which institutions are assumed to operate, seem to be fairly clear, and the criteria used for the exclusion of non-national populations come to be perceived as legitimate and natural. (Of course, even within a national population, deciding who should be included has been a contested terrain: for example, most social scientists in the United States focused on male workers and employers when thinking about relative levels of equity in the 1950s but had to rethink the role of interactions between men and women after the 1960s.)

Can we expect globalization in the future to bring between-country inequality, shaped as we have shown by national citizenship, to an end? Since the eighteenth century, the social sciences have wavered between optimism and pessimism when assessing questions such as this. On the one hand, there have always been those who assert with optimistic certitude that we are moving away from high inequality and rigid systems of social mobility. As we have indicated throughout the book, such certitude has undergirded the constant construction of development panaceas. Some observers today display a similar certainty in predicting that the growing participation of countries such as India and China in world markets represents a final stage in the gradual extension of the virtuous combination of growth, equity, and democracy throughout the world—the holy grail of much of our social sciences.

Others have been more skeptical. Many point out that our past is strewn with panaceas that failed to work as effectively as expected in the midst of the optimism generated by successful experiences of growth. For North (2005, 125), this outcome has been somewhat inevitable, since "policy derived from static theory in a dynamic setting is going to produce unanticipated (and unpleasant) outcomes." Of course, this does not mean that today's successful experiences of growth are inevitably bound to follow on the same path: it does mean, however, that caution should be exercised in judging the likely impact of current developments.

The alternative theoretical and methodological perspective advanced in this book allows us to sort current debates into two principal questions about the future of world-historical inequality. First, are current worldwide trends involving globalization—the relocation of people from poorer to wealthier countries and of jobs from wealthier countries to poorer ones—signaling a dramatic reconfiguration of global inequality? Second, if such a reconfiguration is indeed taking place, what would such a new world look like?

We start with the first question. On the basis of our arguments regarding the relationship of within-country LIE and between-country HIE, we would contend that changes in the existing between-country equilibrium are likely to emerge primarily as a consequence of a rise in the relative bargaining power of the populations of poor nations. As noted several decades ago by Gunnar Myrdal (1957/1964, 70), "benevolence on the part of the richer countries will in this respect be a secondary factor—for the simple reason that, except under the urge of some compulsion, our advanced nations are not prepared to give up privileges and make sacrifices for the poorer countries."

Perhaps we could expect such a shift in bargaining power to emerge as a consequence of the very *market* opportunities generated by between-country inequalities themselves. Similar to the way in which the unequal development of town and country generated the very market forces that in Adam Smith's account would eventually bring such inequality to an end, the incentives generated by the historical growth of the gap between poor and wealthy nations might be leading today to the relocation of people and jobs across the world in a reconfiguration of global inequality. Simultaneously (or, for some, alternatively), such a reconfiguration might involve substantively new institutional arrangements and a shift away from the current primacy of national states to international organizations or transnational networks of regulation.

But we should be careful in inferring from short-term changes in either markets or their political regulation that shifts in equilibria are upon us. As seen in chapter 4, world markets expanded substantively during the late nineteenth and early twentieth centuries, but rising inequality within countries generated "a political backlash" that "led to the reimposition of tariffs and the adoption of immigration restrictions" (O'Rourke and Williamson 1999, 268).[1] As we have shown, in the United States such protective institutional arrangements facilitated this country's low-inequality equilibrium in the interwar and post–World War II periods.[2] But these very same protective arrangements prevented any substantive transformation of the prevailing high-inequality equilibrium between countries. The changes of the last decades of the nineteenth century generated a protective response and forms of market regulation that brought overall global inequality back to its equilibrium. We do not know whether such a protectionist drive could develop in higher-income countries today, or even whether such a drive could have the impact it had in the first half of the twentieth century, since the size of China and India and their linkages to other countries might dampen the impact of a new protectionism by high-income countries. These issues are likely to remain contentious in the immediate future.

Parallel reservations can be made regarding the emergence of new forms of global governance and institutional regulation. Gunnar Myrdal, in the 1960s, noted that a fundamental obstacle for change in this regard is the lack of any accessible institutional mechanism for addressing international inequality.

> The international situation is all the worse and more hopeless, because we have hardly more than the faintest beginnings of anything like an international authority to perform for the world as a whole the task of the national state in an individual country. If from one point of view the explanation of the existing and ever increasing international inequalities is the cumulative tendency inherent in the unhampered play of market forces in a situation where the effectiveness of the spread effects is weak, from another point of view the explanation is the absence of a world state which could interfere in the interest of equality of opportunity. (Myrdal 1957/1964, 63)

In other words, here as before, shifts in equilibria are generally resisted by powerful actors, and the self-perpetuating character of highly uneven distributions of resources and political power provides considerable leverage for such actors. In this regard, once again, political forces in wealthy nations (including relatively less privileged populations within these countries) might strengthen protectionism and exclusion as a way of defending their status.

Today again, as in the nineteenth century, current changes have the potential to transform existing equilibria into something new. But the theoretical standpoint of world-historical inequality directs us to pay attention to the complicated trade-offs and protective backlashes that have a similar potential to return arrangements to their previous equilibrium. This is precisely what the very notion of equilibrium entails: institutional arrangements and the prevailing balance of social and political forces have the ability to transform big changes in patterns of social action into little effective transformation of the overall whole.

This book has provided a framework from which to assess whether we are indeed moving away from the patterns of inequality that have come to prevail over the last two hundred years. Such a transition would involve a shift of between-country inequalities away from their historically high equilibrium. In such a transition, national affiliation would cease to play a crucial role in shaping global social stratification. Such a world is not yet here, and while current trends in "globalization" might continue and eventually bring such a transformation about, the historical record cautions us against imagining a future that simply amplifies current short-term trends.

Our theoretical standpoint also bears upon the second question. For many scholars and policymakers in wealthy countries today, we are in the midst of a growing convergence between nations, a convergence that in the future can only bring about a greater prevalence of economic growth, greater equity, and democracy. But a shift from the prevailing HIE and LIE would bring about a very different world than the one advanced in such visions. From a world-historical perspective, the virtuous combination of economic growth, greater equity, and democracy was always limited to a few areas of the world and a small percentage of the world's population. Moreover, the historical account provided in chapters 2 and 3 indicates that political regimes, patterns of social equity and mobility, and economic growth might not always and inevitably advance all together in harmonious interaction. If the institutional arrangements and the very logic that has shaped global inequality for the past two hundred years come to an end, it is unclear and uncertain how new institutional arrangements would articulate economic growth, equity, and democracy and what the net effects of such arrangements would be for different populations across the world. We should allow for the possibility, for example, that in some not too distant future the combination of growth, equity, and democracy will come to be perceived, even for the few who enjoy it, as a surprising and fleeting moment in history.

Despite these uncertainties about what the future might bring, and doubts about whether markets or political institutions would be most effective in promoting change, we need not be restrained in our efforts to challenge existing forms of inequity. In this regard, we might paraphrase Polanyi (1944/1957: 258b) to argue that "as long as [we] are true to [our] task of creating more abundant freedom for all, [we] need not fear that either power or planning [or competition or markets] will turn against [us] and destroy the freedom [we] are building by their instrumentality. This is the meaning of freedom in a complex society; it gives us all the certainty we need."

The continued importance of nationality in organizing global stratification along ascriptive criteria raises another question: to what extent is our "modern" world substantially different from our "traditional" past? In our traditional past, elites often justified existing inequality as a consequence of the superiority of some races over others, or of men over women, and so forth, and "inferior" peoples were deemed to be in need of guidance and supervision to ensure their own welfare. Thus, today we feel the moral authority to look back to slavery and coercion as practiced two hundred years ago and judge harshly those who at the time justified such severe forms of inequality as a natural state of affairs. But the well-off of our times continue to justify prevalent forms of inequality as an inevitable consequence of a rather natural order, now revolving around national citizenship, arguing that any relative advantages are purely the result of individual effort and that inequalities, now between countries, are a consequence of the failure of poor peoples to advance their own interest (interests that only enlightened social scientists and policymakers can help advance). In both sets of arrangements, so apparently distant in time, the construction of categorical inequality around ascriptive beliefs has played a central role in justifying existing high levels of inequality.

A world-historical perspective unveils the persisting importance of ascription and categorical inequality. Just as shifting the boundaries of the unit of analysis from the nation-state to the world as a whole forces us to reconsider the empirical processes that are relevant to understanding existing inequality, the same shift in boundaries makes it incumbent on us to redefine who is included in the relevant community when we morally assess social justice. Just as we might decide that race or sex should not be a criterion limiting access to opportunity, we must also decide whether the life chances of people should be restricted by the blind luck of their place of birth.

Challenging such arrangements is not easy.[3] As in the past, those who wish to treat categorical inequality concerns as a top priority today are often criticized by enthusiastic adherents of the status quo as failing to understand basic principles of economic rationality. And the critics might be right. Ultimately, world-historical inequality might have to be challenged on moral grounds rather than on the basis of its economic irrationality. In this respect, we might want to consider a historical precedent. At the time of its existence, slavery was seen not merely as a natural state of affairs but also as most conducive to the production of wealth, so abolitionist currents in their origin did not challenge the institution of slavery on the basis of its economic irrationality, but on moral and ethical grounds. We might find ourselves in a similar position today.

From a world-historical perspective, we should challenge the naturalization of national citizenship as a justification for categorical inequality. Such a stance is sure to raise objections. Is the removal of national borders politically viable? Wouldn't such a removal affect the underprivileged and raise inequality in receiving countries? Although we recognize that such questions are inevitable in challenging categorical inequality, it is not the task of this book to provide detailed policy suggestions or ready-made answers. We should note, however, that parallel concerns were raised historically—for example, over the process of removing the institutional arrangements that enforced exclusion based on race.

The more relevant questions are these: Two hundred years from now, how will observers (if still around) think about our age? Was our concern over global inequality a quaint preoccupation of the long twentieth century, since high levels of inequality persisted or even deepened thereafter? Or from a new, truly global low-inequality equilibrium, will future observers be puzzled by our reluctance to acknowledge the deep inequalities of our time and their effects on welfare and be morally outraged at our use of national identity to justify such inequalities as a natural state of affairs?

STATISTICAL APPENDIX

MEASURING INEQUALITY

Many measures of inequality exist, and each carries different assumptions and mathematical properties. A common method of quantifying income dispersion is to calculate ratios of various parts of the distribution—for example, the ratio of the incomes of the bottom 90 percent to the top 10 percent (90/10). Since these measures use only a fraction of the empirical information from the distribution (the income at certain percentile boundaries), they can provide insight into changes in certain parts of the distribution—what is happening to the incomes of the upper strata, or of the middle relative to the upper strata, and so forth—but they do not measure the amount of inequality across the shape of the entire income distribution.

Summary measures of inequality provide a single statistic intended to capture the fluidity of income along the entire distribution. Of the many summary measures that have been proposed, only two—the Gini index and the Theil coefficient—satisfy the five most highly desired properties of an inequality indicator: (1) it is symmetrical; (2) it is income scale–invariant; (3) it is invariant to absolute population levels; (4) it is defined by upper and lower bounds; and (5) it satisfies the Pigou-Dalton principle of transfers (any redistribution from richer to poorer reduces the inequality measure, and vice versa). All other summary measures lack one or more of these properties. The principal distinctions between Gini and Theil concern their sensitivity to income transfers. Mathematically, the Gini coefficient is most sensitive to income transfers around the middle of the distribution, while the Theil coefficient grows increasingly responsive to transfers toward the lower end of the income scale (Allison 1978). In practice, Gini and Theil are highly correlated measures. We use the Gini index in this book for the simple reason that few international data sources report Theil coefficients.

WITHIN-COUNTRY INEQUALITY DATA SET

Accurate and detailed longitudinal data on income inequality within most countries are not easily forthcoming, especially over long periods of time. But even in situations where such data are available, cross-national inequality analysis is often handicapped by differences in survey sources and measurement choices that severely limit the degree of comparability between the indicators (both between countries and within them over time). In particular, there may not be a close correspondence between income concepts and definitions, the scope of the survey coverage, or the methods used for compilation of summary measures and statistics. Inequality summary measures such as the Gini index are extremely sensitive to measurement choices, and comparisons between these indicators are only substantively meaningful by referring to the methods used to derive them. In a previous analysis using the Luxembourg Income Study (LIS), Moran (2003) found that changing certain specifications (the household equivalence scale, gross or net income, and so forth) could make the absolute value of the Gini index vary by as much as 30 to 40 percent *within the same household income survey.* In the inequality literature, comparability problems lead to debates and disagreements about levels and trends, though sometimes the differences being explained are driven by little more than methodological variation.

For this project, we assembled a new and comprehensive data set of percentage distribution data (percentage of income accruing to population deciles) and Gini coefficients to measure inequality within countries. Our data set was carefully assembled to be cross-nationally comparable regarding specification and methodology. Although the reliability of household surveys versus national accounts is debated, as is the question of whether income or consumption is a better indicator of household resources, we assembled the data set to adhere as closely as possible to the recommendations of the Canberra Group's (2001) comprehensive final report on measuring incomes and inequality.

To maximize the size of the sample, we collected data from around the year 2000 (as opposed to a more recent year, when information for fewer countries would be available). The cross-national data set consists of ninety-six countries accounting for over 84 percent of the world's population in 2000. (The decile distribution data used in chapter 5 is available for eighty-five of these countries.) The data set is an aggregation of four primary sources: the Socio-Economic Database for Latin America and the Caribbean (SEDLAC) (CEDLAS and World Bank 2008); the European Commission (2008) for European Union member nations; the Luxembourg Income Study (LIS 2008) for participating countries not covered by SEDLAC or the European Commission; and the World Income Inequality Database (UNU-WIDER 2005), primarily for Asia, Africa, and other developing countries. We employed the following more specific sources to include key countries: for Japan, Otake (2005); for South Africa, Seekings and Nattrass (2005); and for India, Desai et al. (2007). Regarding India, we should note that our data set includes the first Gini index calculated for household income (as opposed to consumption) based on a nationally representative sample.

While combining data from these sources, we paid strict attention to the comparability of the estimates. Across all the sources, the income-receiving unit is the household, and income is defined as net (post-tax, disposable) income, adjusted for household equivalency (for the size of the household) and subjected to top- and bottom-coding (capping at the top and limiting at the bottom reported incomes to correct for possible measurement or sampling errors). We broke from this convention and included estimates based on gross income in order to include sixteen developing countries in South Asia and Africa. Sacrificing an even bigger sample, because of the risk of losing the ability to make meaningful comparisons, we did not include estimates based on individual earnings or consumption and expenditure data. The estimates in our data set are classified as the highest-quality rating by UNU-WIDER (2005); the majority rate a level 1, while a handful of estimates rate a level 2 on the UNU-WIDER 1 to 4 scale. Data from Africa are especially difficult to obtain and trust: so as to include at least a portion of the continent in the sample, seven observations from Africa are classified as level 3 quality. Again at the expense of a broader data set, no level 3 data outside of Africa were included (and the data set includes no level 4 data at all).

Figure 1.3

Figure 1.3 presents all ninety-six countries in the data set by the natural log of per capita gross national income (GNI) in 2000 (Atlas method; World Bank 2008). The high- and low-inequality boundaries were established with the bivariate cross-section using the two-stage, hierarchal clustering algorithm in SPSS, 16.0. More specifically, we employed the two-step cluster procedure in SPSS, applying the default algorithm specification in SPSS—clusters are determined automatically (not fixed) using the log likelihood distance measure applying Schwartz's Bayesian Criteria (BIC). See Norusis (2006) for a full description of these procedures. The three-digit country codes used in figure 1.3 and again in chapter 5 are specified in table A.1.

Figure 1.4

The source of the longitudinal data in figure 1.4 is the same one used to establish the 2000 cross-section estimate—except that data for Finland, the United States, and the United Kingdom are taken from a long-time series published by national statistics offices and reported in UNU-WIDER (2005). To make the historical U.S. data comparable to the specifications outlined here, the long-time series of Gini coefficients reported by the U.S. Census Bureau was indexed to the 2000 figure from the Luxembourg Income Study (2008) used in the cross-section.

BETWEEN-COUNTRY INEQUALITY DATA SET

As discussed in chapter 4, the relative merits of converting national income currencies to a comparable metric have long been debated, and argument has focused specifically on the use of exchange rate (FX) versus purchasing power parity (PPP) data. As we noted, PPP data are intuitively appealing because of their promise of better capturing differences among nations in access to welfare, but they have serious problems that are not usually acknowledged by their users; we have provided considerable discussion elsewhere of the many technical aspects that render such measures much less precise than is usually assumed (see, for example, Korzeniewicz and Moran 2000; Korzeniewicz et al. 2004).

Table A.1   Three-Digit Country Codes

ARG	Argentina	IDN	Indonesia
AUS	Australia	IND	India
AUT	Austria	IRE	Ireland
BEL	Belgium	ISR	Israel
BFA	Burkina Faso	ITA	Italy
BGD	Bangladesh	JAM	Jamaica
BGR	Bulgaria	JOR	Jordan
BLR	Belarus	JPN	Japan
BLZ	Belize	KEN	Kenya
BOL	Bolivia	KOR	Republic of Korea
BRA	Brazil	LKA	Sri Lanka
BWA	Botswana	LSO	Lesotho
CAF	Central African Republic	LTU	Lithuania
CAN	Canada	LUX	Luxembourg
CHE	Switzerland	LVA	Latvia
CHL	Chile	MDA	Moldova
CHN	China	MDG	Madagascar
CMR	Cameroon	MEX	Mexico
COL	Colombia	MLT	Malta
CRI	Costa Rica	MRT	Mauritania
CYP	Cyprus	MYS	Malaysia
CZE	Czech Republic	NGA	Nigeria
DEN	Denmark	NIC	Nicaragua
DEU	Germany	NLD	Netherlands
DOM	Dominican Republic	NOR	Norway
ECU	Ecuador	NPL	Nepal
EGY	Egypt	NZL	New Zealand
ESP	Spain	PAN	Panama
EST	Estonia	PER	Peru
ETH	Ethiopia	PHL	Philippines
FIN	Finland	POL	Poland
FRA	France	PRI	Puerto Rico
GBR	United Kingdom	PRT	Portugal
GHA	Ghana	PRY	Paraguay
GIN	Guinea	ROM	Romania
GMB	Gambia	RUS	Russia
GRC	Greece	SLV	El Salvador
GTM	Guatemala	SVK	Slovak Republic
HAI	Haiti	SVN	Slovenia
HND	Honduras	SUR	Suriname
HRV	Croatia	SWE	Sweden
HUN	Hungary	THA	Thailand
ICE	Iceland	TJK	Tajikistan

(Table continues on p. 128)

Table A.1   (*Continued*)

TUR	Turkey	UZB	Uzbekistan
TWN	Taiwan	VEN	Venezuela
UGA	Uganda	ZAF	South Africa
URY	Uruguay	ZMB	Zambia
USA	United States	ZWE	Zimbabwe

Source: World Bank (2008).

PPP advocates repeatedly appeal to the notion that the foreign exchange–based data are prone to the froth of short-term movements (and references to currency fluctuation are often used to make such a point). In our analysis, the foreign exchange–based data we use are based on the Atlas method, as calculated and disseminated by the World Bank (and are in fact the GNI figures preferred by the bank itself in policy analysis). The method employs a three-year moving average that is explicitly designed to smooth over year-to-year fluctuations in currency values.

It is important to note that critics of FX conversions generally ignore (or minimize) the fact that PPP data are themselves subject to great fluctuations, as shown in table A.2. For example, the latest PPP revision completed by the World Bank in 2005 adjusted downward the estimated income per capita of China by 38 percent (from $6,660 to $4,110) and that of India by 36 percent (from $3,460 to $2,210). Thus, any calculation of trends in world income that was done using the pre-2007 estimates of PPP adjustments would now have to be revised very substantially as an outcome of fluctuations that were introduced, not by changes in foreign exchange rates, but by measurement error involving over 40 percent of the world's population. The impact of this large measurement error is amplified by the fact that new PPP data are published only sporadically (more than ten years can pass between rounds), so researchers working with these data should acknowledge the uncertainties inherent in their numbers.

Moreover, advocates of PPP adjustments often make the assertion that PPP data better reflect the real day-to-day experience of people. If so, we might infer that people would perceive major changes in estimates of PPP, like the significant revisions introduced by the World Bank in 2007, as having deep consequences for their daily lives. Instead, people often react to significant changes in exchange

**Table A.2   Fluctuations in GNI per Capita:
Old and New PPP Estimates
for Selected Countries, 2005**

Country	Old PPP GNI per Capita	New PPP GNI per Capita	Measurement Error (of Old Figures)
Republic of the Congo	$810	$2,450	203% underestimation
Ghana	2,370	1,140	52% overestimation
Ecuador	4,070	6,390	57% underestimation
Venezuela	6,440	9,770	52% underestimation
Nigeria	1,040	1,530	47% underestimation
Bangladesh	2,090	1,120	46% overestimation
China	6,600	4,110	38% overestimation
India	3,460	2,210	36% overestimation
South Africa	12,120	8,300	32% overestimation
Argentina	13,920	10,420	25% overestimation
Turkey	8,420	10,250	22% underestimation
United Kingdom	32,690	32,050	2% overestimation
Japan	31,410	31,010	1% overestimation
United States	41,950	41,680	1% overestimation

Sources: Authors' calculations based on old PPP figures, World Bank (2006); new PPP figures, World Bank (2008).

rates (recall political turmoil in Argentina over the collapse of the Argentine peso in 2001), but major adjustments in PPP estimates at the offices of the World Bank seldom evoke any reaction at all (and often go unnoticed even by their advocates in academia).

Despite these reservations, as well as the additional theoretical considerations we use to justify our methodological decision to privilege FX conversions, we do report all our relevant results using both FX- and PPP-adjusted data. We discuss differences in the resulting trends in chapter 4.

Figures 4.1, 4.5, and 4.6

The historical trends in between-country inequality are based on our calculations employing two data sets. For the 1820 to 1990 series, we estimate inequality between 24 countries using the population and per capita gross domestic product (GDP) data in Maddison (1995). For the contemporary 1975 to 2007 series, we estimate inequality between 107 countries using the population and per capita GNI (Atlas method) data published by the World Bank (2008). The source for figure 4.6 is also per capita GNI (Atlas method) (World Bank 2008).

Figure 4.2

The source of figure 4.2 is Maddison (1995), where per capita GDP estimates are presented in the form of PPP dollars. To obtain comparable FX figures, we index Maddison's trend line to a base year (1992) and apply per capita GNI (Atlas method) (World Bank 2008). Maddison indexed his own trend line to a base year's PPP-adjusted data, so our procedure is essentially the same as his.

GLOBAL STRATIFICATION

The procedures to conceptualize global stratification and mobility employ the country income shares by population decile data from our data set. Taking all the countries in our data set with decile-level income distribution data (the percentage, or share, of income accruing to each one-tenth of the population), we calculated for each of these "country deciles" its average GNI per capita income. For example, the income share accruing to the richest 10 percent of the U.S. population (USA10) is 27.6 percent, which translates into an average income for the decile of $127,517 based on the GNI per capita for the United States in 2007. We then ranked these country deciles from poor to rich to establish global deciles (that is, each decile having 10 percent of the sampled population), their income boundaries, and their composition. For example, the box at the top of figure 5.1, representing the richest 10 percent of our world sample, contains country deciles with an average income above $27,894 (2007 U.S. dollars). Although the population size of each global decile is equivalent, each contains different numbers of country deciles because countries have different national populations (the large number of country deciles in the wealthiest global decile thus reflects the small populations in that part of the world). We replicated these procedures using PPP-adjusted data, and our main findings remained essentially the same. We discuss these results in chapter 5.

The exercise on global stratification and mobility carried out in chapter 5 is difficult to execute owing to the lack of appropriately comparable income data for people and households around the world. Although we fully recognize the shortcomings of our procedures—including the use of per capita GNI as a proxy for the "average" income for people in a given country—our goal is to start an empirically driven discussion around reconceptualizing stratification and mobility as global phenomena. As we note, a more world-historical approach to these issues will require the collection of truly global income and distribution data.

NOTES

INTRODUCTION

1. Of course, such stories are not restricted to the *New York Times:* financial magazines often feature articles reporting that a billion dollars is no longer the fortune it used to be. In "Billionaires Feel the Pinch, Too," *Forbes* reported that it now takes at least $1.3 billion to make its annual list of the four hundred most affluent Americans (September 17, 2008, available at Forbes.com).

2. A review in the *New York Times Book Review* of Robert Frank's *Richistan: A Journey Through the American Wealth Boom and the Lives of the New Rich* (June 10, 2007) notes that "because so many newly enriched entrepreneurs [in the United States] hail from middle-class backgrounds, they hate being called rich" (Alex Beam, "Lifestyles of the Rich").

3. Ibid.

4. Recently, Robert H. Frank reported "consistent survey findings" that "wealthy people are happier, on average, than poor people," indicating "that relative income is a much better predictor of well-being than absolute income" ("Income and Happiness: An Imperfect Link," *New York Times,* March 9, 2008).

5. See American Pet Products Association (APPA) website at: http://www.appma.org/press_industrytrends.asp (accessed July 19, 2008); see also James E. McWhinney, "The Economics of Pet Ownership," available at Investopedia: http://www.investopedia.com/articles/pf/06/peteconomics.asp (accessed July 19, 2008).

6. On the Upper East Side, a private service charges $15 for each forty-five-minute semiprivate dog walk (that is, with up to three other companions): two walks a day, five days a week add up to $150 a week, or an additional $1,800 a year; see NYC Dog Walkers, LC, "Pricing": http://www.nycdogwalkers.com/pricing.html (accessed July 19, 2008). Another service charges $7 for giving a pill and $11 to give an injection to a dog that requires such medication; see Pet-a-Holics, "Rates and Services": http://www.petaholics.com/rateserv.php (accessed July 19, 2008).

7. The comparisons use per capita gross national income (GNI) and per capita health expenditures as reported in World Bank (2007).

8. Charles Tilly (1999, 33) observes that "individualistic analyses of inequality have all the attractions of neoclassical economics: nicely simplified geometric analogies, reassuring references to individual decision-making, insistence on efficiency, avoidance of inconvenient complications such as beliefs, passions, culture, and history. They lend themselves nicely to retroactive rationalization; confronted with unequal outcomes, their user searches the past for individual differences in skill, knowledge, determination, or moral worth that must explain differences in rewards." He goes on to question "any ontology that reduces all social processes to the sentient actions of individual persons" (35) and argues instead that "the crucial causal mechanisms behind categorical inequality . . . operate in the domains of collective experience and social interaction" (24).

9. We should point out that what is created on a global scale are not merely discrepancies in access to wealth but also discrepancies in privilege, and that the construction of the social sciences (as well as that of any kind of knowledge) is an expression of that privilege. This is evident in the very process of the professional development of (and in) the social sciences. Here, as professionals of social science in wealthy countries, we produce through our work (publications, research, conferences) both a privileged knowledge (for example, attributing inequality to what the disadvantaged lack and we have, and seeing both as unrelated) and our very positions in a global social hierarchy (as shaped, for example, by income and status).

10. To some extent, this is somewhat similar to Ira Katznelson's (2005, xv) discussion of "untold history": "a not fully conveyed or altogether disclosed story—one that comes together into full view only when its parts are considered together."

11. Tilly (1999, 36–37) notes that focusing on inequality as a relational outcome tends to produce resistance in the social sciences: "At least in Western countries, people learn early in life to tell stories in which self-motivating actors firmly located in space and time produce all significant changes in the situation through their own efforts. . . . Narratives feature essences, not bonds. They therefore favor individualistic analyses, whether rational-choice, phenomenological, or otherwise. . . . By-products of social interaction, tacit constraints, unintended consequences, indirect effects, incremental changes, and causal chains mediated by nonhuman environments play little or no part in customary narratives of social life. Relational analyses of inequality affront narrative common sense by insisting that just

such subtle ramifications of social interaction produce and sustain unequal relations among whole categories of people." This book argues that such a relational account can be constructed only by embedding it in time and space.

12. This insight has been the methodological heart of what Terence K. Hopkins and Immanuel Wallerstein (1982a) came to call a world-systems approach.

CHAPTER 1

1. For example, Adelman and Morris (1973, 1978); Ahluwalia (1974, 1976a, 1976b); Bollen and Jackman (1985); Bornschier (1983); Bornschier and Ballmer-Cao (1979); Bornschier and Chase-Dunn (1985); Chenery and Syrquin (1975); Crenshaw (1992); Cutright (1967); Evans and Timberlake (1980); Gupta and Singh (1984); Jackman (1974); Kuznets (1963); Meyer (1977); Milner (1987); Muller (1985, 1988, 1989); Paukert (1973); Robinson (1976); Rubinson (1976); Rubinson and Quinlan (1977); Simpson (1990); Srinivasan (1977); Stewart (1978); Teachman (1983); Weede (1982); Weede and Tiefenbach (1981).

2. Criticisms of the inverted U-curve hypothesis developed over time. Some studies challenged the reliability of the cross-sectional data itself in light of wide intercountry variation in data collection methods and possible measurement errors resulting from systematic reporting biases (see, for example, Fields 1980, 1984; Gagliani 1987; Lecaillon et al. 1984; Nugent 1983; Papanek 1978; Papanek and Kyn 1987; Saith 1983; Sundrum 1990). Other studies challenged the use of cross-sectional research to infer longitudinal patterns of change (Datta 1986; Fields 1980, 1984; Gagliani 1987; Papanek 1978; Saith 1983; Stewart 1978; Sundrum 1990). Not until the social and political climate shifted in the 1980s and 1990s did these critiques become accepted and moved out of footnotes and into central arguments to mount a substantive challenge to the assumption that all nations are likely to follow a similar transition regarding patterns of within-country inequality.

3. For a review of the relevant literature and empirical evidence around this topic, see Forsythe, Korzeniewicz, and Durrant (2000).

4. Dovring (1991), IADB (1998), Jha (1996), Milanovic (1994), Nielsen (1994), and Nielsen and Alderson (1995) continue to advocate the existence of the inverted U-curve cross-nationally, while Bourguignon and Morrison (1990), Fishlow (1996), Lantican, Gladwin, and Seale (1996), and Ogwang (1995) offer more cautious or mixed support. In several studies, the cross-sectional inverted U-curve becomes less

robust, "disappears," or even becomes reversed in econometric models by simply including country-level fixed effects (Anand and Kanbur 1993a, 1993b; Bruno, Ravallion, and Squire 1998; Deininger and Squire 1998; Higgins and Williamson 1999; Ram 1997).

5. The data used to estimate the Gini coefficients presented throughout this chapter are carefully assembled to provide a high degree of cross-national comparability. Except where noted in the statistical appendix, all Gini coefficients in this chapter measure inequality of net (post-tax or disposable) household income, estimated using an equivalence scale (to adjust for household size) and top and bottom coding. See the statistical appendix for a more detailed discussion.

6. Bootstrap resampling is a method of using Monte Carlo simulation to obtain an approximation of the sampling distribution of the Gini index (because one is not readily available in theory, as it is for statistics like the mean). Once the sampling distribution is approximated, one can do hypothesis testing in the style of "difference of means" or "t-tests" to ascertain the probability that the difference in two Gini indices is statistically significant or more likely due to sampling error or random chance (see also Moran 2006b).

7. See, for example, Beckfield (2006, 973), where the range of Gini coefficients being compared is quite narrow and an increase from .276 to .301 is labeled "a substantive change."

8. This subfield of literature focusing on relatively narrow differences in inequality in wealthy countries is also driven by the availability of accessible, readily assembled, and easily mined data sets provided by the research offices of the European Commission or the Organization for Economic Cooperation and Development (OECD).

9. Of course, we are grouping under one heading a social mobility literature that conceptualizes the phenomenon in various ways. Some study intergenerational mobility, or the degree to which individuals' station in life can be attributed to their parents. Others study status attainment, or life-cycle (intergenerational) mobility. While particulars matter across these studies, we are emphasizing the consensus inherent in the overall thrust of the literature—that studies of various kinds tend to find evidence of convergence and stability in mobility regimes across the wealthy nations of the world. Also, the empirical links between place-in-time levels of inequality and the patterns of mobility observable in the same place are complex. Measures of overall inequality like the Gini index cannot speak to underlying patterns of social mobility.

10. "Ironically, increases in inequality evolved just as sociologists were developing their strongest case yet for the invariance of core social

mobility patterns over time and across industrialized countries" (Morgan and Kim 2006, 165).

11. This led Jeffrey Williamson (1991, 10) to conclude, with many others, that "the initial Latin inequality may create a path-dependent inegalitarian regime throughout the Latin industrial revolution, just as the initial East Asian equality may create a path-dependent egalitarian regime throughout the East Asian industrial revolution."

12. More specifically, we used the two-step cluster procedure in Statistical Package for the Social Sciences (SPSS), applying the default algorithm specification in SPSS (clusters determined automatically [not fixed] using the log likelihood distance measure applying Schwartz's Bayesian Criteria [BIC]).

13. As noted by Marija Norusis (2006, 367–68), "Different methods for computing the distance between clusters are available and may well result in different solutions . . . [but] that doesn't really matter, since there is no right or wrong answer to a cluster analysis."

CHAPTER 2

1. We use the term "recent institutional literature on inequality" to refer to authors such as Daron Acemoglu, Simon Johnson, and James Robinson (2001, 2002, 2005), Acemoglu and Robinson (2006a, 2006b), David De Ferranti and others (2004), William Easterly (2001, 2006), Sebastian Edwards, Gerardo Esquivel, and Graciela Márquez (2007), and Douglass North (2005), as well as older contributions such as those of, among others, Stanley Engerman (1981), Engerman and Kenneth Sokoloff (1997), North (1981, 1990), and Sokoloff and Engerman (2000).

2. For Acemoglu, Johnson, and Robinson, "the reversal is mostly a late-eighteenth and early nineteenth-century phenomenon, and is closely related to industrialization." Extractive institutions fail to "encourage economic development," as they "are likely to have been designed to maximize the rents to European colonists, not to maximize long-run growth" (2002, 18). Other authors (Coatsworth 1993; Engerman 1981) draw a similar distinction. Acemoglu, Johnson, and Robinson (2005, 4) portray their interpretation as an innovative "marriage between the Marxist thesis linking the rise of the bourgeoisie and the development of the world-economy . . . and the neoclassical emphasis on the development of political institutions and secure property rights in Western Europe," but other authors have formulated similar arguments in the past, putting perhaps an even greater emphasis on the relational aspects of

these developments (see, for example, Wallerstein 1974; or even North 1981).

3. This draws on a much longer tradition in the humanities and social sciences, contrasting the developmental paths of Latin America and North America along various key variables such as land concentration or democracy. But rather than treating these paths as a consequence of initial natural endowments, what we denominate the new consensus on inequality focuses on "social and institutional arrangements" (Garcia Swartz 1993, 67).

4. Thus, De Ferranti and others (2004, 17) indicate that "for as long as data on living standards have been available, Latin America has been one of the regions of the world with the greatest inequality."

5. De Ferranti and others (2004, 110) argue that "people of European descent living in Spanish America benefited from greater wealth, human capital, and political influence than did the rest of the population, and were therefore able to shape policies and institutions to their advantage. These circumstances in turn perpetuated extreme inequality, and conditions changed little after the colonies gained independence."

6. By contrast, "actual legislation putting an official ceiling on black economic opportunities was apparently neither enacted by any law-making body nor even seriously proposed during the era of Jim Crow in the United States. American color bars existed not because government required them but because it did not act, at least until very recently, to prohibit the discriminatory practices of private employers and trade unions" (Fredrickson 1981, 235).

7. Again, this is in contrast to the United States, where "the Fourteenth Amendment and the powerful American commitment to economic *laissez-faire* combined to inhibit the legalization of racial discrimination. Other ways were found to create a high degree of *de facto* residential separation and ghettoization in American cities, but the comprehensiveness and efficiency of a governmentally supported and centrally planned program were never attained" (Fredrickson 1981, 254).

8. Robert Fogel (2003, 15) makes a similar point. For example, George Fredrickson (1981, 86) points out that "the South (in North America) and the Cape (in today's South Africa) were closed societies in comparison to those of the Caribbean and Latin America, where less restrictive manumission requirements enabled more sizable and socially significant free colored groups to develop," but Fredrickson notes that caste boundaries were stronger in the South until much later in the nineteenth century.

9. These categorical differences can be embedded in informal or formal arrangements (as manifested, for example, in the contrasting twentieth-century paths of Brazil and South Africa). The alternative patterns can have contrasting effects. Tilly (1999, 124), for example, notes that "to the degree that a state installs categorical racial distinctions in its laws and institutions, it can use coercive power legally to enforce discrimination. Yet, under changed circumstances, those categories become available as bases of mobilization and demands for rights."

10. The term "suggests systematic and self-conscious efforts to make race or color a qualification for membership in the civil community" (Fredrickson 1981, xi).

11. Thus, Douglas Massey (2007, 23) notes that "categorical inequality results whenever those in power enact policies and practices to give certain groups more access to markets than others; offer competitive advantages to certain classes of people within markets; protect certain groups from market failures more often than others; invest more in the human capital of certain groups than others; and systematically channel social and cultural capital to certain categories of people."

12. As observed by Giovanni Arrighi (1967, 27) in the case of Rhodesia: "To the interest of [white workers and petty bourgeoisie] in limiting racial competition corresponded that of the Africans in eliminating those conditions on which differentials in the standard of living were based."

13. As Tilly (1999, 7–8) points out: "Even where they employ ostensibly biological markers, categories [of inequality] always depend on extensive social organization, belief, and enforcement. Durable inequality among categories arises because people who control access to value-producing resources solve pressing organizational problems by means of categorical distinctions. Inadvertently or otherwise, those people set up systems of social closure, exclusion, and control. *Multiple parties—not all of them powerful, some of them even victims of exploitation—then acquire stakes on those solutions*" (our emphasis).

14. For Daniel Garcia Swartz (1993, 77), these protections for corporate property rights became stronger in the Andean region than in Mexico; he explains that a "higher degree of egalitarianism" prevailed in the former: "The key element here is that the Andean village community, based on the *ayllu,* seems to have been far more widespread, more egalitarian and more resilient in the face of exogenous pressures than its Mexican counterpart, based on the *calpulli.*" The ayllu and the calpulli were the basic social units (groups in which

some but not all members were linked by family ties) of the Incas and Nahuatls, respectively.

15. Of course, while serving to constrain rising inequality, the use of such mechanisms also strengthened and legitimized prevailing institutional arrangements, even while the latter sustained highly unequal arrangements. Thus, John Coatsworth (1993, 18) notes that "revolts from below did not, even in the case of major explosions such as the Tupac Amaru rebellion [1780 to 1784] in the Andes, lead to the abolition of castes but to concessions that reinforced some of the corporate rights of the indigenous communities" ("thus restoring stability to colonial rule at the cost of strengthening institutions inimical to economic growth," the author adds).

16. De Ferranti and others (2004, 119) note that by contrast to the lack of access to education by the poor, "fairly generous support was made available . . . for universities and other institutions of higher learning that were more geared toward the children of the elite."

17. In nineteenth-century Latin America, "new legal frameworks were adopted, beginning with new commercial codes and extending to a wide range of specialized areas such as banking, limited liability, mining, insurance, land, water, and patent legislation. Public lands were privatized, public monopolies abolished, and public property rights in subsoil resources liquidated or attenuated. Internal tariffs and excise taxes disappeared. Tax systems, tariff schedules, and public administration were reformed and streamlined" (Coatsworth 1993, 23). These changes led to "a continent-wide process of entre-preneurial land-grabbing facilitated by the abolition of Indian communal property rights," and thereby "tended to exacerbate inherited inequalities more than in the North Atlantic" (24).

18. "Clientelistic practices enable the poor to make isolated efforts to attain local goods, but these rarely form the basis of broad-based policy initiatives that address the underlying causes of poverty and inequality" (De Ferranti et al. 2004, 126).

19. Populist "incorporation processes simply transferred unequal social structures to the formal political arena by reproducing unequal ver-tical relations at the national political level. Although corporatism is increasingly a phenomenon of the past, its heritage persists in many areas that are relevant to current policy, including widespread vested interests that have accrued to the formal working classes and public sector servants" (De Ferranti et al. 2004, 126).

20. "[Weak state capacity] means, in particular, relative weakness in providing the public with goods such as the rule of law, citizen-ship, and protection of property rights, and with basic services

such as quality primary and secondary education" (De Ferranti et al. 2004, 127).

21. Populism did have redistributive aims—or at least rhetoric—manifested in both authoritarian and democratic regimes, but the movement was also a symptom of unequal, vertical institutions through which charismatic leaders periodically emerged with promises to the masses that were not mediated by institutional structures (De Ferranti et al. 2004, 131).

22. "These economies were not endowed with substantial populations of natives able to provide labor, nor with climates and soils that gave them a comparative advantage in the production of crops characterized by major economies of using slave labor. . . . With abundant land and low capital requirements, the great majority of adult men were able to operate as independent proprietors" (Sokoloff and Engerman 2000, 223).

23. Thus, "Voltaire, for example, considered the conflict in North America between the French and the British during the Seven Years' War (1756–63) to be madness and characterized the two countries as 'fighting over a few acres of snow.' The victorious British were later to engage in a lively public debate over which territory should be taken from the French as reparations—the Caribbean island of Guadeloupe (with a land area of 563 square miles) or Canada" (Sokoloff and Engerman 2000, 217).

24. In the institutional literature generated by economists, gender, the disparities arising therefrom, or the relationship between political discourse and existing gender relations seldom appear as relevant to the origin of these institutional arrangements. Here, the contributions of Julia Adams are invaluable. For example, regarding the issue of equality, Adams (2005b, 251; see also Adams 2005a) writes that it was the consolidation of what she calls "hierarchical paternity" that "opened the discursive door to the possibility of anyone's being considered an equal and a fellow human being—even women, people of other religions, or those who were currently held as slaves."

25. A reader of an earlier version of this manuscript noted that many of these democratic rights were attained by transported Chartists in Australia well before they were attained in Britain itself.

26. We should be careful here about not treating these areas as havens of democracy and social mobility. Rogers Smith (1997, 58) argues that "Colonial America . . . remained in many ways a medieval political world, with power structures defined by titles to estates more than commitments to self-governance." In the Chesapeake colonies of North America, for example, political concerns about the

discontent of dispossessed whites led to a more widespread use of a "rigid and rigorous form of black slavery that seemed to offer greater profits and social stability" (Fredrickson 1981, 68).

27. Along similar lines, many would argue that the establishment of LIE in wealthy countries cannot be separated from European imperialism and its destructive impact on institutions in today's poor countries. Davis (2001, 9) observes that "we are not dealing . . . with 'lands of famine' becalmed in stagnant backwaters of world history, but with the fate of tropical humanity at the precise moment (1870–1914) when its labor and products were being dynamically conscripted into a London-centered world economy. Millions died, not outside the 'modern world system,' but in the very process of being forcibly incorporated into its economic and political structures."

28. We should note that these arrangements differed strongly from the low inequality that prevailed in areas such as China and India, where either growing agricultural productivity or greater freedom of mobility for laborers kept wage differentials from developing in the same way. These are the same characteristics (albeit now, with labor mobility ensured through educational attainment) of the "growth with equity" trajectory followed recently by some countries in Asia (such as South Korea).

29. As discussed by Jeffrey Frieden (2006, 119), in supporting the extension of the welfare state, "labor's central concern was protection against unemployment," and this concern generated pressures to develop unemployment compensation systems more effective than those that existed on a local basis or through mutual aid societies.

30. Wallerstein (1980, 63–64), for example, observes that already in the seventeenth century, "Dutch social welfare . . . aroused the 'unqualified admiration' of foreign visitors" and that social welfare payments ("*higher than elsewhere* in the core states"; emphasis in the original) played an important role in ensuring social peace (but contrast Allen, Bengtsson, and Dribe 2005). Such claims need further research along the world-historical lines we suggest in this book.

31. Similar arguments about a nineteenth-century rise in inequality are made for individual European nations in Dumke (1991), Kaelble and Thomas (1991), Söderberg (1991), and Williamson and Lindert (1980).

32. Henry Gemery (2000, 175–76) notes that "the [U.S.] colonial society, even with its large indentured servant component, was relatively egalitarian, so stature differences between socioeconomic groups (occupations, ethnic background) were largely absent among the soldiers serving in the American Revolution. That absence of socioeconomic effects on stature contrasts dramatically with that of

Europe, where height differences ranging from 8 to 15 centimeters are observed between children drawn from the upper and lower classes."

33. De Ferranti and others (2004, 120) suggest that inequality underwent little change through the twentieth century in Argentina, since the 1930s in Colombia, and since the 1940s in Mexico.

34. As described, for example, by Kenneth Stampp (1956, 6): "Southerners did not create the slave system all at once in 1619; rather, they built it little by little, step by step, choice by choice, over a period of many years."

35. "Earthquake, inundation, fire, revolution, war, plundering the belongings of the rich, reforms, and laws of redistribution of land and capital, progressive taxes, cancellation of debts, expropriation of large profits—such are the forms of the leveling forces" (Sorokin 1927/1959, 47).

36. Observers often note that efforts to provide protection to lagging sectors of the population through market regulation eventually are bound to fail. But Karl Polanyi (1944/1957, 36) reminds us that "such a view seems to miss the point altogether. Why should the ultimate victory of a trend be taken as a proof of the ineffectiveness of the efforts to slow down its progress? And why should the purpose of these measures not be seen precisely in that which they achieved, i.e., in the slowing down of the rate of change? . . . The rate of change is often of no less importance than the direction of the change itself; but while the latter frequently does not depend upon our volition, it is the rate at which we allow change to take place which well may depend upon us."

37. For Smith (1776/1976, I, 74), employers had a clear advantage in their capacity to organize, as "the masters, being fewer in number, can combine much more easily; and the law, besides, authorizes or at least does not prohibit their combinations, while it prohibits those of the workmen." Smith notes that this capacity to organize was often hidden from public view: "We rarely hear, it has been said, of the combinations of masters, though frequently of those of workmen. But whoever imagines, upon this account, that masters rarely combine, is as ignorant of the world as of the subject. Masters are always and every where in a sort of tacit, but constant and uniform combination, not to raise the wage of labor above their actual rate. To violate this combination is every where a most unpopular action, and a sort of reproach to a master among his neighbors and equals. We seldom, indeed, hear of this combination, because it is the usual, and one may say, the natural state of things which nobody ever hears of" (75).

38. Thus, teachers are able to ease competitive pressures among themselves through regulation, and "the discipline of colleges and universities is in general contrived, not for the benefit of the students, but for the interest, or more properly speaking, for the ease of the masters. Its object is, in all cases, to maintain the authority of the master" (Smith 1776/1976, II, 287).

39. John Commons (1934, 69) notes that the concept of institutions is often fraught with uncertainty: "Sometimes an institution seems to be analogous to a building, a sort of framework of laws and regulations, within which individuals act like inmates. Sometimes it seems to mean the 'behavior' of the inmates themselves. Sometimes anything additional to or critical of the classical or hedonistic economics is deemed to be institutional. Sometimes anything that is 'dynamic' instead of 'static,' or a 'process' instead of commodities, or activity instead of feelings, or management instead of equilibrium, or control instead of laissez-faire, seems to be institutional economics."

40. As Rogers Smith (1997, 65) points out, already "by the early eighteenth century free blacks were widely denied rights to hold office, to vote, to testify against whites, to assemble, and to serve in the militia; and the colonies almost universally banned interracial sexual relations."

41. In the rise of the welfare state under the New Deal, for example, "tax rates on the rich were increased, and the resulting revenues were used to support the expansion of the federal government into a range of new domains—regulating markets, managing industrial relations, assisting workers, protecting consumers, increasing education, promoting research, and erecting a rudimentary but functional safety net for the elderly and the poor" (Massey 2007, 29).

42. Katznelson (2005, 103) also notes: "If, for Jews and Catholics, the war marked the first moment of full inclusion via the pathway of military service and benefits, for blacks, the war was the last moment of formal exclusion from equal citizenship by the federal government."

43. According to Katznelson (2005), there were three specific mechanisms through which southern legislators shaped New Deal programs to strengthen white privilege. "Racially laden" provisions excluded African Americans from key programs: for example, farmworkers and maids—who constituted "more than 60 percent of the black labor force in the 1930s and nearly 75 percent of those who were employed in the South—were excluded from the legislation that created modern unions, from laws that set minimum wages and regulated the hours of work, and from Social Security until the 1950s" (Katznelson 2005,

22). In addition, the administration of these programs was "placed in the hands of local officials who were deeply hostile to black aspirations" (23). And finally, southern representatives "prevented Congress from attaching any sort of antidiscrimination provisions to a wide array of social welfare programs" (23).

44. At the heart of these arrangements was the unequal distribution of political power accruing to whites and blacks from the South: "Since blacks counted in the numbers reported by the census, their large presence combined with their frequent inability to vote allowed white citizens to gain representation in higher proportions than their population in the House of Representatives. The Senate, with its distribution of two seats for each state, conferred on its seventeen racially segregated states a veto on all legislative enactments they did not like. When this power was deployed, as it was in matters of relief and social insurance, it seriously widened the racial gap. Federal social welfare policy operated, in short, not just as an instrument of racial discrimination but as a perverse formula for affirmative action" (Katznelson 2005, 51).

45. In this regard, there is some evidence "that some Native Americans were remarkably ingenious, adaptive, and successful in the face of exceptional demographic stress" (Steckel and Prince 2001, 287).

46. Thus, "from the revolution to the passage of the Homestead Act during the Civil War greater weight was given to the popular demand for access to land than to the élite's desire to keep profit and control in its own hands" (Clark 1993, 202).

47. As noted by Tilly (1999, 29), "any unified, fixed model of inequality—and, *a fortiori*, of stratification—that we impose on social life caricatures a dynamic reality, etches a Gillray portrait of social interaction. As with other useful caricatures, then, the secret is to sketch a model that brings out salient features of its object, but never to confuse the model with reality." James Gillray (1756–1815) was a noted English caricaturist whose engravings satirized current political events.

CHAPTER 3

1. There have been long and complicated debates on whether slavery represented a form of capitalism or an efficient form of organizing labor (some iterations can be found in Fogel and Engerman 1974; Genovese 1965; Stampp 1956). As noted by Robert Fogel (2003), some of the assumptions shaping these debates can be traced to the nineteenth-century portrayal of slavery by opponents as an inefficient set of arrangements that produced backwardness and to the

twentieth-century persistence of such a portrayal among scholars both more and less sympathetic to planters.

2. Discussing this synthesis in sugar production, Mintz (1985, 47) notes, for example, that "the specialization by skill and jobs, and the division of labor by age, gender, and condition into crews, shifts, and 'gangs,' together with the stress upon punctuality and discipline, are features associated more with industry than with agriculture—at least in the sixteenth century."

3. "The industrial discipline, so difficult to bring about in the factories of free England and free new England, was achieved on sugar plantations more than a century earlier—partly because sugar production lent itself to a minute division of labor, partly because of the invention of the gang system, which provided a powerful instrument for the supervision and control of labor, and partly because of the extraordinary degree of force that planters were allowed to bring to bear on enslaved black labor" (Fogel 1989, 26).

4. "Over the three and a half centuries between [the early 1500s and the 1860s] about 9,900,000 Africans were forcibly transported across the Atlantic. Brazil was by far the largest single participant in the traffic, accounting for 41 percent of the total. British- and French-owned colonies in the Caribbean and the far-flung Spanish-American empire were the destination of 47 percent. Dutch, Danish and Swedish colonies took another 5 percent. The remaining 7 percent represent the share of the . . . colonies that eventually became the United States" (Fogel 1989, 18).

5. Other candidates for such an explanation have included the contrasts between British and Spanish institutions (Coatsworth 1993; North 1981) and, as noted in our review later, local rates of European mortality (Acemoglu, Johnson, and Robinson 2001).

6. George Fredrickson (1981, 172) argues that white farmers in South Africa "had little to gain from turning their workers into commodities to be bought and sold, because they lacked a plantation system and a developed commercial economy. What they absolutely required was political control over their relationships with the indigenous people."

7. Immanuel Wallerstein (1989b, 145), for example, points out that in Europe "slave trading was sufficiently attractive in the second half of the eighteenth century to attract some investors *away from* textile production."

8. See Alexander von Humboldt at the turn of the eighteenth century: "Travelling along the ridges of the Andes, or the mountainous part of Mexico, we everywhere see the most striking examples of the

beneficial effects of mines on agriculture. Were it not for the establishments formed for the working of the mines, how many places would have remained deserted? How many districts uncultivated in the four intendancies of Guanajuato, Zacatecas, San Luis Potosí and Durango?" (cited in Frank 1978, 115).

9. Fogel (2003, 30) notes his surprise in the 1960s when his research data on the 1860s challenged long-standing assumptions regarding the comparative disadvantages of slave agriculture: "We had to confront the discomforting reality that, although American slavery was deeply immoral and politically backward, it might, nevertheless, have been a highly efficient form of economic organization that was able to sustain high rates of economic growth and yield substantial profits to its ruling class."

10. Likewise, apparently drawing on Angus Maddison's data but also on his own historical research, Coatsworth (1993, 10) argues that "it seems likely that Mexico's income per capita roughly equaled that of Great Britain and the thirteen British North American colonies at the end of the seventeenth century."

11. Wallerstein (1980, 170) argues that the prevalence of absentee landlords in the English sugar islands "came about because successful entrepreneurs were profiting from their good fortune, and it is evidence of the strength of their enterprise."

12. Among slaves in the United States, for example, "infant death rates were exceedingly high, running about 30 percent, and partly because of poor weaning diets, about 20 percent of the survivors died between ages one and five" (Fogel 2003, 36).

13. Fogel and Engerman (1974, 249) point out that "if we treat the North and South as separate nations and rank them among the countries of the world, the South would stand as the fourth most prosperous nation of the world in 1860. The South was richer than France, richer than Germany, richer than Denmark, richer than any of the countries of Europe except England."

14. "Slaveowners accumulated wealth in a form that had no counterpart in nonslave societies, a form that vanished when slavery was forcibly ended" (Wright 2006, 61). Indeed, "slavery retarded regional economic growth by absorbing the savings of slaveowners, 'crowding out' investment in physical capital. But there was no reason for slaveowners to adopt that point of view, since even small owners were wealthy men by national standards" (Wright 2006, 61).

15. Thus, the promise of easy access to wealth attracted contemporary Europeans to these areas. For example, "during the Prussian time, some families of Neuchâtel were engaged in slave labor. David de

Pury was a Hoffactor for the Portuguese Monarch. Jean-Pierre de Pury, who founded Purrysburg, South Carolina, owned and traded with slaves. Jacques Louis Poutales became a slave owner in Grenada. Pierre Alexandre DuPeyrou became a slave owner in the Dutch colony [of] Surinam. Charles Daniel de Meuron became a slave owner in South Africa. Other slave owners and producers of tobacco were from the Neuchâtel family Coulon. The activities of these families made Neuchâtel rich. Members of the slave owner families tried to keep Neuchâtel Prussian, when it became part of Switzerland"; see Wikipedia entry on "Canton of Neuchâtel," available at: http://en.wikipedia.org/wiki/Canton_of_Neuch%C3%A2tel (accessed May 13, 2008).

16. Even world-systems approaches often engage in a similar type of exercise, assuming that wealth is more truly characteristic of some activities than others (for example, manufacturing rather than mining) or conflating the production of wealth with its distribution (for example, since gold and silver did not stay where they were produced, they did not constitute true wealth).

17. There is then a subsequent tendency (often by policymakers) to further translate such formulas into development panaceas that purport to have identified paths that all nations should find easy to attain growth, democracy, and equity.

18. In fact, Acemoglu, Johnson, and Robinson (2001, 1) eventually move from focusing on institutional arrangements as key to different degrees of inequality to arguing that "*better* institutions" are characterized by "secure property rights, and less distortionary policies," rallying as evidence "the divergent paths of North and South Korea, or East and West Germany, where one part of the country stagnated under central planning and collective ownership, while the other prospered with private property and a market economy."

19. Examples of such treatment abound. Kevin O'Rourke and Jeffrey Williamson (1999, 54) casually mention that the "combination of declining transport costs and a dramatic switch to free trade created powerful globalization forces in Japan. Other Asian nations followed this liberal path, most forced to do so by colonial dominance or gunboat diplomacy. . . . India went the way of British free trade in 1846, and Indonesia mimicked Dutch liberalism. . . . Asian commitment to globalization started more than a century ago." But institutional arrangements such as those entailed in colonial dominance or gunboat diplomacy are not distinct from "free markets": these markets are embedded in such institutional arrangements. Moreover, "efficiency is not a synonym for good and it is a disservice to the struggle for a moral society to make it a synonym" (Fogel 1989, 411).

20. Albeit these circles often bring a rather antiseptic tone to their description of the arrangements at hand. In a World Bank publication, for example, David De Ferranti and others (2004, 109) tell us that on plantations "there were very few European[s] among much larger populations of indigenous peoples and slaves, but they were greatly advantaged by their higher levels of human capital (that is, knowledge of technology and the sorts of legal and economic institutions established in the colonies), wealth, and legal standing." Clearly, the description only hints at the advantages derived by elites from control of the means of violence and, more generally, power. After all, as indicated by Fogel (1989, 34), the main feature that led planters to prefer slaves to free labor was "the enormous, almost unconstrained degree of force available to masters who wanted and needed to transform ancient modes of labor into a new industrial discipline."

21. Glenn Firebaugh (2003, 16) criticizes what he calls "the Trade Protest Model": globalization → global inequality. By contrast, he develops a "theoretical" model that he represents as: globalization → narrowing of institutional differences across nations → reduction in between-nation inequality → reduction in global inequality (194).

22. Illustrating such assumptions, Wallerstein (1974, 127) writes that "free labor is indeed a defining feature of capitalism, but not free labor throughout the productive enterprises. Free labor is the form of labor control used for skilled work in core countries whereas coerced labor is used for less skilled work in peripheral areas. The combination thereof is the essence of capitalism. When labor is everywhere free, we shall have socialism."

23. The religious basis of antislavery sentiment did not give way until the midnineteenth century, when the issue of how to organize property rights in new territories, in a context of growing economic growth and immigration, generated new political coalitions that perceived slaveholders to be promoting a "far-reaching plot against American freedom, a plot aimed ultimately at the complete subjugation of free people" (Fogel 1989, 338).

24. A compatible point is made by Mintz (1985, 41, emphasis added), who notes that in the development of the sugar plantation system, "the whole process—from the establishment of colonies, the seizure of slaves, the amassing of capital, the protection of shipping, and all else to actual consumption—took shape under the wing of the state, [and hence,] *such undertakings were at every point as meaningful politically as they were economically.*"

25. For an excellent account of this process in Africa, see Cooper (1996).

26. "Imagine . . . the arrival of a new technology, for example, the opportunity to industrialize. If the elite could undertake industrial investments without losing its political power, we may expect them to take advantage of these opportunities. However, in practice there are at least three major problems. First, those with the entrepreneurial skills and ideas may not be members of the elite and may not undertake the necessary investments, because they do not have secure property rights and anticipate that they will be held up by political elites once they undertake those investments. Second, the elites may want to block investments in new industrial activities, because it may be these outside groups, not the elites themselves, who will benefit from these new activities. Third, they may want to block these new activities, fearing political turbulence and the threat to their political power that these new technologies will bring" (Acemoglu, Johnson, and Robinson 2002, 24–25).

27. This has been a point of significant contention. Past studies often explained growing divergence between nations, particularly after the nineteenth century, as the outcome of the lack of innovative entrepreneurial spirit among the traditional type of elites prevalent in peripheral areas. José Ocampo (1981, 105), for example, argues that capitalist elites in Colombia "invested in production only when prices were extremely high, and then only to enjoy what can be called the 'speculative gain' associated with great scarcity. Consequently, they had no interest in the reinvestment of profits for building productive capacity. Their interest lay only in making easy profits under conditions in which almost every type of production would do." Similar arguments can be found earlier in Genovese (1965, 17): "Southern slavery directed reinvestment along a path that led to economic stagnation." But it is not clear that coercive labor arrangements always constrained innovation. In Cuba, for example, sugar production rose rapidly in tandem with slavery following the fall of Saint-Domingue and, more broadly, with stagnation in the British West Indies. Dale Tomich (2004, 84) points out that in the nineteenth century "the Cuban sugar mill developed on a giant scale, and the technology of sugar production there attained the most advanced level known under slavery."

28. In a sense, this is the point made by Barrington Moore (1966).

29. This is what Gunnar Myrdal (1957/1964, 41) probably had in mind when he noted that "generally speaking, on a low level of economic development with relatively weak spread effects, the competitive forces in the markets will, by circular causation, constantly be tending towards regional inequalities, while the inequalities themselves

will be holding back economic development, and at the same time weakening the power basis for egalitarian policies. A higher level of development will strengthen the spread effects and tend to hamper the drift towards regional inequalities; this will sustain economic development, and at the same time create more favorable conditions for policies directed at decreasing regional inequalities still further. The more effectively a national state becomes a welfare state— motivated in a way which approaches a more perfect democracy, and having at its disposal national resources big enough to carry out large-scale egalitarian policies with bearable sacrifices on the part of the regions and groups that are relatively better off—the stronger will be both the urge and the capacity to counteract the blind market forces which tend to result in regional inequalities; and this, again, will spur economic development in the country, and so on and so on, in circular causation."

30. A similar interpretation, albeit with a different account of the intervening mechanisms at hand, has been advanced more recently by William Baumol (2002, viii), who argues that "what differentiates the prototype capitalist economy most sharply from all other economic systems is free-market pressures that force firms into a continuing process of innovation, because it becomes a matter of life and death for many of them. The static efficiency properties that are stressed by standard welfare economics are emphatically not the most important qualities of capitalist economies." For a related perspective, see also North (1981, 57): "The major source of changes in an economy over time is structural change in the parameters held constant by the economist—technology, population, property rights, and government control over resources."

31. Kuznets (1940) was critical in his own review of Schumpeter's work on business cycles, indicating that he had doubts about the empirical accuracy of Schumpeter's account in regard to the clustering of innovations in cycles. A vast literature and extensive debates have been devoted to the existence of periodic cycles of innovation and to their causes and implications (see, for example, Aghion and Howitt 1992, 1998; Dinopoulos and Segerstrom 1999; Forbes 2000; Francois and Lloyd-Ellis 2003; Goldstein 1988; Maddison 1982; Mansfield 1983; Rostow 1978; Thompson 1990). Although these debates are important, whether the type of innovations emphasized in this chapter can be observed in cycles is not central to our argument regarding the impact of change on inequality.

32. In recent decades, Schumpeter has had a major impact across the social sciences. His ideas have been incorporated in research ranging

from the workings of democracy to outsourcing and other "global-ization" issues. Endogenous growth theory, for example, brought renewed attention to the "virtuous cycles" (for example, those involving investments in either human capital or research and development) that enhance the ability of wealthy nations to continue to grow through technological innovations. For various formulations of such arguments, see Aghion and Howitt (1992, 1998), Barro and Sala-i-Martin (1995), and Romer (1990).

33. This is why Giovanni Arrighi and Jessica Drangel (1986, 20) suggest that Schumpeter's arguments can be read "as a description of core-periphery relations in space, instead of a description of A-B phases in time."

34. In fact, the kind of institutional divergence that authors such as Coatsworth and Acemoglu, Johnson, and Robinson emphasize was itself a product of the world-economy as it developed between the fifteenth and eighteenth centuries. This is recognized to some extent by Coatsworth (1993, 26–27), who notes that "Latin America's external economic relations did not retard growth, but they did contribute to a growth trajectory characterized by extreme concentration of wealth and income."

35. Besides the prevailing inequalities between European and non-European peoples constructed around coercive forms of labor control, "the persistence and stability of elites, as well as of inequality generally, were also certainly aided by the restrictive immigration policies applied by Spain to her colonies, and by laws throughout Spanish America requiring that a citizen (a status entailing the right to vote and other privileges) own a substantial amount of land (qualifications that were modified in post-independence constitutions to require literacy and a specific economic standing)" (Sokoloff and Engerman 2000, 222).

36. For Wallerstein (1974, 87), slavery "is only profitable if the market is large so that the small per capita profit is compensated by the large quantity of production. . . . Slaves . . . are not useful in large-scale enterprises whenever skill is required."

37. Among such multiple and overlapping transitions, those characterized by the most unbalanced growth are, of course, the most likely to result in rapidly rising inequality (Williamson 1991).

38. There is a long-standing debate over whether growing polarization between poor and wealthy countries began in the nineteenth century (see, for example, Pomeranz 2000) or centuries earlier (see, for example, Wallerstein 1974). A precise answer is not easily available, as data are lacking and there is no agreement yet on the criteria that

should be used to select the appropriate measures. The interpretation advanced here emphasizes continuities from the sixteenth to the twenty-first centuries regarding the existence of a single world-economy but opens the door to the possibility that significant shifts in patterns of inequality took place around the eighteenth and nineteenth centuries.

39. This effect varies depending on the extent of political competition: "Both political elites that are subject to competition [and thus more likely to be replaced] and those that are highly entrenched [and thus not afraid of losing power] are likely to adopt new technologies. . . . It is elites that are somewhat entrenched but still fear replacement that will block innovation" (Acemoglu and Robinson 2006a). According to the same authors, a lower prevalence of rents creates greater probability of elite change, and so does a greater prevalence of human capital, and the presence of external threats.

40. For example, as summarized by Paget Henry (2004, 160), plantations "were very definitely economies that produced what they did not consume, and consumed what they did not produce."

41. This is why mobility (for example, as discussed in chapter 2 in the context of shifts in between-country inequality) often goes hand in hand with the adoption of innovative practices. In this sense, the notion of creative destruction leads us to expect some degree of shift over time in the "leading" sectors. This is another way of stating what can be found in Henri Pirenne: "I believe that, for each period into which our economic history may be divided, there is a distinct and separate class of capitalists. In other words, the group of capitalists in a given epoch does not spring from the capitalist group of the preceding epoch. At every change in economic organization we find a breach of continuity. It is as if the capitalists who have up to then been active recognize that they are incapable of adapting themselves to conditions which are evoked by needs hitherto unknown and which call for methods hitherto unemployed. They withdraw from the struggle and become an aristocracy, which if it again plays a part in the course of affairs, does so in a passive manner only" (cited in Wallerstein 1974, 124).

CHAPTER 4

1. See World Bank, International Comparison Program (ICP), "2005 International Comparison Program: Results," available at: http://web.worldbank.org/WBSITE/EXTERNAL/DATASTATISTICS/ICPEXT/0,,pagePK:62002243~theSitePK:270065,00.html (accessed October 28, 2007).

2. There are alternative ways of conceptualizing world inequality; see, for example, the three concepts explored by Branko Milanovic (2005). We should note that the data required to estimate what Milanovic calls "Concept 3" inequality—in which observations on within-country distributions are combined with between-country income estimates—are scarcely available today and are altogether absent for the longer period of time discussed in this book. That is why our historical estimates in this regard are limited to the stylized representations used here and in chapter 3. Regarding the more contemporary period, as we noted earlier, we are less interested in adjudicating between arguments debating whether overall global inequality is rising or falling and more in developing an argument on how to understand the forces driving these changes.

3. Milanovic (n.d., 27), for example, notes that "the current dollar inequality . . . reaches a Gini of 80 [sic] in 1993 . . . , the highest income or expenditure Gini coefficient ever reported."

4. Of course, there are persistent debates as to whether the gap in wealth between Europe and areas such as China and India developed before the nineteenth century (as stated in a classical eighteenth-century statement by Adam Smith) or closer to the twentieth (as indicated in some more recent approaches). Arguing that gaps developed rather later in China, Kenneth Pomeranz (2000, 2005) focuses primarily on the living standards of the "poor majority," and Boxhong Li (2005) assesses rural labor productivity. On India, again focusing on standards of living among workers, see Parthasarathi (2005). These arguments are challenged by Stephen Broadberry and Bishnupriya Gupta (2006), who maintain that divergence was already pronounced prior to the 1800s. More world-historical research is needed to ascertain whether it is in the process of becoming more fully incorporated into the world-economy, and under the pressure of European colonialism and empire or not, that major parts of the world such as China and India underwent the institutional transformations and competitive erosion emphasized by authors such as Mike Davis (2001) and Immanuel Wallerstein (1989).

5. Most often, the gap between wealthy and poor nations is presented as the outcome of the uneven spread of the industrial revolution (see, for example, Bairoch 1977, 1979, 1981, 1993; and more recently, Pritchett 1997 and Milanovic 2005).

6. For a simple example of this type of argument, see Firebaugh (2003, 174), for whom the rise (through most of the nineteenth century and the first half of the twentieth century) and decline (in the second half of the twentieth century) of inequalities between nations are

explained primarily by the uneven "spread of industrialization to poor nations. . . . Because industrialization took root first in richer nations, the spread of industrialization has boosted inequality across nations. . . . Now, however, the diffusion of industrialization works to compress inequality across nations."

7. As noted by Wallerstein (1989, 4), "the continued development of the capitalist world-economy has involved the unceasing ascension of the ideology of national economic development as the primordial collective task, the definition of such development in terms of national economic growth, and the corresponding virtual axiom . . . that the route to affluence lies by way of an industrial revolution."

8. We assume that Sala-i-Martin used the default range provided by Excel when making a figure out of the relevant data.

9. William Easterly (2001), for example, goes to great lengths to rightly criticize economic theories of development for assuming that investments in capital equipment or human capital would have the same impact in both poor and wealthy countries, but then he goes on to make extensive use of PPP-adjusted data without considering that such adjustments often have been based on precisely the same type of assumption. For example, for a long time educational expenditures and capital equipment were assumed to have equal values across poor and wealthy nations.

10. Peter Lindert and Jeffrey Williamson (2001) observe rising inequality between nations, but argue that the forces usually identified as "globalization" have tended to reduce rather than enhance such inequality.

11. Frank (1967, 3) traced this relationship to "four centuries of capitalist development" and called for studying "the historical development of the single world capitalist system" (1979, xii). For Frank (1979, 22–23), "three centuries of unequal exchange on the basis of unequal values . . . drained most of the 'new' world's colonies and colonialized peoples of vast amounts of capital that the European metropolis invested in the economic development, which in the nineteenth century was, in turn, to consolidate Latin America's underdevelopment."

12. Illustrating these divergent interpretations, contrast Adam Smith's (1776/1976, 16) assertion in the 1770s that "the accommodation of an European prince does not always so much exceed that of an industrious and frugal peasant, as the accommodation of the latter exceeds that of many an African king," to Mike Davis's (2001, 16) recent observation that until the latter half of the nineteenth century, "the differences in living standards, say, between a French sans-culotte

and Deccan farmer were relatively insignificant compared to the gulf that separated both from their ruling classes."

13. For example, John Coatsworth (1993, 15–16) argues that high transaction cost (due, for example, to "the capacity of conquered peoples to resist authoritative demands for revenues") limited the amount of revenue that colonial powers could extract from Latin America.

14. Terence Hopkins (1982a, 21) writes: "As process, then, unequal exchange works through an extraordinarily wide array of historical forms and arrangements to reproduce continually the basic core-periphery division and integration—despite massive changes over the centuries in the actual organization of production processes and despite continual shifts in the areas and processes forming the system's core, semiperiphery and periphery."

15. Emmanuel (1972, 130) distinguishes an original, "accidental" divergence between countries from that which ensues from unequal exchange: "Once a country has got ahead, through some historical accident, even if this be merely that a harsher climate has given men additional needs, this country starts to make other countries pay for its high wage through unequal exchange. From that point onward, the impoverishment of one country becomes an increasing function of the enrichment of another, and vice versa. The superprofit from unequal exchange ensures a faster rate of growth. This brings with it technological and cultural development. In order to deal with increasingly complicated production tasks, the ruling class is obliged to raise the people's educational level. The conditions favoring trade-union organization are created; and so forth in cycles reinforcing over time"; as a result, "*wealth begets wealth*" (Emmanuel 1972, 131, emphasis added). The opposite happens in poor countries, with unequal exchange depriving the means of accumulation, limiting the market, discouraging investment, enhancing unemployment, and further reducing wages, so that "*poverty begets poverty*" (131, emphasis added).

16. For reviews of some of these panaceas from very different perspectives, see Easterly (2001) and Escobar (1995).

17. As summarized by Charles Tilly (1999, 36, 81): "Established solutions generally have the advantage over innovations in the short run because the transaction costs of devising, perfecting, installing, teaching, and integrating new solutions to problems exceed the cost of maintaining old ways, more so to the extent that old ways articulate well with a wide range of adjacent beliefs and practices." In this sense, "most organizations . . . take shape and change not as

efficiency-driven designs but as mosaics of established models and exterior social structure."

18. "The inhabitants of a town, being collected into one place, can easily combine together. The most insignificant trades carried on in towns have accordingly, in some place or another, been incorporated; and even where they have never been incorporated, yet the corporation spirit, the jealousy of strangers, the aversion to take apprentices, or to communicate the secret of their trade, generally prevail in them, and often teach them, by voluntary associations and agreements, to prevent that free competition which they cannot prohibit by byelaws" (Smith 1776/1976, I, 141).

19. "Whatever stock, therefore, accumulated in the hands of the industrious part of the inhabitants of the country, naturally took refuge in cities, as the only sanctuaries in which it could be secure to the person that acquired it" (Smith 1776/1976, I, 427).

20. And such critical perspectives developed early on. Sorokin (1927/1959, 31), after reviewing data on the decline of population in the Pacific islands through the nineteenth century, argued that "such facts show that, instead of improvement, the level of economic and social welfare in the nineteenth century went down and led to the extinction of these peoples; and that European economic improvement in the nineteenth century was due in part to their exploitation and plundering. What was good for one group was disastrous to others. To ignore these other groups—hundreds of millions of people of India, Mongolia, Africa, China, the natives of all non-European continents and islands, at least some of whom the European progress cost a great deal and who scarcely have improved their standard of living for the last century—to ignore them and to advance 'the permanent spiral progress' theory only on the basis of some European countries is to be utterly subjective, and partial, and fantastic."

21. Of course, not all is exclusion. The institutions of within-country LIE exclude important sectors of the population of other nations from some markets, but seek to include them in other markets (such as the one constituted by intellectual property).

22. We should remember that "it was not until the 1840s that voluntary European migration first exceeded the volume of the slave trade" (Wright 2006, 21). Walter Willcox and Imre Ferenczi (1929, 83) argue that mass movements of people in Europe became a significant phenomenon after the 1840s removal of "legal obstacles to emigration. . . . One of the seldom mentioned outcomes of the French Revolution, for example, was the declared freedom of the individual to migrate within and from her or his country." Our discussion on immigration

draws on Foner (2005), Frieden (2006), Kaelble (1985), Soysal (1994), and Woytinsky and Woytinsky (1953).

23. In the United States, it is estimated that in the 1910 to 1914 period, there was an average yearly arrival of 1,035,000 legal migrants, as compared to 714,000 in the mid-1990s (Meissner et al. 1993, 28, 91). For Fredrickson (1981, 202), "the phenomenal rate of capital formation and industrial growth in nineteenth- and early twentieth-century America was due in part to the seemingly inexhaustible supply of low-paid immigrant workers who were in a weak position for improving their collective situation."

24. Alan Dowty (1987, 62) notes that "there was [in the 1890s] even serious debate over whether states had the right to restrict emigration." On the other hand, Stephen Castles (2007, 33) challenges the notion that there was "an era of laissez-faire in migration that ended with World War II" and argues that throughout the nineteenth century states were exploiting various ways of controlling migration flows.

25. As noted by Kevin O'Rourke and Jeffrey Williamson (1999, 15), this is "mostly a story about labor-abundant Europe with lower workers' living standards catching up with the labor-scarce New World with higher workers' living standards."

26. A parallel to freedom of movements of people can be found in the permeability of leading technological areas at the turn of the century: enterprises in some core countries could leapfrog to capture the lead in new technologies (Hikino and Amsden 1994).

27. According to Jeffrey Frieden (2006, 52), "while there was no impact [of migration] on the wages of artisans, the effects on American unskilled workers was appreciable: Every percentage point increase in the foreign-born depressed laborers wages by 1.6 percent."

28. Race and sex would remain two important categorical axes used to justify exclusion well into the twentieth century, but they eventually became increasingly challenged (in the United States, for example, by the civil rights movements and the women's movement).

29. But Ashley Timmer and Jeffrey Williamson (1998, 760) argue that "there is no evidence of the influence of racism or xenophobia, once underlying economic variables are taken into account."

30. The main slogan of the Workingmen's Party, the main political force pushing to restrict Asian migration in the 1870s, was "The Chinese Must Go!"; the party and its leaders had other targets as well: they "claimed that the city's wealthiest people were plotting to overthrow the American republic, destroy freedom, and replace white American workingmen with oriental slaves" (Shumsky 1991, 9), and the party's statement of principle promised to "wrest the government from the

hands of the rich and place it in those of the people where it properly belongs" (quoted in Shumsky 1991, 20).

31. The further U.S. restrictions on immigration that were implemented in the 1880s, supported by both Democrats and Republicans, "den[ied] admission to prostitutes and alien convicts (and) prohibiting the immigration of the mentally ill, or persons likely to become public charges" (Woytinsky and Woytinsky 1953, 80; Ahmad 2007).

32. John Higham (1956, 217) points out that "a growing company of reformers sounded alarms at the polarization of American society. Protestant advocates of a Social Gospel, a new generation of German-trained economists, and a host of municipal reformers charged immigration with increasing the rift of classes, complicating the slum problem, causing boss-rule, and straining the old moralities. . . . Many of the reformers who raised these issues were questioning the hallowed principles of *laissez-faire.* Immigration restriction, therefore, appealed to them as a simple way of using the power of the state to combat many interlocking social problems."

33. For example, "in 1891, the leading citizens of New Orleans led a lynching party into the parish prison and systematically slaughtered eleven Italians who had just been found not guilty of a murder charge. When the Italian government reacted indignantly, there was feverish talk in the United States of a war with Italy. The incident proved second only to the Haymarket Affair in stimulating restrictionist sentiment" (Higham 1956, 219).

34. For example, as noted by O'Rourke and Williamson (1999, 93), "the major event in Europe was the invasion of cheap New World and Ukrainian grain, which threatened to reduce agricultural incomes, while there were two major events that mattered in the New World: mass migration from Europe, which threatened to lower workers' living standards, and the competition that European manufactured exports gave to New World infant industries."

35. Among wealthier countries, according to O'Rourke and Williamson (1999, 93–94), "there were four political responses to [competitive pressures in the late nineteenth and early twentieth centuries]: (1) the continental European response, which typically involved imposing tariffs on the New World's agricultural exports; (2) the British, Irish, and Danish response, which meant holding firm to free trade in agricultural goods; and, in the New World, (3) a gradual escalation in immigration restrictions and (4) the creation of high tariffs protecting manufacturers. These four political responses have left scars that remain visible today."

36. In short, the rise of inequality in wealthy countries produced a retreat from open markets: far from being destroyed by unforeseen and exogenous political events, globalization, at least in part, destroyed itself" (O'Rourke and Williamson 1999, 268). For O'Rourke and Williamson, the experience entails lessons about globalization: "History shows that globalization can plant the seeds of its own destruction. Those seeds were planted in the 1870s, sprouted in the 1880s, grew vigorously around the turn of the century, and then came to full flower in the dark years between the two world wars" (93). Thus, "the record suggests that unless politicians worry about who gains and who loses, they may be forced by the electorate to stop efforts to strengthen global economy links, and perhaps even to dismantle them" (268).

37. Restrictions on immigration, together with growing regulations on international trade, were critical in reversing the Atlantic convergence of the late nineteenth century. In the United States, a comparative wage advantage reasserted itself at the turn of the century, a consequence of rapid industrialization. But more broadly, "between 1914 and 1934, real wage dispersion did not fall at all, implying that the secular convergence that had been at work since the middle of the nineteenth century stopped completely during these two decades. Following 1934, real wage gaps in the Atlantic economy widened so much that measures of global labor market (dis)integration retreated all the way back to the levels of the late 1870s . . . real wage divergence took place after 1934 and up through World war II, and it took place everywhere: within Europe, within the New World, and between the two" (O'Rourke and Williamson 1999, 25–26).

38. In this sense, it is important to recognize (as Adam Smith certainly did) that for some disadvantaged populations, greater access to markets becomes an effective strategy for challenging existing inequalities.

39. For Prebisch (1950, 14), moreover, this helped explain differential rates of economic growth: "The greater ability of the masses in the cyclical centers to obtain rises in wages during the upswing and to maintain the higher level during the downswing and the ability of the centers, by virtue of the role they play in production, to divert cyclical pressure to the periphery (causing a greater reduction in income of the latter than that in the centers) explain why income at the centers persistently tends to rise more than in the countries of the periphery, as happened in the case of Latin America."

40. Moreover, Lewis (1954, 177) notes, "the export of capital is therefore a much easier way out for the capitalists, since trade unions are

quick to restrict immigration, but much slower in bringing the export of capital under control."

41. Of course, Kuznets is not the only theorist who bounded these processes nationally. Rawls (1971, 8) writes that his theory of justice applies to a national society conceived "as a closed system isolated from other societies." The world-systems perspective adopted in this book provides an alternative understanding (particularly insofar as equal citizenship is not forthcoming globally, as Rawls assumes it is at a national level).

42. We have shown this in our previous work (Korzeniewicz and Moran 1997). In a detailed combination of within- and between-country data, Milanovic (2005) calculates that inequality between countries accounted for roughly two-thirds of overall world inequality in 1993.

CHAPTER 5

1. This is what Immanuel Wallerstein (1982, 99) aims at in arguing that "if you were to sit down and do a content analysis of books of history, to see if political conflicts were between or within classes, I think you would find on any rapid checklist that about 95 percent of the conflicts within the world are in fact *within* classes."

2. This effort to produce a more global picture of the distribution of income worldwide updates the analysis we first presented in Korzeniewicz and Moran (1997).

3. For the country deciles in figure 5.1, the correlation between the country decile and the global decile is only .36, meaning that country decile numbers explain only about 13 percent of the variance in global decile numbers. This quite dramatically shows the importance of national boundaries in determining one's relative place in the world.

4. For example, Douglas Massey (2007, 36) notes that "an accurate understanding of any system of stratification necessarily begins with the identification of which social groups experience the categorical mechanisms of exploitation and exclusion," but in studying the historical evolution of stratification in the United States, he ignores nationhood as the basis of categorical inequality.

5. The same points apply here as in other forms of categorical inequality. For example, in relation to race relations in the United States in the twentieth century, Massey (2007, 53) notes that "although most whites are reluctant to admit it, the simple fact of the matter is that categorical mechanisms of racial inequality worked to their advantage for most of

the twentieth century. Ending racial stratification, therefore, not only requires the direct expenditure of public resources but also imposes significant costs on people who benefited under the old racial regime."

6. For Massey (2007, 36), "under capitalism categorical mechanisms of inequality, in addition to existing outside the market, are often built into the very organization of the market itself—they are embedded within its laws, regulations, conventions, understandings, and institutions, both formal and informal."

7. Thus, "when we address ourselves to distributions without remembering to see them as summaries of conditions continually resulting from processes among the units, we give up our central focus on relations and perforce become eclectic and ad hoc in our efforts to set forth coherent accounts of 'distributions' " (Hopkins 1982b, 150).

8. Using the PPP-adjusted data alters these findings only slightly. For Mexico, all country deciles below MEX8 (instead of MEX9) are upwardly mobile to USA2. For Guatemala, the results are the same. For Argentina, all country deciles below ARG7 (instead of ARG9) are upwardly mobile into ESP2. For Bolivia, all country deciles below BOL7 (instead of BOL8) are upwardly mobile into ARG2.

9. Charles Tilly (1999, 91) refers to such strategies of exclusion as "opportunity hoarding": "When members of a categorically bounded network acquire access to a resource that is valuable, renewable, subject to monopoly, supportive of network activities, and enhanced by the network's modus operandi, network members regularly hoard their access to the resource, creating beliefs and practices that sustain their control. As in exploitation, a boundary separates beneficiaries from others, while unequal relations across the boundary connect them."

10. These institutions also provided opportunities for some (but not other) rural populations to rapidly enhance their incomes by moving to urban areas, thereby contributing further to declines in within-country inequality in wealthier nations.

11. Williamson (1991, 17), for example, argues that declining inequality in industrialized countries after the 1930s was chiefly the outcome of pre-fisc forces that altered returns to skilled and unskilled sectors of the labor force in favor of the latter, and he notes that key to these forces was "an erosion in the premium on . . . skills, and [a] relative increase in unskilled labor scarcity."

CHAPTER 6

1. Hence, "the record suggests that unless politicians worry about who gains and who loses, they may be forced by the electorate to stop

efforts to strengthen global economy links, and perhaps even to dismantle them" (O'Rourke and Williamson 1999, 268).

2. Massey (2007, 30) summarizes this period, which was part of a broader trend in wealthy countries: "Standards of living rose rapidly . . . , median incomes increased, inequality fell, and average citizens came to know the benefits of what John Kenneth Galbraith (1958) called 'the affluent society' and Lane Kenworthy (2004) has labeled 'egalitarian capitalism.'"

3. C. Wright Mills (1959, 176) had similar points in mind when he wrote: "I do not know the answer to the question of political irresponsibility in our time. . . . But is it not clear that no answers will be found unless these problems are at least confronted? Is it not obvious that the ones to confront them, above all others, are the social scientists of the rich societies? That many of them do not now do so is surely the greatest human default being committed by privileged men in our times."

References

Abbott, Andrew. 2006. "Mobility: What? When? How?" In *Mobility and Inequality: Frontiers of Research in Sociology and Economics,* edited by Stephen L. Morgan, David B. Grusky, and Gary S. Fields. Stanford, Calif.: Stanford University Press.

Acemoglu, Daron. 2002. "Technical Change, Inequality, and the Labor Market." *Journal of Economic Literature* 40(1): 7–72.

Acemoglu, Daron, Simon Johnson, and James A. Robinson. 2001. "The Colonial Origins of Comparative Development: An Empirical Investigation." *American Economic Review* 91(December): 649–61.

———. 2002. "Reversal of Fortune: Geography and Institutions in the Making of the Modern World Income Distribution." *Quarterly Journal of Economics* 117(November): 1231–94.

———. 2005. "The Rise of Europe: Atlantic Trade, Institutional Change, and Economic Growth." *American Economic Review* 95(June): 546–79.

Acemoglu, Daron, and James A. Robinson. 2000. "Why Did the West Extend the Franchise? Democracy, Inequality, and Growth in Historical Perspective." *Quarterly Journal of Economics* 115(November): 1167–99.

———. 2006a. "Economic Backwardness in Political Perspective." *American Political Science Review* 100(1): 115–31.

———. 2006b. *Economic Origins of Dictatorship and Democracy.* Cambridge: Cambridge University Press.

Adams, Julia. 2005a. *The Familial State: Ruling Families and Merchant Capitalism in Early Modern Europe.* Ithaca, N.Y.: Cornell University Press.

———. 2005b. "The Rule of the Father: Patriarchy and Patrimonialism in Early Modern Europe." In *Max Weber's Economy and Society: A Critical Companion,* edited by Charles Camic, Philip S. Gorski, and David M. Trubek. Stanford, Calif.: Stanford University Press.

Adelman, Irma, and Cynthia Taft Morris. 1973. *Economic Growth and Social Equity in Developing Countries.* Stanford, Calif.: Stanford University Press.

———. 1978. "Growth and Impoverishment in the Middle of the Nineteenth Century." *World Development* 6(3): 245–73.

Aghion, Phillippe, and Peter Howitt. 1992. "A Model of Growth Through Creative Destruction." *Econometrica* 60(2): 323–51.

———. 1998. *Endogenous Growth Theory*. Cambridge, Mass.: MIT Press.

Ahluwalia, Montek S. 1974. "Income Inequality: Some Dimensions of the Problem." In *Redistribution with Growth*, edited by Hollis Chenery, Phillippe Aghion, and Peter Howitt. London: Oxford University Press.

———. 1976a. "Income Distribution and Development: Some Stylized Facts." *American Economic Review* 66(2): 128–35.

———. 1976b. "Inequality, Poverty, and Development." *Journal of Development Economics* 3(4): 307–42.

Ahmad, Diana L. 2007. *The Opium Debate and Chinese Exclusion Laws in the Nineteenth-Century American West*. Reno: University of Nevada Press.

Alderson, Arthur A., and François Nielsen. 2002. "Globalization and the Great U-Turn: Income Inequality Trends in Sixteen OECD Countries." *American Journal of Sociology* 107(55): 1244–99.

Allahar, Anton L. 2004. "Sugar and the Politics of Slavery in Midnineteenth-Century Cuba." In *Sugar, Slavery, and Society: Perspectives on the Caribbean, India, the Mascarenes, and the United States*, edited by Bernard Moitt. Gainesville: University Press of Florida.

Allen, Robert C., Tommy Bengtsson, and Martin Dribe. 2005. *Living Standards in the Past: New Perspectives on Well-being in Asia and Europe*. Oxford: Oxford University Press.

Allison, Paul D. 1978. "Measures of Inequality." *American Sociological Review* 43(December): 865–80.

Anand, Sudir, and S. M. R. Kanbur. 1993a. "The Kuznets Process and the Inequality-Development Relationship." *Journal of Development Economics* 40(1): 25–52.

———. 1993b. "Inequality and Development: A Critique." *Journal of Development Economics* 41(1): 19–43.

Anand, Sudir, and Paul Segal. 2008. "What Do We Know About Global Income Inequality?" *Journal of Economic Literature* 46(1): 57–94.

Andersen, Margaret L., and Patricia Hill Collins. 2007. *Race, Class, and Gender: An Anthology*, 6th ed. Belmont, Calif.: Wadsworth Publishing.

Arrighi, Giovanni. 1967. *The Political Economy of Rhodesia*. The Hague: Mouton & Co.

Arrighi, Giovanni, and Jessica Drangel. 1986. "The Stratification of the World-Economy: An Exploration of the Semiperipheral Zone." *Review: A Journal of the Fernand Braudel Center* 10(1): 9–74.

Arts, Wil, and John Gelissen. 2002. "Three Worlds of Welfare Capitalism or More? A State of the Art Report." *Journal of European Social Policy* 12(2): 137–58.

Atkinson, Anthony B. 1970. "On the Measurement of Inequality." *Journal of Economic Theory* 2: 244–63.

Bairoch, Paul. 1977. "Estimations du revenu national dans les sociétés occidentales pré-industrielles et au XIXe siècle." *Revue Economique* 28(2): 177–208.

———. 1979. "Escarts internationaux des niveaux de vie avant la révolution industrielle." *Annales, ESC* 34(1): 145–71.

———. 1981. "The Main Trends in National Economic Disparities Since the Industrial Revolution." In *Disparities in Economic Development Since the Industrial Revolution,* edited by Paul Bairoch and Maurice Lévy-Leboyer. New York: St. Martin's Press.

———. 1993. *Economics and World History.* Chicago: University of Chicago Press.

Barro, Robert J., and Xavier Sala-i-Martin. 1995. *Economic Growth.* Cambridge, Mass.: MIT Press.

Baumol, William J. 2002. *The Free-Market Innovation Machine: Analyzing the Growth Miracle of Capitalism.* Princeton, N.J.: Princeton University Press.

Beckfield, Jason. 2006. "European Regional Integration and Income Inequality." *American Sociological Review* 71(6): 964–85.

Berman, Eli, John Bound, and Zvi Griliches. 1994. "Changes in the Demand for Skilled Labor Within U.S. Manufacturing: Evidence from the Annual Survey of Manufacturers." *Quarterly Journal of Economics* 109(2): 367–97.

Birdsall, Nancy, David Ross, and Richard Sabot. 1997. "Education, Growth, and Inequality." In *Pathways to Growth: Comparing East Asia and Latin America,* edited by Nancy Birdsall and Frederick Jasperson. Washington, D.C.: Inter-American Development Bank.

Blau, Francine D., and Lawrence M. Kahn. 1996. "International Differences in Male Wage Inequality: Institutions Versus Market Forces." *Journal of Political Economy* 104(2): 791–837.

Blau, Peter M., and Otis Dudley Duncan. 1967. *The American Occupational Structure.* New York: Wiley.

Bluestone, Barry, and Bennett Harrison. 1982. *The Deindustrialization of America.* New York: Basic Books.

Blyth, Mark. 2002. *Great Transformations: Economic Ideas and Institutional Change in the Twentieth Century.* Cambridge: Cambridge University Press.

Bollen, Kenneth A., and Robert W. Jackman. 1985. "Political Democracy and the Size Distribution of Income." *American Sociological Review* 50(4): 438–57.

Bornschier, Volker. 1983. "World Economy, Level of Development, and Income Distribution: An Integration of Different Approaches to the Explanation of Income Inequality." *World Development* 11: 11–20.

Bornschier, Volker, and Thanh-Huyen Ballmer-Cao. 1979. "Income Inequality: A Cross-National Study of the Relationships Between

MNC-Penetration, Dimensions of the Power Structure, and Income Distribution." *American Sociological Review* 44: 487–506.

Bornschier, Volker, and Christopher Chase-Dunn. 1985. *Transnational Corporations and Underdevelopment.* New York: Praeger.

Boserup, Ester. 1989. *Woman's Role in Economic Development.* London: Earthscan. (Orig. pub. in 1970.)

Bound, John, and George Johnson. 1992. "Changes in the Structure of Wages in the 1980s: An Evaluation of Alternative Explanations." *American Economic Review* 82(3): 371–92.

Bourguignon, François, and Christian Morrisson.1990. "Inequality and Development: The Role of Dualism." *Journal of Development Economics* 57(2): 233–57.

Bowles, Samuel, and Herbert Gintis. 1976. *Schooling in Capitalist America: Educational Reform and the Contradictions of Economic Life.* New York: Basic Books.

Bradley, David, Evelyne Huber, Stephanie Moller, François Nielsen, and John D. Stephens. 2003. "Distribution and Redistribution in Postindustrial Democracies." *World Politics* 55(2): 193–230.

Brady, David. 2003. "The Politics of Poverty: Left Political Institutions, the Welfare State, and Poverty." *Social Forces* 82(2): 557–88.

Broadberry, Stephen, and Bishnupriya Gupta. 2006. "The Early Modern Great Divergence: Wages, Prices, and Economic Development in Europe and Asia, 1500–1800." *Economic History Review* 59(1): 2–31.

Bruno, Michael, Martin Ravallion, and Lyn Squire. 1998. "Equity and Growth in Developing Countries: Old and New Perspectives on the Policy Issues." In *Income Distribution and High-Quality Growth,* edited by Uiro Tanzi and Ke-Young Chu. Cambridge, Mass.: MIT Press.

Campbell, John L. 2004. *Institutional Change and Globalization.* Princeton, N.J.: Princeton University Press.

Canberra Group. 2001. "Expert Group on Household Income Statistics: Final Report and Recommendations." Ottawa: Canberra Group.

Carlsson, Gösta. 1958. *Social Mobility and Class Structure.* Lund: Gleerup.

Castles, Francis G. 2004. *The Future of the Welfare State.* Oxford: Oxford University Press.

Castles, Stephen. 2007. "The Factors That Make and Unmake Migration Policies." In *Rethinking Migration: New Theoretical and Empirical Perspectives,* edited by Alejandro Portes and Josh DeWind. New York: Berghahn Books.

CEDLAS (Center for Distributional, Labor, and Social Studies) and World Bank. 2008. Socio-Economic Database for Latin America and the Caribbean (SEDLAC). Available at: www.depeco.econo.unlp.edu.ar/cedlas/sedlac (accessed January 23, 2008).

Chenery, Hollis, and Moises Syrquin. 1975. *Patterns of Development, 1950–1970.* London: Oxford University Press.

Clark, Christopher. 1993. "Agrarian Societies and Economic Development in Nineteenth-Century North America." In *Development and Underdevelopment in America: Contrasts of Economic Growth in North and Latin America in Historical Perspective,* edited by Walther L. Bernecker and Hans Werner Tobler. Berlin: Walter de Gruyter.

Coatsworth, John H. 1993. "Notes on the Comparative Economic History of Latin America and the United States." In *Development and Underdevelopment in America: Contrasts of Economic Growth in North and Latin America in Historical Perspective,* edited by Walther L. Bernecker and Hans Werner Tobler. Berlin: Walter de Gruyter.

Commons, John R. 1934. *Institutional Economics: Its Place in Political Economy.* New York: Macmillan.

Cooper, Frederick. 1996. *Decolonization and African Society: The Labor Question in French and British Africa.* Cambridge: Cambridge University Press.

Crenshaw, Edward. 1992. "Cross-National Determinants of Income Inequality: A Replication and Extension Using Ecological-Evolutionary Theory." *Social Forces* 71(2): 339–63.

Cutright, Philips. 1967. "Inequality: A Cross-National Analysis." *American Sociological Review* 32(4): 562–78.

Danziger, Sheldon H., and Peter Gottschalk, eds. 1993. *Uneven Tides: Rising Inequality in America.* New York: Russell Sage Foundation.

Datta, Anindya. 1986. *Growth with Equity: A Critique of the Lewis-Kuznets Tradition.* Calcutta: Oxford University Press.

Davis, Mike. 2001. *Late Victorian Holocausts: El Niño Famines and the Making of the Third World.* London: Verso.

———. 2007. *Planet of Slums.* New York: Verso.

De Ferranti, David, Guillermo E. Perry, Francisco H. G. Ferreira, and Michael Walton. 2004. *Inequality in Latin America: Breaking with History?* Washington: World Bank.

Deininger, Klaus, and Lyn Squire. 1998. "New Ways of Looking at Old Issues: Inequality and Growth." *Journal of Development Economics* 57(2): 259–87.

Desai, Sonalde, Amaresh Dubey, B. L. Joshi, Mitali Sen, Abusaleh Shariff, and Reeve Vanneman. 2007. India Human Development Survey (IHDS) (computer file). ICPSR22626-v1. University of Maryland and National Council of Applied Economic Research, New Delhi (producers), Inter-University Consortium for Political and Social Research, Ann Arbor, Mich. (distributor).

Dinopoulos, Elias, and Paul Segerstrom. 1999. "A Schumpeterian Model of Protection and Relative Wages." *American Economic Review* 89(3): 450–72.

Dovring, Folke. 1991. *Inequality: The Political Economy of Distribution.* New York: Praeger.

Dowty, Alan. 1987. *Closed Borders: The Contemporary Assault on Freedom of Movement.* New Haven, Conn.: Yale University Press.

Du Bois, W. E. B. 1903. *The Souls of Black Folk.* Available at: http://en.wikisource.org/wiki/The_Souls_of_Black_Folk (accessed August 14, 2008).

Dumke, Rolf. 1991. "Income Inequality and Industrialization in Germany, 1850–1913: The Kuznets Hypothesis Reexamined." In *Income Distribution in Historical Perspective,* edited by Y. S. Brenner, Hartmut Kaelble, and Mark Thomas. Cambridge: Cambridge University Press.

Durkheim, Émile. 1997. *The Division of Labor in Society.* New York: Free Press. (Orig. pub. in 1893.)

Easterly, William. 2001. *The Elusive Quest for Growth: Economists' Adventures and Misadventures in the Tropics.* Cambridge, Mass.: MIT Press.

———. 2006. *The White Man's Burden.* New York: Penguin Books.

Edwards, Sebastian, Gerardo Esquivel, and Graciela Márquez, eds. 2007. *The Decline of Latin American Economies: Growth, Institutions, and Crises.* Chicago: University of Chicago Press.

Emmanuel, Arghiri. 1972. *Unequal Exchange: A Study of the Imperialism of Trade.* New York: Monthly Review Press.

Engerman, Stanley L. 1981. "Notes on the Patterns of Economic Growth in the British North American Colonies in the Seventeenth, Eighteenth, and Nineteenth Centuries." In *Disparities in Economic Development Since the Industrial Revolution,* edited by Paul Bairoch and Maurice Lévy-Leboyer. New York: St. Martin's Press.

Engerman, Stanley L., and Kenneth L. Sokoloff. 1997. "Factor Endowments, Institutions, and Differential Paths of Growth Among New World Economies." In *How Latin America Fell Behind: Essays on the Economic Histories of Brazil and Mexico, 1800–1914,* edited by Stephen Haber. Stanford, Calif.: Stanford University Press.

Erikson, Robert, and John Goldthorpe. 1992. *The Constant Flux: A Study of Class Mobility in Industrial Societies.* Oxford: Oxford University Press.

Escobar, Arturo. 1995. *Encountering Development: The Making and Unmaking of the Third World.* Princeton, N.J.: Princeton University Press.

Esping-Anderson, Gøsta. 1990. *The Three Worlds of Welfare Capitalism.* Princeton, N.J.: Princeton University Press.

European Commission. 2008. Statistical tables. Luxembourg: Eurostat, Statistical Office of the European Communities. Available at: http://epp.eurostat.ec.europa.eu.

Evans, Peter, and Michael Timberlake. 1980. "Dependency, Inequality, and the Growth of the Tertiary: A Comparative Analysis of Less Developed Countries." *American Sociological Review* 45(4): 531–52.

Fei, John C. H., Gustav Ranis, and Shirley W. Y. Kuo. 1979. *Growth with Equity: The Taiwan Case.* New York: Oxford University Press.

Fields, Gary S. 1980. *Poverty, Inequality, and Development.* Cambridge: Cambridge University Press.

———. 1984. "Assessing Progress Toward Greater Equality of Income Distribution." In *The Gap Between the Rich and the Poor,* edited by Mitchell A. Seligson. Boulder, Colo.: Westview Press.

Findlay, Ronald, and Stanislaw Wellisz. 1993. *Five Small Open Economies.* Oxford: Oxford University Press.

Firebaugh, Glenn. 2003. *The New Geography of Global Income Inequality.* Cambridge, Mass.: Harvard University Press.

Firebaugh, Glenn, and Brian Goesling. 2004. "Accounting for the Recent Decline in Global Income Inequality." *American Journal of Sociology* 110(2): 283–312.

Fishlow, Albert. 1996. "Inequality, Poverty, and Growth: Where Do We Stand?" In *Annual World Bank Conference on Development Economics 1995,* edited by Michael Bruno and Boris Pleskovic. Washington: World Bank.

Fogel, Robert W. 1989. *Without Consent or Contract.* New York: W. W. Norton.

———. 2003. *The Slavery Debates, 1952–1990: A Retrospective.* Baton Rouge: Louisiana State University Press.

———. 2004. *The Escape from Hunger and Premature Death, 1700–2100.* Cambridge: Cambridge University Press.

Fogel, Robert W., and Stanley L. Engerman. 1974. *Time on the Cross: The Economics of American Negro Slavery.* Boston: Little, Brown and Co.

Foner, Nancy. 2005. *In a New Land: A Comparative View of Immigration.* New York: New York University Press.

Forbes, Kristin J. 2000. "A Reassessment of the Relationship Between Inequality and Growth." *American Economic Review* 90(4): 869–87.

Forsythe, Nancy, Roberto Patricio Korzeniewicz, and Valerie Durrant. 2000. "Gender Inequalities and Economic Growth: A Longitudinal Evaluation." *Economic Development and Cultural Change* 48(3): 573–617.

Francois, Patrick, and Huw Lloyd-Ellis. 2003. "Animal Spirits Through Creative Destruction." *American Economic Review* 93(3): 530–50.

Frank, Andre Gunder. 1967. *Capitalism and Underdevelopment in Latin America: Historical Studies of Chile and Brazil.* New York: Monthly Review Press.

———. 1978. *World Accumulation 1492–1789.* New York: Monthly Review Press.

———. 1979. *Dependent Accumulation and Underdevelopment.* New York: Monthly Review Press.

Fredrickson, George M. 1981. *White Supremacy: A Comparative Study in American and South African History.* New York: Oxford University Press.

Freeman, Richard B. 1993. "How Much Has De-unionization Contributed to the Rise in Male Earnings Inequality?" In *Uneven Tides: Rising Inequality in America,* edited by Sheldon H. Danziger and Peter Gottschalk. New York: Russell Sage Foundation.

Freeman, Richard B., and Lawrence F. Katz, eds. 1995. *Differences and Changes in Wage Structures.* Chicago: University of Chicago Press.

Frieden, Jeffrey A. 2006. *Global Capitalism.* New York: W. W. Norton.

Friedman, Thomas L. 2000. *The Lexus and the Olive Tree.* NY: Farrar, Straus and Giroux.

Furubotn, Eirik, and Svetozar Pejovich. 1972. "Property Rights and Economic Theory: A Survey of Recent Literature." *Journal of Economic Literature* 10(4): 1137–62.

Gagliani, Giorgio. 1987. "Income Inequality and Economic Development." *Annual Review of Sociology* 13(1): 313–34.

Galbraith, James K. 1998. *Created Unequal: The Crisis in American Pay.* New York: The Free Press.

Galbraith, John Kenneth. 1958. *The Affluent Society.* Boston: Houghton Mifflin.

Garcia Swartz, Daniel D. 1993. "Economic Growth and Stagnation in the Colonial Americas: An Exploratory Essay." In *Development and Underdevelopment in America: Contrasts of Economic Growth in North and Latin America in Historical Perspective,* edited by Walther L. Bernecker and Hans Werner Tobler. Berlin: Walter de Gruyter.

Gemery, Henry A. 2000. "The White Population of the Colonial United States, 1607–1790." In *A Population History of North America,* edited by Michael R. Haines and Richard H. Steckel. New York: Cambridge University Press.

Genovese, Eugene. 1965. *The Political Economy of Slavery.* New York: Pantheon Books.

Glass, David V., ed. 1954. *Social Mobility in Britain.* London: Routledge & Kegan Paul.

Goldstein, Joshua. 1988. *Long Cycles: Prosperity and War in the Modern Age.* New Haven, Conn.: Yale University Press.

Gornick, Janet C., and Jerry A. Jacobs. 1998. "Gender, the Welfare State, and Public Employment: A Comparative Study of Seven Industrialized Countries." *American Sociological Review* 63(5): 688–710.

Gupta, Gar S., and Ram D. Singh. 1984. "Income Inequality Across Nations over Time: How Much and Why?" *Southern Economics Journal* 51(1): 250–77.

Gustafsson, Björn, and Mats Johansson. 1999. "In Search of Smoking Guns: What Makes Income Inequality Vary over Time in Different Countries?" *American Sociological Review* 64(4): 585–605.

Harrison, Bennett, and Barry Bluestone. 1988. *The Great U-Turn.* New York: Basic Books.

Hasenbalg, Carlos A. 1985. "Race and Socioeconomic Inequalities in Brazil." In *Race, Class, and Power in Brazil,* edited by Pierre-Michel Fontaine. Los Angeles: Center for Afro-American Studies.

Henry, Paget. 2004. "The Caribbean Plantation: Its Contemporary Significance." In *Sugar, Slavery, and Society: Perspectives on the Caribbean, India, the Mascarenes, and the United States,* edited by Bernard Moitt. Gainesville: University of Florida.

Higgins, Matthew, and Jeffrey G. Williamson. 1999. "Explaining Inequality the World Round: Cohort Size, Kuznets Curves, and Openness." Working paper 7224. Cambridge, Mass.: National Bureau of Economic Research (July).

Higham, John. 1956. "American Immigration Policy in Historical Perspective." *Law and Contemporary Problems* 21(2): 213–35.

Hikino, Takashi, and Alice H. Amsden. 1994. "Staying Behind, Stumbling Back, Sneaking Up, Soaring Ahead: Late Industrialization in Historical Perspective." In *Convergence of Productivity: Cross-National Studies and Historical Evidence,* edited by William J. Baumol, Richard R. Nelson, and Edward N. Wolff. Oxford: Oxford University Press.

Hoffman, Kelly, and Miguel Angel Centeno. 2003. "The Lopsided Continent: Inequality in Latin America" *Annual Review of Sociology* 29(1): 363–90.

Hopkins, Terence K. 1982a. "The Study of Capitalist World-Economy: Some Introductory Considerations." In *World-Systems Analysis: Theory and Methodology,* edited by Terence K. Hopkins and Immanuel Wallerstein. Beverly Hills, Calif.: Sage Publications.

———. 1982b. "World-Systems Analysis: Methodological Issues." In *World-Systems Analysis: Theory and Methodology,* edited by Terence K. Hopkins and Immanuel Wallerstein. Beverly Hills, Calif.: Sage Publications.

Hopkins, Terence K., and Immanuel Wallerstein, eds. 1982. *World-Systems Analysis: Theory and Methodology.* Beverly Hills, Calif.: Sage Publications.

Huber, Evelyne, and John D. Stephens. 2001. *Development and Crisis of the Welfare State: Parties and Policies in Global Markets.* Chicago: University of Chicago Press.

Inter-American Development Bank (IADB). 1998. *Facing Up to Inequality in Latin America.* Washington, D.C.: IADB.

Jackman, Robert W. 1974. "Political Democracy and Social Inequality." *American Sociological Review* 39(1): 29–45.

Janoski, Tomas, and Alex M. Hicks, eds. 1994. *The Comparative Political Economy of the Welfare State.* Cambridge: Cambridge University Press.

Jencks, Christopher, Marshall Smith, Henry Acland, Mary Jo Bane, David Cohen, Herbert Gintis, Barbara Heyns, and Stephanie Michelson. 1972. *Inequality: A Reassessment of the Effect of Family and Schooling in America.* New York: Basic Books.

Jenkins, Stephen. 1991. "The Measurement of Income Inequality." In *Economic Inequality and Poverty: International Perspectives,* edited by Lars Osberg. Armonk, N.Y.: M. E. Sharpe.

Jha, Sailesh K. 1996. "The Kuznets Curve: A Reassessment." *World Development* 24(4): 773–80.

Kaelble, Hartmut. 1985. *Social Mobility in the Nineteenth and Twentieth Centuries: Europe and America in Comparative Perspective.* Dover, N.H.: Berg.

Kaelble, Hartmut, and Mark Thomas. 1991. "Introduction." In *Income Distribution in Historical Perspective,* edited by Y. S. Brenner, Hartmut Kaelble, and Mark Thomas. Cambridge: Cambridge University Press.

Kalecki, Michal. 1942. "A Theory of Profits." *Economic Journal* 52(206–207): 258–67.

Katz, Lawrence F., and David Autor. 2000. "Changes in the Wage Structure and Earnings Inequality." In *The Handbook of Labor Economics,* vol. 3, edited by Orley Ashenfelter and David Card. Amsterdam: Elsevier.

Katz, Lawrence F., and Kevin M. Murphy. 1992. "Changes in Relative Wages, 1963–1987: Supply and Demand Factors." *Quarterly Journal of Economics* 107(1): 35–78.

Katznelson, Ira. 2005. *When Affirmative Action Was White.* New York: W. W. Norton.

Kelly, Nathan J. 2004. "Does Politics Matter? Policy and Government's Equalizing Influence in the United States." *American Politics Research* 32(3): 264–84.

Kenworthy, Lane. 2004. *Egalitarian Capitalism.* New York: Russell Sage Foundation.

Korpi, Walter. 2003. "Welfare-State Regress in Western Europe: Politics, Institutions, Globalization, and Europeanization." *Annual Review of Sociology* 29: 589–609.

Korzeniewicz, Roberto Patricio, and Timothy Patrick Moran. 1997. "World-Economic Trends in the Distribution of Income, 1965–1992." *American Journal of Sociology* 102(4): 1000–1039.

———. 2000. "Measuring World Income Inequalities." *American Journal of Sociology* 106(1): 209–14.

Korzeniewicz, Roberto Patricio, and William C. Smith. 2000. "Growth, Poverty, and Inequality in Latin America: Searching for the High Road." *Latin American Research Review* 35(fall): 7–54.

Korzeniewicz, Roberto Patricio, Angela Stach, Vrushali Patil, and Timothy Patrick Moran. 2004. "Measuring National Income: A Critical Assessment." *Comparative Studies in Society and History* 46(3): 535–86.

Kozol, Jonathan. 1992. *Savage Inequalities.* New York: HarperCollins.

Kuznets, Simon. 1940. "Schumpeter's Business Cycles." *The American Economic Review* 30(2): 257–271.

———. 1955. "Economic Growth and Income Inequality." *American Economic Review* 45(1): 1–28.

———. 1963. "Quantitative Aspects of the Economic Growth of Nations: Distribution of Income by Size." *Economic Development and Cultural Change* 11(2): 1–80.

Lambert, Peter J., Daniel L. Millimet, and Daniel Slottje. 2003. "Inequality Aversion and the Natural Rate of Subjective Inequality." *Journal of Public Economics* 87(5–6): 1061–90.

Lantican, Clarita P., Christina H. Gladwin, and James L. Seale Jr. 1996. "Income and Gender Inequalities in Asia: Testing Alternative Theories of Development." *Economic Development and Cultural Change* 44(2): 236–63.

Lecaillon, Jacques, Felix Paukert, Christian Morrisson, and Dimitri Germidis. 1984. *Income Distribution and Economic Development: An Analytical Survey.* Geneva: International Labor Organization.

Lewis, W. Arthur. 1954. "Economic Development with Unlimited Supplies of Labor." *Manchester School of Economic and Social Studies* 22(2): 139–91.

———. 1958. "Unlimited Labor: Further Notes." *Manchester School of Economic and Social Studies* 26(1): 1–31.

———. 1960. *The Theory of Economic Growth.* London: Allen and Unwin. (Orig. pub. in 1955.)

———. 1976. "Development and Distribution." In *Employment, Income Distribution, and Development Strategy: Problems of the Developing Countries,* edited by Alec Cairncross and Mohinder Puri. New York: Holmes and Meier.

Li, Boxhong. 2005. "Farm Labor Productivity in Jiangnan, 1620–1850." In *Living Standards in the Past,* edited by Robert C. Allen, Tommy Bengtsson, and Martin Dribe. Oxford: Oxford University Press.

Lindert, Peter H., and Jeffrey G. Williamson. 2001. "Does Globalization Make the World More Unequal?" Paper presented to the National Bureau of Economic Research "Globalization in Historical Perspective" conference. Santa Barbara, Calif. (March).

Lipset, Seymour Martin, and Reinhard Bendix. 1959. *Social Mobility in Industrial Society.* Berkeley: University of California Press.

Luxembourg Income Study (LIS). 2008. Restricted database. Available at: http://www.lisproject.org (accessed March 15, 2008).

Maddison, Angus. 1982. *Phases of Capitalist Development.* New York: Oxford University Press.

———. 1995. *Monitoring the World Economy, 1820–1992.* Paris: Organization for Economic Cooperation and Development.

Mandle, Jay R. 1981. "The Economic Underdevelopment of the United States in the Post-Bellum Era." In *Disparities in Economic Development Since the Industrial Revolution,* edited by Paul Bairoch and Maurice Lévy-Leboyer. New York: St. Martin's Press.

Mansfield, Edwin. 1983. "Long Waves and Technological Innovation." *American Economic Review* 73(2): 141–45.

Marx, Karl, and Friedrich Engels. 1848. *The Communist Manifesto.* Available at: http://www.marxists.org/archive/marx/works/1848/communist-manifesto/index.htm (accessed November 5, 2006).

Massey, Douglas S. 2007. *Categorically Unequal: The American Stratification System.* New York: Russell Sage Foundation.

Meissner, Doris M., Robert D. Hormats, Antonio Garrigues Walker, and Shujuro Ogata. 1993. *International Migration Challenges in a New Era.* New York: Trilateral Commission.

Meyer, John W. 1977. "The Effects of Education as an Institution." *American Journal of Sociology* 83(1): 55–77.

Milanovic, Branko. 1994. "Determinants of Cross-Country Income Inequality: An 'Augmented' Kuznets Hypothesis." Working paper 1246. Washington: World Bank, Policy Research Department, Transition Economics Division.

———. 2003. "The Two Faces of Globalization: Against Globalization as We Know It." *World Development* 31: 667–83.

———. 2005. *Worlds Apart: Measuring International and Global Inequality.* Princeton, N.J.: Princeton University Press.

———. N.d. "True World Income Distribution, 1988 and 1993: First Calculation Based on Household Surveys Alone." Washington: World Bank, Development Research Group.

Mill, John Stuart. 1936. *Principles of Political Economy.* London: Longmans, Green and Co. (Orig. pub. in 1848.)

Mills, C. Wright. 1959. *The Sociological Imagination.* Oxford: Oxford University Press.

Milner, Murray, Jr. 1987. "Theories of Inequality: An Overview and a Strategy for Synthesis." *Social Forces* 65(4): 1053–89.

Mintz, Sidney. 1985. *Sweetness and Power: The Place of Sugar in Modern History.* New York: Viking.

Moitt, Bernard. 2004a. "Introduction." In *Sugar, Slavery, and Society: Perspectives on the Caribbean, India, the Mascarenes, and the United States,* edited by Bernard Moitt. Gainesville: University Press of Florida.

————. 2004b. "Sugar, Slavery, and *Maronnage* in the French Caribbean." In *Sugar, Slavery, and Society: Perspectives on the Caribbean, India, the Mascarenes, and the United States,* edited by Bernard Moitt. Gainesville: University Press of Florida.

Moitt, Bernard, and Horace L. Henriques. 2004. "Social Stratification and Agency in a Sugar Plantation Society." In *Sugar, Slavery, and Society: Perspectives on the Caribbean, India, the Mascarenes, and the United States,* edited by Bernard Moitt. Gainesville: University Press of Florida.

Moore, Barrington. 1966. *Social Origins of Dictatorship and Democracy. Lord and Peasant in the Making of the Modern World.* Boston: Beacon Press.

Moran, Timothy Patrick. 2003. "On the Theoretical and Methodological Context of Cross-National Inequality Data." *International Sociology* 18(2): 351–78.

————. 2005. "Kuznets's Inverted U-Curve Hypothesis: The Rise, Demise, and Continued Relevance of a Socioeconomic Law." *Sociological Forum* 20(2): 209–43.

————. 2006a. "Statistical Inference and Patterns of Inequality in the Global North." *Social Forces* 84(3): 1799–1818.

————. 2006b. "Statistical Inference for Measures of Inequality with a Cross-National Bootstrap Application." *Sociological Methods and Research* 34(3): 296–333.

Morgan, Stephen L. 2006. "Past Themes and Future Prospects on Social and Economic Mobility." In *Mobility and Inequality: Frontiers of Research in Sociology and Economics,* edited by Stephen L. Morgan, David B. Grusky, and Gary S. Fields. Palo Alto, Calif.: Stanford University Press.

Morgan, Stephen L., and Young-Mi Kim. 2006. "Inequality of Conditions and Intergenerational Mobility." In *Mobility and Inequality: Frontiers of Research in Sociology and Economics,* edited by Stephen L. Morgan, David B. Grusky, and Gary S. Fields. Palo Alto, Calif.: Stanford University Press.

Morley, Samuel A. 1995. *Poverty and Inequality in Latin America: The Impact of Adjustment and Recovery in the 1980s.* Baltimore: Johns Hopkins University Press.

Mueller, Dennis C., and Thomas Stratmann. 2003. "The Economic Effects of Democratic Participation." *Journal of Public Economics* 87(9): 2129–55.

Muller, Edward N. 1985. "Income Inequality, Regime Repressiveness, and Political Violence." *American Sociological Review* 50(1): 47–61.

————. 1988. "Democracy, Economic Development, and Income Inequality." *American Sociological Review* 53(1): 50–68.

————. 1989. "Democracy and Inequality." *American Sociological Review* 54(5): 868–71.

Murphy, Kevin M., and Finis Welch. 1992. "The Structure of Wages." *Quarterly Journal of Economics* 107(1): 285–326.

Myrdal, Gunnar. 1964. *Economic Theory and Under-Developed Regions.* London: Gerald Duckworth & Co. (Orig. pub. in 1957.)

Nickell, Stephen, and Brian Bell. 1996. "The Collapse in Demand for the Unskilled and Unemployed Across the OECD." *Oxford Review of Economic Policy* 11(1): 40–62.

Nielsen, François. 1994. "Income Inequality and Industrial Development Revisited." *American Sociological Review* 59: 654–77.

Nielsen, François, and Arthur S. Alderson. 1995. "Income Inequality, Development, and Dualism: Results from an Unbalanced Cross-National Panel." *American Sociological Review* 60(5): 674–701.

North, Douglass C. 1981. *Structure and Change in Economic History.* New York: W. W. Norton.

———. 1990. *Institutions, Institutional Change, and Economic Performance.* Cambridge: Cambridge University Press.

———. 2005. *Understanding the Process of Economic Change.* Princeton, N.J.: Princeton University Press.

Norusis, Marija. 2006. *SPSS 15.0 Statistical Procedures Companion.* New York: Prentice-Hall.

Nugent, Jeffrey B. 1983. "An Alternative Source of Measurement Error as an Explanation of the Inverted-U Hypothesis." *Economic Development and Cultural Change* 31(2): 385–96.

Nurkse, Ragnar. 1953. *Problems of Capital Formation in Underdeveloped Countries.* New York: Oxford University Press.

Ocampo, José Antonio. 1981. "Export Growth and Capitalist Development in Colombia in the Nineteenth Century." In *Disparities in Economic Development Since the Industrial Revolution,* edited by Paul Bairoch and Maurice Lévy-Leboyer. New York: St. Martin's Press.

Ogwang, Tomson. 1995. "The Economic Development–Income Inequality Nexus: Further Evidence on Kuznets's U-Curve Hypothesis." *American Journal of Economics and Sociology* 54(2): 217–29.

O'Rourke, Kevin H., and Jeffrey G. Williamson. 1999. *Globalization and History: The Evolution of a Nineteenth-Century Atlantic Economy.* Cambridge, Mass.: MIT Press.

Otake, Fumio. 2005. *Inequality in Japan (Nihon no Fubyodo).* Tokyo: Nihon Keizai Shinbun Sha.

Papanek, Gustav F. 1978. "Economic Growth, Income Distribution, and the Political Process in Less Developed Countries." In *Income Distribution and Economic Inequality,* edited by Zvi Griliches, W. Krelle, H. J. Krupp, and O. Kyn. New York: Halsted Press.

Papanek, Gustav F., and Oldrich Kyn. 1987. "Flattening the Kuznets Curve: The Consequences for Income Distribution of Development Strategy, Government Intervention, Income, and the Rate of Growth." *Pakistan Development Review* 26(1): 1–54.

Parthasarathi, Prassanan. 2005. "Agriculture, Labor, and the Standard of Living in Eighteenth-Century India." In *Living Standards in the Past,* edited by Robert C. Allen, Tommy Bengtsson, and Martin Dribe. Oxford: Oxford University Press.

Paukert, Felix. 1973. "Income Distribution at Different Levels of Development: A Survey of the Evidence." *International Labor Review* 108(23): 97–125.

Pierson, Paul, ed. 2001. *The New Politics of the Welfare State.* Oxford: Oxford University Press.

Plotnick, Robert D., Eugene Smolensky, Eirik Evenhouse, and Siobhan Reilly. 2000. "The Twentieth-Century Record of Inequality and Poverty in the United States." In *The Twentieth Century,* edited by Stanley L. Engerman and Robert E. Gallman. Cambridge: Cambridge University Press.

Polanyi, Karl. 1957. *The Great Transformation: The Political and Economic Origins of Our Time.* Boston: Beacon Press. (Orig. pub. in 1944.)

Pomeranz, Kenneth. 2000. *The Great Divergence: China, Europe, and the Making of the World Economy.* Princeton, N.J.: Princeton University Press.

———. 2005. "Standards of Living in Eighteenth-Century China: Regional Differences, Temporal Trends, and Incomplete Evidence." In *Living Standards in the Past,* edited by Robert C. Allen, Tommy Bengtsson, and Martin Dribe. Oxford: Oxford University Press.

Prebisch, Raúl. 1950. *The Economic Development of Latin America and Its Principal Problems.* Lake Success, N.Y.: United Nations, Department of Economic Affairs, Economic Commission for Latin America.

Pritchett, Lant. 1997. "Divergence, Big Time." *Journal of Economic Perspectives* 11(3): 3–17.

Ram, Rati. 1989. "Level of Development and Income Inequality: An Extension of Kuznets-Hypothesis to the World-Economy." *Kyklos* 42(1): 73–88.

———. 1997. "Level of Economic Development and Income Inequality: Evidence from the Postwar Developed World." *Southern Economic Journal* 64(2): 576–83.

Rawls, John. 1971. *A Theory of Justice.* Cambridge, Mass.: Belknap Press of Harvard University Press.

Robinson, Sherman. 1976. "A Note on the U-Hypothesis Relating Income Inequality and Economic Development." *American Economic Review* 66(3): 437–40.

Rogoff, Natalie. 1953. *Recent Trends in Occupational Mobility.* Glencoe, Ill.: Free Press.

Romer, Paul. 1990. "Endogenous Technological Growth." *Journal of Political Economy* 98(5): 71–102.

Rostow, Walt W. 1978. *The World Economy: History and Prospect.* Austin: University of Texas Press.

Rubinson, Richard. 1976. "The World-Economy and the Distribution of Income Within States: A Cross-National Study." *American Sociological Review* 41(4): 638–59.

Rubinson, Richard, and Dan Quinlan. 1977. "Democracy and Social Inequality: A Reanalysis." *American Sociological Review* 42(4): 611–23.

Sachs, Jeffrey. 2005. *The End of Poverty: Economic Possibilities for Our Time.* New York: Penguin Press.

Saith, Ashwani. 1983. "Development and Distribution: A Critique of the Cross-Country U-Hypothesis." *Journal of Development Economics* 13(4): 367–82.

Saito, Osamu. 2005. "Wages, Inequality, and Pre-Industrial Growth in Japan, 1727–1894." In *Living Standards in the Past: New Perspectives on Well-Being in Asia and Europe,* edited by Robert Allen, Tommy Bengtsson, and Martin Dribe. Oxford: Oxford University Press.

Sala-i-Martin, Xavier. 2006. "The World Distribution of Income: Falling Poverty and . . . Convergence, Period!" *Quarterly Journal of Economics* 121(2): 351–97.

Schumpeter, Joseph A. 1942. *Capitalism, Socialism, and Democracy.* New York: Harper & Row.

Seekings, Jeremy, and Nicoli Nattrass. 2005. *Class, Race, and Inequality in South Africa.* New Haven, Conn.: Yale University Press.

Shavit, Yossi, and Hans-Peter Blossfeld, eds. 1993. *Persistent Inequality: Changing Educational Attainment in Thirteen Countries.* Boulder, Colo.: Westview Press.

Shumsky, Neil Larry. 1991. *The Evolution of Political Protest and the Workingmen's Party of California.* Columbus: Ohio State University Press.

Silva, Nelson do Valle. 1985. "Updating the Cost of Not Being White in Brazil." In *Race, Class, and Power in Brazil,* edited by Pierre-Michel Fontaine. Los Angeles: Center for Afro-American Studies.

Simpson, Miles. 1990. "Political Rights and Income Inequality: A Cross-National Test." *American Sociological Review* 55(5): 682–93.

Smeeding, Timothy. 2002. "Globalization, Inequality, and the Rich Countries of the G-20: Evidence from the Luxembourg Income Study." Working paper 320. Luxembourg City: Luxembourg Income Study.

Smith, Adam. 1976. *An Inquiry into the Nature and Causes of the Wealth of Nations.* Chicago: University of Chicago Press. (Orig. pub. in 1776.)

Smith, Rogers M. 1997. *Civic Ideals: Conflicting Visions of Citizenship in U.S. History.* New Haven, Conn.: Yale University Press.

Söderberg, Johan. 1991. "Wage Differentials in Sweden, 1725–1950." In *Income Distribution in Historical Perspective,* edited by Y. S. Brenner,

Hartmut Kaelble, and Mark Thomas. Cambridge: Cambridge University Press.

Sokoloff, Kenneth L., and Stanley L. Engerman. 2000. "Institutions, Factor Endowments, and Paths of Development in the New World." *Journal of Economic Perspectives* 14(3): 217–32.

Sorokin, Pitirim. 1959. *Social Mobility.* New York: Harper & Brothers. (Orig. pub. in 1927.)

Soysal, Yasemin N. 1994. *Limits of Citizenship: Migrants and Postnational Membership in Europe.* Chicago: University of Chicago Press.

Srinivasan, T. N. 1977. "Development, Poverty, and Basic Human Needs: Some Issues." *Food Research Institute Studies* 16(2): 11–28.

Stampp, Kenneth M. 1956. *The Peculiar Institution: Slavery in the Ante-Bellum South.* New York: Vintage Books.

Steckel, Richard H. 1995. "Stature and the Standard of Living." *Journal of Economic Literature* 33(4): 1903–40.

Steckel, Richard H., and Joseph M. Prince. 2001. "Tallest in the World: Native Americans of the Great Plains in the Nineteenth Century." *American Economic Review* 91(1): 287–94.

Stephens, John D. 1989. "Democratic Transition and Breakdown in Western Europe, 1870–1939: A Test of the Moore Thesis." *American Journal of Sociology* 94(5): 1019–76.

Stewart, Frances. 1978. "Inequality, Technology, and Payment Systems." *World Development* 6(3): 275–93.

Stiglitz, Joseph E., and Andrew Charlton. 2005. *Fair Trade for All: How Trade Can Promote Development.* Oxford: Oxford University Press.

Sundrum, R. M. 1990. *Income Distribution in Less Developed Countries.* London: Routledge.

Teachman, Jay D. 1983. "State Power, Socioeconomic Characteristics, and Income Inequality: A Cross-National Analysis." *Human Organization* 42(3): 205–13.

Terreblanche, Sampie. 2002. *A History of Inequality in South Africa, 1652–2002.* Scottsville: University of Natal Press.

Thompson, William R. 1990. "Long Waves, Technological Innovation, and Relative Decline." *International Organization* 44(2): 201–33.

Thornton, Russell. 2000. "Population History of Native North Americans." In *A Population History of North America,* edited by Michael R. Haines and Richard H. Steckel. New York: Cambridge University Press.

Tilly, Charles. 1999. *Durable Inequality.* Berkeley: University of California Press.

Timmer, Ashley S., and Jeffrey G. Williamson. 1998. "Immigration Policy Prior to the 1930s: Labor Market, Policy Interactions, and Globalization Backlash." *Population and Development Review* 24(4): 739–71.

Tomich, Dale. 2004. *Through the Prism of Slavery: Labor, Capital and World Economy.* New York: Rowman and Littlefield Publishers.

United Nations University, World Institute for Development Economics Research (UNU-WIDER). 2005. World Income Inequality Database (WIID). Version 2.0a. Available at: http://www.wider.unu.edu/research/Database/en_GB/database/(accessed June 24, 2008).

U.S. Bureau of the Census. 2006. "Median Income Levels." Available at: http://www.census.gov/hhes/www/income/incomestats.html (accessed April 28, 2006).

Wade, Robert Hunter. 2004. "Is Globalization Reducing Poverty and Inequality?" *World Development* 32(4): 567–89.

———. 2008. "Globalization, Growth, Poverty, Inequality, Resentment, and Imperialism." In *Global Political Economy,* edited by John Ravenhill. Oxford: Oxford University Press.

Wallerstein, Immanuel. 1974. *The Modern World System: Capitalist Agriculture and the Origins of the European World-Economy in the Sixteenth Century.* New York: Academic Press.

———. 1980. *The Modern World-System II: Mercantilism and the Consolidation of the European World-Economy, 1600–1750.* New York: Academic Press.

———. 1982. "World-Systems Analysis: Theoretical and Interpretative Issues." In *World-Systems Analysis: Theory and Methodology,* edited by Terence K. Hopkins and Immanuel Wallerstein. Beverly Hills, Calif.: Sage Publications.

———. 1989a. "Dependence in an Interdependent World: The Limited Possibilities of Transformation within the Capitalist World-Economy." In *The Capitalist World-Economy,* edited by Immanuel Wallerstein. Cambridge: Cambridge University Press.

———. 1989b. *The Modern World-System III: The Second Era of Great Expansion of the Capitalist World-Economy, 1730–1840s.* San Diego: Academic Press.

Weber, Max. 1996. *The Protestant Ethic and the Spirit of Capitalism.* Los Angeles: Roxbury Publishing Co. (Orig. pub. in 1905.)

Weede, Erich. 1982. "The Effects of Democracy and Socialist Strength on the Size Distribution of Income: Some More Evidence." *International Journal of Comparative Sociology* 23(34): 151–65.

Weede, Erich, and Horst Tiefenbach. 1981. "Some Recent Explanations of Income Inequality: An Evaluation and Critique." *International Studies Quarterly* 25(2): 255–82.

Wellenreuther, Hermann. 1993. "The Impact of the Colonial Heritage on the Economic Development in the Nineteenth and Twentieth Century: North America." In *Development and Underdevelopment in America:*

Contrasts of Economic Growth in North and Latin America in Historical Perspective, edited by Walther L. Bernecker and Hans Werner Tobler. Berlin: Walter de Gruyter.

Willcox, Walter F., and Imre Ferenczi. 1929. *International Migrations*. New York: National Bureau of Economic Research.

Williamson, Jeffrey G. 1991. *Inequality, Poverty, and History: The Kuznets Memorial Lectures of the Economic Growth Center, Yale University*. New York: Basil Blackwell.

Williamson, Jeffrey G., and Peter H. Lindert. 1980. *American Inequality: A Macro-Economic History*. New York: Academic Press.

World Bank. 1993. *The East Asian Miracle*. New York: Oxford University Press.

———. 2006, 2007, 2008. *World Development Indicators*. Washington: World Bank.

Woytinsky, Wladimir S., and Emma S. Woytinsky. 1953. *World Population and Production: Trends and Outlook*. New York: Twentieth-Century Fund.

Wright, Eric Olin. 1979. *Class Structure and Income Determination*. New York: Academic Press.

Wright, Gavin. 2006. *Slavery and American Economic Development*. Baton Rouge: Louisiana State University Press.

INDEX

Boldface numbers refer to figures and tables.